INTERNATIONAL POLITICAL ECONOMY SERIES

General Editor: Timothy M. Shaw, Professor of Political Science and International Development Studies, and Director of the Centre for Foreign Policy Studies, Dalhousie University, Nova Scotia, Canada

Recent titles include:

Pradeep Agrawal, Subir V. Gokarn, Veena Mishra, Kirit S. Parikh and Kunal Sen
ECONOMIC RESTRUCTURING IN EAST ASIA AND INDIA: Perspectives on Policy Reform

Solon L. Barraclough and Krishna B. Ghimire
FORESTS AND LIVELIHOODS: The Social Dynamics of Deforestation in Developing Countries

Jerker Carlsson, Gunnar Köhlin and Anders Ekbom
THE POLITICAL ECONOMY OF EVALUATION: International Aid Agenicies and the Effectiveness of Aid

Steve Chan
FOREIGN DIRECT INVESTMENT IN A CHANGING GLOBAL POLITICAL ECONOMY

Edward A. Comor (*editor*)
THE GLOBAL POLITICAL ECONOMY OF COMMUNICATION

Paul Cook and Frederick Nixson (*editors*)
THE MOVE TO THE MARKET? Trade and Industry Policy Reform in Transitional Economies

O. P. Dwivedi
DEVELOPMENT ADMINISTRATION: From Underdevelopment to Sustainable Development

John Healey and William Tordoff (*editors*)
VOTES AND BUDGETS: Comparative Studies in Accountable Governance in the South

Noeleen Heyzer, James V. Riker and Antonio B. Quizon (*editors*)
GOVERNMENT–NGO RELATIONS IN ASIA: Prospects and Challenges for People-Centred Development

George Kent
CHILDREN IN THE INTERNATIONAL POLITICAL ECONOMY

Laura Macdonald
SUPPORTING CIVIL SOCIETY: The Political Role of Non-Governmental
Organizations in Central America

Gary McMahon (*editor*)
LESSONS IN ECONOMIC POLICY FOR EASTERN EUROPE FROM
LATIN AMERICA

Juan Antonio Morales and Gary McMahon (*editors*)
ECONOMIC POLICY AND THE TRANSITION TO DEMOCRACY: The Latin
American Experience

Paul J. Nelson
THE WORLD BANK AND NON-GOVERNMENTAL ORGANIZATIONS:
The Limits of Apolitical Development

Archibald R. M. Ritter and John M. Kirk (*editors*)
CUBA IN THE INTERNATIONAL SYSTEM: Normalization and Integration

Ann Seidman and Robert B. Seidman
STATE AND LAW IN THE DEVELOPMENT PROCESS: Problem-Solving and
Institutional Change in the Third World

Tor Skålnes
THE POLITICS OF ECONOMIC REFORM IN ZIMBABWE: Continuity and
Change in Development

John Sorenson (*editor*)
DISASTER AND DEVELOPMENT IN THE HORN OF AFRICA

Howard Stein (*editor*)
ASIAN INDUSTRIALIZATION AND AFRICA: Studies in Policy Alternatives
to Structural Adjustment

Deborah Stienstra
WOMEN'S MOVEMENTS AND INTERNATIONAL ORGANIZATIONS

Larry A. Swatuk and Timothy M. Shaw (*editors*)
THE SOUTH AT THE END OF THE TWENTIETH CENTURY: Rethinking the
Political Economy of Foreign Policy in Africa, Asia, the Caribbean and Latin
America

Sandra Whitworth
FEMINISM AND INTERNATIONAL RELATIONS

Debating Development Discourse

Institutional and Popular Perspectives

Edited by

David B. Moore
Lecturer in Politics
Flinders University of South Australia

and

Gerald J. Schmitz
Senior Research Officer
Library of Parliament, Ottawa

Foreword by Colin Leys

First published in Great Britain 1995 by
MACMILLAN PRESS LTD
Houndmills, Basingstoke, Hampshire RG21 6XS
and London
Companies and representatives
throughout the world

A catalogue record for this book is available
from the British Library.

ISBN 0–333–61753–3

 First published in the United States of America 1995 by
ST. MARTIN'S PRESS, INC.,
Scholarly and Reference Division,
175 Fifth Avenue,
New York, N.Y. 10010

ISBN 0–312–12886–X

Library of Congress Cataloging-in-Publication Data
Debating development discourse: institutional and popular
perspectives/ edited by David B. Moore and Gerald J. Schmitz.
p.   cm. — (International political economy series)
includes bibliographical references and index.
ISBN 0–312–12886–X
1. Economic development—Case studies.   2. Sustainable
development—Case studies.   3. Political participation—Case
studies.   I. Moore, David B.   II. Schmitz, Gerald J.   III. Series.
HD75.D43   1995
338.9—dc20   95–33046
                                                  CIP

10   9   8   7   6   5   4   3   2   1
04   03   02   01   00   99   98   97   96   95

Printed and bound in Great Britain by
Ipswich Book Co Ltd, Ipswich, Suffolk

This book is dedicated to the memory of **Otto Roesch**, 5 November 1951–7 June 1994, who died in a car accident near Xai-Xai, Mozambique, on his way to a UN humanitarian project site. Otto's anthropological and solitary work with the Mozambican people exemplifies what this book is attempting to encourage.

Contents

Contents

Foreword

The 1980s turn to economic neo-liberalism, making 'the market' the chief, if not the sole, agent of economic progress, put in question the whole concept of 'development' as something collectively willed, planned and state-directed. This posed a serious difficulty for the 'development community' (as it likes to call itself – or 'development industry', as James Ferguson, a contributor to this volume, prefers to call it). On the one hand, the development community depends overwhelmingly for its funding on the major OECD countries, most of whose governments have become fully committed to global neo-liberalism. On the other hand, it depends *morally* on the acute needs and deepening despair – or cynicism – of millions of ordinary people in underdeveloped countries whose plight has been sharply aggravated by 'structural adjustment' and the inexorably mounting burden of debt service. The development community has been caught in the middle; and one of the ways in which it has responded to its predicament has been to wrap its activities in thicker and thicker layers of rhetoric, in which the words 'sustainability', 'equity' and 'participation' figure prominently.

The buzzwords of development tend to have a relatively short product cycle and have usually been replaced by the time they are subjected to any systematic critique. On this occasion, however, a group of experienced scholars has been provoked by the seriousness of what is at stake in the contemporary crisis of 'development' to make such a critique while these terms are still very much current. Their aim has not been to offer a philosophical analysis of the concepts of sustainability, equity and participation (although Gerald Schmitz's dissection of 'governance', the illegitimate offspring of neo-liberalism and democracy, would be hard to improve upon – the pin is finally through that particular beetle). What they undertake is, rather, to explore the real relationships and policies to which these words – however misleadingly or even, at times, hypocritically – refer.

David Moore's highly condensed but rich and provocative overview of the evolution of the development discourse that has spawned these terms ought to be an important focus of debate and teaching for several years to come; and the same can be said for Manfred Bienefeld's powerful analysis of the opposition between 'structural adjustment' and democracy, and for James Ferguson's sharp delineation of the opposition between the pseudo-amoralism of 'scientific capitalism' and the pervasive moral humanism of ordinary Africans' economic thinking. Equally persuasive are the three

case-studies, drawn from South Africa, Zimbabwe and Costa Rica, of
what 'participation' and 'equity' mean in practice; and – last but not least
– one from northern Alberta, where some also ordinary but determined
people showed that both 'sustainability' and 'participation' were in
irresoluble conflict with commercially based notions of 'development'.

In short, this book is a boost for intellectual honesty at a time when we
badly need it.

COLIN LEYS

Queen's University
Kingston, Ontario, Canada

Preface and Acknowledgements

This book had its origins while Pierre Sané, then Director of the International Development Research Centre's Central and West African Region, was pacing the halls during a break in an IDRC Regional Director's meeting in Ottawa. He was wondering whether anyone at the IDRC really knew what was meant by the organization's new mission statement's main concepts – sustainable growth, participation, and equity. He decided that a study should be done on the origins and meanings of these notions. On the suggestion of Marc van Ameringen (then in the Social Science Division of the IDRC, now the director of its South Africa office) Pierre approached David Moore to carry out a review of the literature. The result may be far from what Pierre and Marc envisaged, but here it is.

The review was presented in a preliminary form as 'The Crisis in Developmental Discourse and the Concepts of Sustainability, Equity, and Participation. A Way out of the Impasse?' at the Canadian Political Science Association Annual Meeting in June of 1991, at Queen's University, Kingston, Ontario, where Timothy Shaw was kind enough to take note of it and ask David Moore to consider organizing a panel around the theme at the next meeting of the Canadian Association for the Study of International Development (CASID), with a view to working on the proceedings for a book in his International Political Economy series. Gerald Schmitz, who was putting the finishing touches on his and David Gillies' *The Challenge of Democratic Development: Sustaining Democratization in Developing Societies*, also took note of the paper and began communicating with David Moore. Moore, eager to share Shaw's challenge, proposed a working partnership with Schmitz.

We invited all this book's contributors and a wide variety of discussants – Katherine Pearson, Development Policy Unit, Canadian Council for International Co-operation; Scott Sinclair, York University and University of Prince Edward Island, and a tireless worker in the popular movement opposing the North American 'free trade' agreements; Jean-Michel Labatut, Programme Officer, Social Policy Programme, IDRC; and Roger Ehrhardt, Africa and Middle East Desk, Canadian International Development Agency – to the 1992 CASID Conference at the Learned Society's meeting at the University of Prince Edward Island in Charlottetown, where we made up a vivid day-long mini-conference of our own. The IDRC and Athabasca

University sponsored the conference participation of David Moore and the participants who lived outside of Canada. The Canadians owe thanks to their universities and institutions for that memorable day. Gerald Schmitz was unable to attend the meeting, but prevailed upon Roy Culpepper of the North–South Institute to present his 'Why Words Matter: Some Thoughts on the "New" Development Agenda' in his absence.

David Moore's chapter has benefitted from the comments of many. Before the CASID meeting, it was presented to a seminar sponsored by the Zimbabwe Institute of Development Studies and the Department of Political and Administrative Studies at the University of Zimbabwe, at an IDRC meeting in Ottawa, and at the place for which it was originally commissioned – the IDRC's Senegal office, as Pierre inaugurated a comprehensive restructuring process.[1] After the CASID meeting, various other versions of the paper were presented at Planact in Johannesburg, the Canada–Asia Project Summer School in Athabasca, at a seminar at Flinders University in Adelaide, and at a meeting of the Canadian Research Consortium on Southern Africa. Henry Bernstein made very helpful suggestions in writing (which led to his very fruitful stay as a distinguished visitor to Athabasca University in September 1993, where he shared his knowledge of distance education with the faculties, and his keen intellect on and commitment to development and Africa with a smaller and even more privileged group of us). If all the good suggestions had been incorporated, it would be a much better (and even longer) paper than it is now. As it was, it took much of the time of the Athabasca University President's Award for Research and Scholarly Excellence to rewrite it and prepare the rest of the volume, for which Moore owes yet more thanks to 'AU.' Gerald Schmitz's chapter has been enriched by many discussions of the relationship of democracy to development and 'governance,' and has benefitted in particular from its presentation to the 1993 CASID meeting at Carleton University in Ottawa. It also owes much to the stimulating environment at the North–South Institute during his several years there directing a research programme on human rights and democratic government.

We are both extremely grateful to all the people and institutions mentioned above, to each other for the mutual and comradely support necessary for such a project, to the encouragement and patience of Tim Shaw, for the fortitude of editors Clare Andrews, Gráinne Twomey and Keith Povey at Macmillan, and to Tanya Lyons for assistance with proof-reading, indexing and gender awareness – but most of all to the contributors to the book. We were harsh in our requirements, but they were always exceeded. We hope we will be able to meet again, because the debates, like the struggles from which they grow, will continue.

DAVID B. MOORE
GERALD J. SCHMITZ

Note

1.   The IDRC paper is entitled 'Concepts and Strategies of Development – Sustainable Growth–Participation–Equity: An Exploration of Their Meaning', ROF 3-A-89-5713.

List of Abbreviations

ACORDE	Asociación Costarricense de Organismos de Desarrollo
AID	United States Agency for International Development (also USAID)
ANC	African National Congress
CECADE	Centro de Capacitación y Desarrollo
CIA	Central Intelligence Agency (USA)
CIDA	Canadian International Development Agency
COSATU	Congress of South African Trade Unions
CROD	Concertación Regional de Organismos de Desarrollo
CRS	Catholic Relief Services
CST	Colonialism of a Special Type (South Africa)
CUFTA	Canada–US Free Trade Agreement
CZI	Confederation of Zimbabwean Industries
DBSA	Development Bank of Southern Africa
DFA	Development Fund for Africa (American)
DRC	Domestic Resource Costs
DTZ	Development Trust of Zimbabwe
ECA	Economic Commission for Africa (UNECA)
ECLA(C)	Economic Commission for Latin America and the Caribbean
EIA	Environmental Impact Assessment
ESAP	Economic Structural Adjustment Programme
FINCA	Fundación Integral Campesina
GATT	General Agreement on Tariffs and Trade
GDP	Gross Domestic Product
IDRC	International Development Research Centre (Ottawa)
IDT	Independent Development Trust (South Africa)
IFIs	International Financial Institutions (IMF, World Bank, etc.)
IMF	International Monetary Fund
ILO	International Labour Organization
ISP	Industrial Strategy Project
MERG	Macro-Economic Research Group (South Africa)
NAFTA	North American Free Trade Agreement
NAL	Non-Adjustment Lending (Country)
NGOs	Non-Governmental Organizations
NHF	National Housing Forum (South Africa)
NICs	Newly Industrializing (or -ed) Countries

NIEO	New International Economic Order
OECD	Organization of Economic Cooperation and Development
OEF	(International) formerly Overseas Education Fund
OGIL	Open General Import Licence (Zimbabwe)
PACT	Private Agencies Collaborating Together
PEP	Programme for Education in Participation
PF-ZAPU	Patriotic Front – Zimbabwe African Peoples Union (during the liberation war: ZAPU)
PVOs	Private Voluntary Organizations
RDP	Reconstruction and Development Programme (ANC)
QUANGO	Quasi Non-Government Organization
RENAMO	National Resistance Movement of Mozambique
SACP	South African Communist Party
SADCC	Southern African Development Coordination Conference
SAL	Structural Adjustment Lending
SAP	Structural Adjustment Programme
SIDA	Swedish International Development Authority
SANCO	South African National Civic Organization
TANU	Tanzanian African National Union
UB	Urban Foundation (South Africa)
UNCTAD	United Nations Conference on Trade and Development
UNDP	United Nations Development Program
UNTCR	United Nations Truth Commission Report
UNHCR	United Nations High Commission for Refugees
UNICEF	United Nations Children's Fund
UPA	UPANACIONAL – Costa Rica's largest peasant union
WIB	Women in Business
WID	Women in Development
ZANU-PF	Zimbabwe African National Union – Patriotic Front (during the Liberation War: ZANU)
ZCTU	Zimbabwe Congress of Trade Unions
ZIDCO	Zimbabwe Development Corporation
ZINASU	Zimbabwe National Students' Union
ZIPA	Zimbabwe People's Army

Notes on the Contributors

Patrick Bond worked at the Johannesburg development NGO Planact from 1990 to 1994, and served SANCO and the ANC as an editor of the Reconstruction and Development Programme and of the government's RDP White Paper. He presently teaches social policy at Johns Hopkins University.

Manfred A. Bienefeld is a Professor in the School of Public Administration at Carleton University, after having spent many years at the University of Dar es Salaam in Tanzania and at the Institute of Development Studies at Sussex University in England. He has written and edited books ranging from *Economics for Business* (1964) to *The Struggle for Development: National Strategies in an International Context* (1982) and *Production, Space, Identity: Political Economy Faces the 21st Century* (1993), and published with journals such as the *Review of African Political Economy* and *Studies in Political Economy*. His consulting work has included teaching for the Asian Development Bank, and from 1992 to 1994 working as senior advisor to the Green Industrial Strategy Group in the Ontario Ministry of Energy and Environment.

James Ferguson is Associate Professor of Anthropology at the University of California at Irvine. He is the author of *The Anti-Politics Machine: 'Development', Depoliticization and Bureaucratic Power in Lesotho* (1994). He has published articles in journals including the *Journal of Southern African Studies*, *American Anthropologist* and *Cultural Anthropology*, and is the co-editor of a special issue of *Cultural Anthropology* on the theme 'Space and Place'.

Michael Gismondi is Associate Professor of Sociology and Global Studies at Athabasca University, Alberta, Canada. He has published extensively on religion and revolution in Nicaragua and on the politics and language of the environment in Northern Alberta. **Mary Richardson** is Associate Professor of Philosophy at Athabasca University. She approaches environmental issues from the perspective of an applied ethicist. **Joan Sherman** is an editor at Athabasca University and an organic farmer. All are members of the Friends of the Athabasca River, a grassroots organization developed to organize the pulp mill hearings under study in this book (among other democratic acts of resistance), and which is now working to keep

Alberta-Pacific Forest Products to the environmental promises it made as
a result of the hearing process documented in their chapter. Together, they
have written *Winning Back the Words: Confronting Experts in an Environmental Public Hearing*, in *Capitalism, Nature, Socialism*, and in the
Participatory Development Review. They are also organizers of the Canada–
Asia Partnership summer school, working with community development
practitioners from Thailand, the Philippines, Nepal, and Canada to explore
community-based responses to the EIA and public hearing processes.

Laura Macdonald holds a doctorate in political science from York University and is Assistant Professor in the Department of Political Science,
Carleton University, Ottawa, Canada. She has published several articles
related to NGOs, civil society and Canadian foreign policy. Her forthcoming
book *Supporting Civil Society: The Political Role of Non-Governmental
Organizations in Central America* will be published by Macmillan Press
as part of the International Political Economy Series.

David B. Moore is Visiting Lecturer in Politics at The Flinders University of South Australia, in Adelaide. He has published on the liberation
war in Zimbabwe (on which he is continuing research), in publications
including the *Journal of Southern African Studies* and *Third World Quarterly*. He is a regular contributor to the *Southern African Review of Books*.
While working on this book he taught Political Science at Athabasca
University, Alberta, Canada, from where he is currently on leave.

Lloyd M. Sachikonye, Research Fellow in Labour and Agrarian Studies
at the Institute of Development Studies, University of Zimbabwe, holds
Bachelor's and Master's degrees in Politics from Ahmadu Bello University,
Nigeria and a doctorate in Politics from Leeds University. He co-edited
and contributed a chapter to *The One Party State and Democracy: The
Zimbabwean Debate*, and has published in the *Review of African Political
Economy*, the *African Journal of Political Economy* and many other jour-
nals. He is a regular contributor to the *Southern African Political and
Economic Monthly*.

Gerald J. Schmitz is a senior parliamentary research analyst specializing
in governance and international policy issues. He holds degrees in economics and political science from the University of Saskatchewan, and a
doctorate in political science from Carleton University. From 1991 to
1993 he was Programme Director for Human Rights and Democratic
Government at the Ottawa-based North–South Institute. Among other works

he is the author, with David Gillies, of *The Challenge of Democratic Development: Sustaining Democratization in Developing Societies*, published by the Institute in 1992. The chapter in this book reflects solely his personal views.

Introduction

Debates intensify during crises. The discourse of development practitioners and scholars is very much in crisis, regardless of the fact that one of
the initiating influences behind this book now claims it is well on the road
'beyond the impasse.'[1] Half a century after the first promise of 'modernization' was held out for the 'third world', it is obvious that very little of
that ambition has been realized. Neither the academies nor the agencies
are forthcoming with coherent explanations of or comprehensive answers
to the impasse. Academics are mired in a neo-classical versus state interventionist stalemate (while at the left end of the spectrum, marxists, who
never did resolve the dependency/progressive capitalist debate, are dis-
enchanted by the demise of state socialism and its affects on their prospects) and workers in the agencies are trapped in the dead-ends of macro
'structural adjustment' policy panegyrics or an endless array of directionless
and context-devoid projects. Where the 'people' do have promising projects
and meaningful aspirations, local states and global capitals – the roots of
the real crisis – conspire against them.

An apparent consensus that a way out of the impasse (or perhaps of
evading the crisis) can be found through the operationalization of the
terms 'sustainable development, participation, and equity' has appeared.
Development discourse (the symbols, actions and institutions concurrent
with economic, social, and political transformation in 'underdeveloped'
parts of the world) now encompasses environmental, democratic, and distributional concerns along with the traditional – and still paramount –
attention to 'growth.' Since the unabashed espousal of naked neo-classical
policies in the early eighties appears to have passed, the rhetoric of the
international financial institutions most concerned with the fate of the
third world appears to pay credence to democratic and accountable 'good
governance,' environmental correctness, and social programmes as well as
'getting the prices right.' And to the left of the citadels of finance capital,
the language of 'new social movements' pays more heed to rainbow coalitions of ecologists, students, women and autonomy seeking ethnic groups
than to the vanguards and popular classes of vintage red hues. The conceptual triad seems to speak to all of their concerns.

The essays in this volume are all concerned with this question: can this
consensus mean anything but that the new development discourse is meaningless? Can the concepts 'sustainability, participation and equity' have
any intellectual and practical weight if such divergent interests can make

use of them? The essays, starting with theoretical, conceptual, historical and analytical concerns and proceeding to focus on concrete case studies in southern Africa, Central America and northern Canada, are united in answering a definitive no to that query. But at the same time, they answer 'yes' if the terms can be re-articulated to a project of the left, from where they were lifted and nearly denuded of their radical potential.

This collection will demonstrate that there is indeed a crisis within a development discourse which seeks to be all things to all people. The seeming consensus on 'sustainability, participation and equity' is a fragilely constructed one, serving to mask the fundamental contradictions with the dominant perception of 'growth' and the interests this ideology serves. The theoretical analyses and case studies within *Debating Development Discourse* illustrate that the current, crisis-ridden conjuncture of the global political economy has thrown the post-war consensus on 'development' into disarray. The organizers of capitalist hegemony have attempted to lift the language of 'development's' challengers into the dominant discourse, but have not altered their basic practice, or, more importantly, the dynamics of the global economy.

But as the case studies illustrate, local actions in southern Africa, Central America, and northern Canada can present fundamental challenges to the dominant notions of development. In spite of the efforts of the dominant classes to neutralize the resistance-laden discourse centred around class, race, gender, and the environment, the papers illustrate that a fundamental dichotomy of class interests remains – at global and local levels. There is no crisis in the analysis of the urban South Africans who kept the housing agenda clear while the ANC's Reconstruction and Development Programme was being hammered out, the Costa Rican peasant organizations who see the wide ramifications of their struggles for 'community self-reliance,' and the northern Albertans who spoke out against the corporate understanding of 'sustainable development' so widely touted in the Alberta-Pacific Pulp Mill's slick newspaper-style advertisements dropped in resident's mailboxes and legitimized by its 'expert' scientists.

Thus the essays make it clear that 'participation' is the most tension-laden of all the notions in the triad of 'sustainability, participation, and equity.' If full and substantively democratic participation is allowed to flourish in the 'third world' (whether it be in its traditional geographical place or in part of the once 'first' world), then technocratic and elitist solutions to the problems of 'sustainability and equity' will be denied. The *real* meanings of the words could be pulled back. Democracy, then, is the 'nub' of the new discourse. This probably accounts for the current flurry of academic and policy-making activity on 'governance' emanating from the agencies and their intellectuals – and for the importance of their demystification.

The following chapters pursue this quest. David Moore's essay traces the emergence of development discourse in the last few decades through the development agencies and universities, using the Gramscian notion of hegemony to relate the shifts in development practice and theory to the international political economy and the rise of fall of social movements. Gerald Schmitz's extended evaluation of the current international development agency and academic writing on 'good governance' develops a critique of imposed notions of democracy in the third world derived from an uncritical acceptance of liberal democracy in the West – in deep crisis itself. Manfred Bienefeld's trenchant critique of structural adjustment ideology, using World Bank documents themselves to illustrate that the policies are doomed to failure *in their own terms*, is at the same time a chilling analysis of the democratic shortfalls of the global neo-liberal trend and a considered appraisal for a democratic re-beginning. More closely approaching popular, as opposed to institutionalized agency perspectives, James Ferguson juxtaposes well-established traditions of indigenous political discourse at various levels of African societies which link economic processes directly to the moral ordering of the world with the World Bank's 'amoral' language of 'scientific capitalism,' and asks how those of us who 'sent the market' might reorder the international ethical order.

Getting even closer to the ground of actually existing popular and participatory democracy, Patrick Bond demonstrates the very clear ways in which the urban associations have articulated a critique of South African capitalism through a grassroots discourse of basic needs and community control on the housing question. This may well have its effects on the more rarefied modes of development discourse he outlines. Lloyd Sachikonye's case study of the changes within the Zimbabwean state's development discourse parallels the international shifts from radical and social-democratic concatenations to those of neo-liberal order, documenting the roots of and resistance to these changes in internal class struggles. Laura Macdonald takes us further into the dynamics of participatory discourse in Costa Rica, exposing its illusions and deftly bringing us to the recognition that the popular saying 'think globally' has very real local application. Finally, Michael Gismondi, Joan Sherman, and Mary Richardson's piece illustrates that 'development discourse' is in no way restricted to the so-called 'third world,' and that the forms of participation exported through the development agencies from north to south are fraught with the tensions of liberal democracy. The eloquent realism of the critiques of maldevelopment which emerged from the floors of northern Alberta's community halls made initial impact on the processes of transnational capital accumulation, but were halted before they gathered sufficient momentum. The lesson to be learned from the experience is shared by the other contributions in the book: sustained political participation – that which strives for the democratization of both civil society relationships and state/public institutions – is necessary to turn the current critical conjuncture into opportunities for equitable, humane and truly sustainable development. It is hoped that this collection will make some contribution to the quest for democratic alternatives inherent in such processes of social contestation and deliberative debate. It is in that democratic crucible, moreover, that the test of *any* development discourse ultimately lies.

DAVID B. MOORE
GERALD J. SCHMITZ

Note

1. David Booth's 'Marxism and Development Sociology: Interpreting the Impasse,' *World Development,* 13, 7 (July 1985), pp. 761–787, was one of the primary inspirations to this book. In his 'Development Research: From Impasse to New Directions,' in Frans Schuurman (ed.), *Beyond the Impasse: New Directions in Development Theory* (London: Zed Press, 1993) however, he indicates that development studies are well on the road to recovery. This may be, but in the world of neo-liberal dominated development *practice*, we contend that the crisis is still with us. Therefore it still must be so in the realm of the academy.

1 Development Discourse as Hegemony: Towards an Ideological History – 1945–1995

David B. Moore

> The bourgeoisie . . . compels all nations, on pain of extinction, to adopt the bourgeois mode of production . . . to become bourgeois themselves. In one word, it creates a world after its own image.[1]

INTRODUCTION

This essay constitutes an attempt to begin an ideological history of development discourse[2] as a component of hegemony – as one of the means by which a dominant social class organizes its rule so it seems 'natural'[3] to its subjects. The process of hegemonic construction and maintenance is by no means easy. It displays many fluctuations as the material base of the political economy changes, and as social and political struggles among classes, nations, genders, and ethnic groups – as well as among groups within the ruling classes – ebb and flow. It takes on as many guises as the multitudinous manifestations of capitalism can support; as many strands of oppositional discourse as it can co-opt. As we witness the early stages of hegemony for global capital and the classes riding on top of its accumulation processes, it widens its reach – and narrows its common denominator – as never before.[4] And as global expansion of and shifts in hegemony go, so follows, albeit unevenly, with its own institutional and ideological rhythms, development discourse, perhaps one of the most derivative discourses there are.[5]

There are two main themes running through this essay. They will be united by a common analytical strand suggesting that the way to investigate and chart oscillations in the theory and practice of development is by unravelling the relationships among institutional discourses on development

1

(that is, within agencies and the academy), and how these forms of knowledge and practice have reflected and affected the much larger spheres of international political economy and social movements.

The first theme is that there have been two main phases of development discourse in the post-war era, coinciding with the major eras in the global political economy in this time. The first period was that of international Keynesianism and state-mediated capitalism based on 'Fordist' production in the west[6] (with stronger planning and welfarist tendencies in the United Kingdom and Europe[7] than in the United States), American international dominance (somewhat politically and ideologically challenged by the Soviet bloc, especially in the 'third world'[8]), and the decolonization and emergence of the third world. The second main phase of the post-war global political economy is that of the neo-liberal, de-regulated capitalism which emerged during the 1970s and is with us still.[9] It is a world of 'flexible production' and footloose capital in which the market reigns supreme. In the latter years of this phase the challenges of state socialism and an ideologically uncertain third world have disappeared. The former crashes towards a mixture of its past and a mafia-led market future.[10] Whatever socialist and national capitalist pretensions that the latter had have been drummed out of it, while its split into 'Newly Industrialized Countries' (NICs) and fourth worlds widens – nationally, regionally, and socially. In the west, the mediating agencies of welfarism, unionism and international humanitarianism[11] have been blown away by the gales of global competition, swept asunder with the nostalgic mists of the 'golden age of capitalism,'[12] to be replaced only by soup kitchens and new social movements.

In between these two phases was 'the sixties.' In retrospect these short years can be seen as a transitional phase, in which the freedoms promised by regulated capitalism threatened to turn into those which could only be assured by more constraints than capitalism could abide. Thus 'liberty' has quickly become moored to the market – to which, now, 'there is no alternative'[13] – although many of freedom's earlier tinges live on to occasionally irritate the apostles of the new order. Echoes of third world liberation inspired by Cuba and Vietnam still resound with Chiapas rebellions, South African civic associations, and alternative non-governmental development organizations.[14] They may point to the possibilities of a left-leaning future, but the resonances are weak in the face of the globalization of commodity fetishism.

The second theme running through this paper is a consideration of how today's developmental 'buzzwords' have evolved during the last half-century. Equity, democracy, and sustainability[15] have emerged during the last fifty years as the core triad of ideological concepts within development discourse. They hold within them a vast array of meanings from left to right, thus allowing them to be used with remarkable facility by a multitude of institutions, agents and social movements and to take on notably different hues in various hegemonic eras. This triad addresses issues of economic growth and distribution (equity), debates around political participation, order and governance (democracy), and concerns about the viability of the societies and environments upon which the developmental project is imposed (sustainability). They are thus at the core of development debates and the struggles they grow out of. They are loose enough to hold varying, even opposing, interpretations: essentially contested concepts, they are the arenas for ideological battles. They hold within them both the possibility of preserving what we know of development through the present crisis, but also have the potential of reforming, transforming or even transcending the current system of orthodoxy.[16] They thus deserve unravelling.

The best way to observe how the notions of equity, democracy and sustainability have taken on varying ideological moorings is to assess them historically; relating them to the political-economic and ideological eras outlined above, and tracing the ways in which discourses in the agencies and the academy interact between themselves and with the world around them. It is fairly easy to discern the rough outlines of such a schemata.

The notion of equity can be split into two main elements within the capitalist hegemonic order: those of state indicated growth, industrial planning, and social welfarism versus the neo-liberal monolith of economic reasoning which sees the state as the source of inequitable deviations from the impartiality of the invisible hand – as a refuge for corrupt rent-seekers impinging on the evenhanded honesty of entrepreneurs. This latter notion of equity is paramount today, if the term exists at all (it may simply refer to what is swapped for the reduction of national debt while a state's citizens face the devaluation of their currencies and wages, the elimination of subsidies, and rampant privatization). As David Slater's words suggest, neo-liberal equity means differentiation, dismissal and discipline as the market has been (re)invested with the 'sign of the sacred,'[17] and any 'political' or collective interventions on this sacrosanct terrain are seen as denying the sovereign individual equal and inalienable access to it.

Since 1945 the shades of meaning around 'equity' can be related to the epochs outlined above: to see the general picture contrast Kennedyesque and British Labour Party language, replete with the promise of quick 'modernization' for the third world, with that of Reagan, Thatcher and the concurrent, crisis-laden Berg Report.[18] Then separate these images by some of the radical moments of the sixties and early seventies, when, among other things the World Bank attempted to stave off a 'new international economic order' with the watered-down radicalism of 'basic needs,'[19] and one can perceive the way in which today's notion of (neo-)liberalism has been stripped down from its former version.

The discourse around democracy follows a slightly more complicated path (perhaps because political scientists prevail in this discourse, and they are less prone to unidimensionality than economists), but is nevertheless amenable to this form of analysis. In general terms, the early hopes that liberal democracy (even if they were based on an idealist rendering of its history in the west) would ride on the back of exponential growth were dashed when it was discovered that 'order' was just as often as not rent asunder in such circumstances, and that even in the west the participation of the untutored masses was unpalatable.[20] The brief break of the sixties promised a democratic flowering into 'participation.' Today, the proponents of 'order' have taken the word 'democracy' back on board with their new terminology of 'good governance,' hoping that a resurrection of the formal aspects of liberal democracy can alleviate the strains of newly unleashed market freedoms through a combination of good management principles and enough space for public elite competition[21] – and that such pyrotechnics will hide the fact that political freedom is restricted to those who play to the rules established by the international financial institutions.[22]

Finally, the language of sustainability is older than it appears. Today, the meanings jostling within it stretch from deep ecology to preserving the market from the dangers of environmentalism, 'excess' democracy – and even from pushing the market too fast for its own good.[23] During the latter part of the first post-war phase – not long ago – the term was almost synonymous with 'order:' the hope was for 'sustained growth,' meaning economic growth that would not be destroyed in the entrails of the social chaos it engendered.[24] That meaning has remained, but it has been added to by the environmentalism which emerged in the 1960s and 1970s: today, 'greenwashing' may be the most sustained activity in global capitalism's hegemonic arsenal, as one reads of attempts to keep the environment in a good enough condition to maintain economic growth well into the future – to develop in such a way that the next generations' developmental capacities are not impinged.[25]

Of course, all of these 'buzzwords' can be moored to a conceptual framework outside of the one which has dominated the post-war world: a democratic socialist one, in which public and participatory control over production, surplus, and consumption would enable equality of condition instead of equality of opportunity in the economic sphere, regular and substantive democratic access to politico-economic apparatuses, and careful, non-profit dominated approaches to the delicacy of nature and our relations with it. These notions did make some headway in the transitional period of the sixties – but as many have noted, the ambiguities of that age may well have added to the legitimacy of neo-liberalism as much as they led to a degree of socialism.[26] As neo-liberalism frays at the edges today, there may be a resurgence of such polarities and choices. We just *may* be entering a new transitional phase.

CONTEMPORARY CAPITALISM, 'DEVELOPMENT', AND HEGEMONY

Before further elaborating the above themes it may be wise to remember Marx's and Engels' words marking the start of this chapter. The discourse of institutions devoted to development in the 'third world' are part and parcel of the movement these two 'participant observers' so forcefully described many years ago. International development agencies and university programmes in development studies have made no small contribution to the hegemony of capitalism on a global scale.[27] Most of the people who work within them have promoted the 'moral and intellectual leadership,'[28] of the classes who preside over the global political economy. They are a segment of capital's 'intellectuals,'[29] and with their class-peers in other sectors of society have also organized many of the dull, compulsory economic forces 'freeing' billions from their means of production and reproduction and drawing them into the commodification of everyday life. They have also assisted the orchestration of often brutal political domination accompanying the protracted globalization process. It may well be that the simple insertion of the word 'development' into the lexicon of legitimacy for global capitalism is the single most important facet of its hegemonic project: the notion of development adds much luster to the dream pursued by most of the world today. Coupled with its derivative, 'modernization,' it may well define that illusive image.

Of course, there is a huge difference between the alluring portrayal of capitalism drawn by the development agencies and the picture sketched by Marx and Engels. Lest post-modernists assume that the latter vision is the same as the consumerist cornucopia masquerading as the American dream, let them return to the days in which the words of *The Communist Manifesto* were written: then the 'bourgeois world' – or rather, the world the bourgeoisie was ruling – was not that of leafy off-campus suburbia, but a living hell for most of its partakers. It was only in the very brief post-World War II era that the fruits of capitalism came close to being eaten by all of those fortunate enough to be living in the west. Now that fantasy has dissipated.[30] The real bourgeois world is closer to Calcutta than northern California.[31] Observations and predictions in the Marxist tradition – about uneven and combined development, crises, over-production, the tendency for the rate of profit to fall, capital's obsessive search for new sources of cheap labour and re-valorization,[32] and most importantly of all the struggles waged around and against these processes – have turned out to be surprisingly accurate. In the days when the 'first world' is taking on the attributes of unevenness we have been used to attributing to the 'third world,' it is foolish to place Marx and Rostow on the same intellectual footing.[33] As Giovanni Arrighi has put it, most of the world's people have been proletarianized in the last fifty years, but precious little of the west's wealth has trickled down to them.[34] As far as poverty and inequality go, the first world is becoming more like the third – as is the former 'second,' state-socialist, world. Actually existing capitalism(s)[35] come nowhere near the apparitions offered by the mainstream of western enlightenment.

But the lure of benign and munificent capitalism is still held out. Most of those who work in the many offices and agencies of development are still busily extending the bait to the third world. Even if, as André Gunder Frank has written, 'development' can no longer be a viable buzzword,[36] it still informs the activities of a good number of politicians, bureaucrats, field-workers and grass-roots activists – not to mention the captains of private enterprise and the people who work for them.[37] Those who analyze its discourse should not yet consider themselves archaeologists.[38] As long as capitalism exists and lays ruin to much in its wake, so too will its development agencies. As one might borrow from James Ferguson's *The Anti-Politics Machine*, these agencies will continue to generate their own kinds of discourse, will construct objects of knowledge on them, and intervene accordingly. And in spite of often 'failing,' the machine will continuously expand.[39] While one may wish to start a *history* of development, one should not bury it: development might be entering a new era after its first fifty years and severe indications of crisis, but it is far from dead. Indeed, the neo-liberal wave may have even given orthodox development discourse added impetus. That sort of development discourse is not at an impasse.[40] We are far from entering an era of post-development.[41]

The apparatuses of development will continue to proliferate along with the capitalism of which they are an integral part. Yet while considering this reality it should be remembered that just as capitalism is rife with struggles – indeed, is *formed out* of struggles – so is 'development.' Ferguson illustrates not only that the results of 'development' are the entrenchment of bureaucratic state power and the depoliticization of 'every-thing it touches,' but also that this is a very political and ideological process.[42] This is especially the case as one goes from the 'project' level to that of country level macro-economic programmes – informed by global strategies – which are now the realm of the most important of the development agencies. Indeed, as one surveys the development discourse of the last half-century one can perceive an ideological and political battlefield – carried on inside and outside of development agencies, within and between nations, and by those for and against capitalism. It would be wise not to ignore these battles and their protagonists. It would be astute to pay special attention to struggles for and against 'reform' within the dominant discourses of development,[43] because both reform and reaction are born of clear challenges to orthodoxy and thus imply, in their own ways, revolution.

THE DEVELOPMENT APPARATUSES: CLASS, LOCATION, AND INTERNATIONAL POLITICAL ECONOMY

This chapter proposes to begin an ideological history of development discourse which takes seriously the struggles within it. The framework in which this truncated history will be embedded is outlined in the words of the previous pages: development discourse will be conceived as an integral part of capitalism's organizers' ongoing attempts to gain and maintain hegemony – to make capitalism seem the natural order of things – all over the world. Such a process is inherently contradictory for at least three reasons.

Firstly, all the efforts to make capitalism natural must work to make it appear to be genuinely universal in scope: as long as it promises to improve life-chances for the majority of those under its control, it must deliver. It must be developmental.[44] Secondly, and closely related to the first point, capitalism must be able to incorporate struggles against its worst effects and make its antagonists all the better for it: this is the essence of reform and 'passive revolution.'[45] Otherwise, these struggles must be delegitimized or brutal repression must be resorted to. Part of this second task in the process of gaining and maintaining capitalist hegemony is guiding capitalism out of its many inherent crises, else capitalists and their subordinates alike self-destruct.

The third factor leading to the contradictions of the process of hegemony is the fact that the people who work at its organization do not necessarily make up a coherent and cohesive group. Most hegemonic organizers occupy the social space of what has been vaguely labelled as 'middle class' – that volatile, yet ironically largely bureaucracy-bound, social group occupying an uncomfortable position between capital and labour, core and periphery, powerful and marginalized. The very task of moderating the contradictions between these antagonistic forces is complicated by the fact that the mediating social group is not straightforwardly one or the other. Its alliances cannot be guaranteed – especially during times of crisis – even though most of the time they serve capital's interests very well indeed.[46]

It is not quite enough, then, to nestle a discussion of post-World War II agency and academy development discourse straightforwardly within the vicissitudes of the global political economy. When examining how these ebbs, flows, and crises effect the policies and theories of men and women working in the institutions of development practice and theory, their class position must be accounted for. If the institutional struggles resulting in policy (and even theory) have to be seen as ideological battlefields, the class and spatial context of the terrain must be mapped. Development workers, administrators and teachers are indeed Gramsci's intellectuals, but they are not necessarily of one class. Nor do they come from one place.

Ralph Miliband's analysis can help make sense of the different classes within the corps of development intellectuals.[47] He does not hesitate to use the term 'power elite' – which has lain in disuse among Marxists for quite some time – to describe those at the top of the 'dominant class.' These are the men (and usually they are men) who in the private sector direct the commanding heights of industry and finance. In the public sector they are the presidents, prime ministers, military commanders and directors of development agencies. This conception is compatible with the Gramscian notion that there must be an elite among the members of the fundamental class which can organize society in general and manage the state. It also matches his perception that *most* intellectuals correspond to junior officers in the military.[48] The Barber Conables and Maurice Strongs of the world seem much closer to the category of 'power elite' than they do to the middling intellectual branch of the division of developmental labour.

Miliband, however, has problems with labelling the 'junior officers' of the dominant class as members of anything but the bourgeoisie. Miliband's bourgeoisie is found in the private and public sectors, and many of them appear to fit in with the Gramscian notion of capital's intellectuals. Alongside the owners of medium sized industries are 'professionals' such as 'lawyers, scientists, architects, doctors, middle-rank civil servants and military personnel, senior teachers and administrators in higher education, public relations experts, and many others.' For Miliband these latter make up the 'upper levels of the "credentialized" part of the social structure' and work in the state or the public sector, or independently of either.[49] In the world of development, one would likely put senior administrators, policy analysts, and many highly paid consultants (and are they in the private or public sector?) in this category.

The aspect of 'credentialization' and the fact that many of its members work for a salary suggest to many analysts that this group is not quite 'bourgeois.'[50] However, Miliband is adamant that these people *not* be considered 'middle class' or 'petty bourgeois,' because they have too much power and wealth. It would seem that the lawyers who defend workers, the development administrator who advocates rural revolution, the doctor who is a member of the Communist Party, and the red/green professor are in these spaces through ideology alone – although their slightly ambivalent class position may make it easier for them to identify downward.

For Miliband, the 'petty-bourgeois' members of the salariat are much more likely to have radical propensities. A substantial part of this 'large and constantly growing subclass of semi-professional supervisory men and women . . . social workers, local government officials, and the like' are prone to 'leftist disposition.'[51] Where do we find them in the development apparatuses? They may well take the bottom rung on the ladder, because 'real' workers do not seem to play a very large role in the production of this particular form of activity. The petty-bourgeois or 'middle class' employees of the development business are 'supervisors' as their projects transform the places and people in which and on whom they are implemented, but they are hardly the originators of its rules. Their very physical proximity to the people whose lives they are transforming just may incline them to radical positions, too.

Miliband may well be too cavalier in placing his 'bourgeois' public servants alongside the captains (as opposed to the generals) of medium-sized enterprise. The facts that the conditions of their existence are not contingent upon direct capitalist competition, and that their employees' associations are somewhat related to unions, must make a difference. Perhaps in the current neo-liberal ideological climate, in which the state is being dismantled, the differences will overshadow the similarities within this 'bourgeois' group. In any case, it seems clear that the class nature of the institutions of development are not very different from those of any government agency. However, the very fact that one of their original purposes was of a 'welfarist' nature may lend their workers slightly more left-leaning tendencies than the average governmental agency – at the same time as having less power.[52]

Of course, when one is considering the international nature of the development apparatuses, the usual national basis of class analysis must be modified. As Robert Cox would have it, investigations of development must take into account the internationalization of the state and the 'trans-national managerial class' he teases out of this process.[53] As well, one must also situate development apparatuses – especially 'non-governmental' ones and the lower levels of the official institutions – within the logic of the internationalization of social movements.[54]

When one considers how the global political economy affects class analysis, one must turn to the proximity of development agencies to imperial power. Regardless of their national class composition, the Economic Commissions for Latin America and Africa are bound by their political-geographical situation to be in a relationship of at least some antagonism to institutions emanating from the metropole.[55] To deny this would be to make the baseless assertion that all intellectuals on the periphery are compradors. To assert it is only to suggest that a very large part of the project of western development discourse is to bring third world intellectuals on side.[56] In the west, too, the fact that the World Bank and the International Monetary Fund are located only two blocks away from the White House is no accident and has real consequences.[57] The distance of Swedish and Canadian agencies (for example) from Washington may have some bearing on their discourse, too – especially when the spatial dimension is tied in with their differing political and ideological histories. The various histories of agencies within countries also must be considered: there may be significant contrasts between the United States Agency for International Development (USAID) and the World Bank (not only because the latter is a multi-lateral agency), as there undoubtedly are between the United Nations Development Programme (UNDP) and the same UN's Food and Agriculture Organization. Similarly, in Canada and Sweden the more research oriented International Development Research Centre (IDRC) and the Swedish Agency for Research Cooperation with Developing Countries (SAREC) may have focus at considerable odds with their countries' larger and more orthodox 'aid' agencies, the Canadian International Development Agency (CIDA) and SIDA, its Swedish counterpart. The class make-up of these organizations cannot account for all of their differences, although it certainly can explain much else about them.

As Erik Olin Wright has warned us, political and ideological processes cannot be directly deduced from the class location of their protagonists: the more 'fine grained and concrete the object of explanation . . . the more likely it is that relatively contingent causal processes . . . will loom large in the explanation.'[58] And as one gets closer to the slippery sands of development discourse, it is essential to discern the differences between its academic and policy-making institutions, although there is certainly a great degree of similarity and cross-over between them.[59] It might be instructive to see academic development discourse (ADD in Figure 1.1) as constituting a 'meta-discourse.' In many ways, it has attempted to systematize the practice in the agencies (development agency discourse, or DAD) so that it can be transmitted to new recruits. However, there are certain particularities within the academic realm which militate against a direct conveyance of development agency practice to its apprentices. These specificities may contribute to discursive modification.

The academic intellectual is often mythologized in 'common sense.' He or she is supposed to be aloof from material concerns. Thus the scholar of development studies should be able to distil whatever truths are resident in vulgar development discourse, while weeding out its contradictions and falsities. Fortunately, this ideal does have a small base in reality: as long as academic freedom remains intact, those academics who choose to side with truths residing in social bases outside of the hegemonic blocs will be able to maintain the minimal conditions for reconstructive intellectual activity. Radical academics will be able to discern the contradictions of orthodox development discourse and distil the antagonisms of counter-hegemony, just as do their colleagues down the hall for a much different constituency – the purveyors of passive revolution, the manufacturers of minimal hegemony – in very different ways.

A significant part of the former's task is to take away the clothes of emperor development in order to see that what lies underneath them is the body politic of the global capitalist economy. Some of these insights may work themselves back up through the development apparatuses, especially when the global political economy is in crisis. There, they may be absorbed and deprived of their transformative content, or they may contribute to the popular challenges from which they emerge. This does not mean that the academic intellectual is autonomous, but that he or she studies and distils the social movements' discourse, the forces in the international political economy, and the policy analysis emanating from the development agencies (which in turn reflect and refract the same global transformations) in unique ways – some of which are related to the class position and ideological propensity of the academics, some to the proximity to various development agencies, and some to the rigour and rhythm of the formal process of knowledge production and disciplinary frameworks themselves.

Those who work in the development agencies are much closer than academics to Gramsci's concept of capital's 'organic intellectuals' who plan and organize its encroachments when its hand cannot remain invisible. This function gives them less autonomy than their class peers in the academy (with whom, to be sure, they interact and even change roles). Yet because they must maintain their masters' legitimacy, they must appear to

Figure 1.1 The dynamics of development discourse: international political economy, development agency discourse and academic development discourse

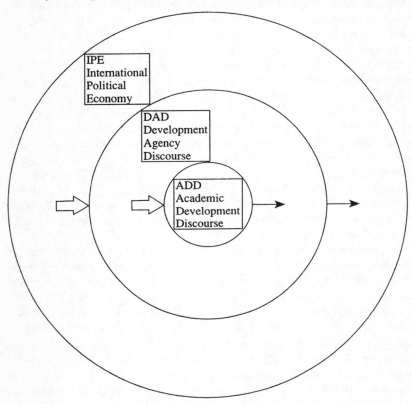

Note: The arrows indicate strength of influence: in general, the global economy and social movements have more influence on agency and academic discourse than *vice versa*, but in some rare instances the flow is altered. In peripheral social formations, for example, the power of DAD is substantial, e.g. structural adjustment loans. And in times of crisis, ADD may have moments of significant power over the direction of DAD, e.g. basic needs and dependency in the 'sixties.'

Source: Thanks to Margaret Anderson, Media Services, Athabasca University, for this diagram.

bend more flexibly with the ebbs and flows of social movements and crisis: with the 'civics' in Alexandria,[60] with human rights advocates in Congress, with the Chipkos in the forests of India,[61] with the protagonists of bread riots and revolutions, with the makers of a New International Economic Order,[62] with the consequences of 'post-Fordism'[63] and the liberalization of international finance.[64]

Thus when one considers the autonomy and power of the development agencies, it is wise to revert more closely to classical imperial and class analysis than when looking at the academy. In that respect it is also wise to remember that if in the west the agencies may seem relatively insubstantial, on the periphery they can rule: if seventy-five per cent of a national economy is derived from 'aid,' its agencies 'call the shots.'[65] If the international financial institutions (IFIs) did indeed 'persuade' more than 25 countries to privatize $137.8 billion worth of assets from 1988 to 1991, if in 1990 they had 60 countries under the discipline of 187 structural adjustment loans, and if they plan to make more loans conditional on 'democratic good governance,'[66] then the IFIs are the orchestrators of many national hegemonies. And if the battles within such agencies are at all decisive, they warrant tracing in their own terms. So do the skirmishes among the academic interpreters of these wars and the larger ones among and between the agencies, the imperial and peripheral states, and the captains of international production and finance. In such a light, the difference between global Keynesianism and neo-liberalism, between an emphasis on human rights and democracy versus the firm hand of authoritarian support for capitalist development, and between 'sustainable' development as opposed to *laissez-faire* environmental disregard could spell the difference between life and death for millions. The logical poles between such alternatives are *usually* not as far apart in the agencies, bound as they are by the pragmatics of every-day hegemonic adjustment, as they are in the academy. During times of crisis, however, the agencies take on a much more ideological hue – while academic discourse, as it reassesses the battleground, takes on the nature of an impasse.[67] The protagonists of combat in the agencies have higher – or at least more immediate – stakes than do their academic counterparts. In the 'real' world of the global political economy, of course, the antithetical forces are furthest apart and the consequences of the fallout are harshest.[68]

SEQUENCES AND FUTURES OF DEVELOPMENT DISCOURSE

It is not enough, then, to situate the shifts in development discourse within transformations in the global political economy. One must analyze *how* both development agency discourse and academic development discourse develop in response to, and affect, the larger realms of society. In any institution, this process is much more complicated than mechanical 'reflection,'[69] but when one considers the interaction between two or more spheres of discourse and practice to see how they affect each other, the process is even more complex. To be sure, a crucial aspect in the analysis of the emergence of a discourse within any one system of institutions will be conditioned by its distance from the 'market,' imperial power, and civil society. The World Bank will be more proximate to the first two segments of global society than the Canadian University Services Overseas (CUSO – an NGO which emerged in the 'sixties' and still has a radical and grassroots approach) will be, but CUSO's access to local civil societies may lend a certain weight, in certain contexts, to its discourse. Universities, with elements of their customary (but diminishing) detachment from all three realms – but well-positioned to quickly extract abstractions from social, political, economic and ideological shifts – should exhibit a unique rhythm of discourse. It should be remembered, too, that no matter what the distance from capital and popular classes, each institutional matrix, and each institution within it, will have its own particular history and dynamic.

The time and space devoted to this chapter disallow such intense scrutiny: such is the work of archival analysis, interviews with crucial actors, deconstruction of academic and institutional texts, and much theoretical fine-tuning. Midway through the first century of 'development discourse' is probably the right historical moment to begin such work. This chapter, however, can only draw a rough scheme for such a task, by attempting to periodize the post-war variations – and continuities – in development discourse in relation to the waxing and waning of the golden age of capitalism.

Arturo Escobar is correct to assert that the very 'system' of development discourse which has emerged in the past fifty years has remained largely invariant[70] – flexible, but bounded by the process of the hegemonic construction and reconstruction of capitalism as well as by its own rules of the technification and de-politicization of the many 'problems' it defines. We are still within the era of 'modernization' in spite of its perpetual postponement. In this chapter, however, it will be assumed that the variegations within the system are worthy of disentanglement – not least because the most promising of these modifications came about because of challenges to the system. Thus, the concern will be with the content of the flexible moments of development discourse.

As outlined in this chapter's introduction, it is possible to ascertain two main phases of development discourse since the end of the second world war, with a transitional one symbolised best by reminiscences of the 'sixties.' Perhaps as the current phase is fraying one can see the beginnings of a new one – bearing many traces from the 1960s – in which 'new social movements' challenge neo-liberalism. These eras do not follow upon each other in clear stages, of course, nor does one phase ever come to a clear end: the later phases maintain many of their predecessors' elements in a subordinated way.

The dominant phases take up almost all of development discourse's history. They follow each other sequentially, and take up roughly equal periods within the last half-century. They can be called 'state-led' and 'market-led,' although these terms simply indicate a shift of balance in emphasis on the public and private sectors, since in each era they are unabashedly capitalist and they imply and rely upon each other.[71] In the era of 'planning' the market was always at the core, just as in spite of its self-abnegating ideology the state is an essential component of any strategy of neo-liberalism. Even though during the market-led era the state is no longer seen as the harbinger of modernization – indeed is seen as its antithesis – it is still relied upon to bulldoze the way to market freedom.[72]

For purposes of rough periodization, the 'state-led' phase can be said to have occurred from 1945 to the early 1970s, while the 'market-led' or neo-liberal phase can be said to have emerged from the crisis beginning in the late 1960s to take steam in the mid-1970s. It gathered full steam in 1980 to continue on to, and probably past, 1995. In the midst of the transition between Phase I and Phase II came the moment of basic needs, participation, and environmental concern.[73] Radical 'dependency' theories in the academy preceded the shift in the central agencies: but these theories grew out of a form of structural-international Keynesianism in a peripheral agency – the Economic Commission for Latin America – as it combined with popular radicalism, so can not be considered a *total* break with the dominant trend.[74] Yet this transitional phase did represent real challenges to the dominant discourse – even though the 'sixties' challenge could be called 'populist.' The imperial agencies were threatened by social movements and political transformation in both the north and south.

Today, some analysts suggest we are on the edge of a 'post-development' era.[75] There is a mix of pessimism and optimism in these projections: grand aspirations for socialism, capitalism or any form of western-style 'development' have been dashed, so it is wise to celebrate the 'marginals' who are able to organize abstemious respite from the global crisis.[76] There is some doubt over whether or not such concerns are new: Ivan Illich, from whom much of this sentiment evolves, has been hovering on the critical margins of development discourse for many decades. In many ways the concerns raised by this convivialist critique hark back to the strain of thought in the 'sixties' which was more dismissive of mass consumerism than the political and economic structures which denied the choice of tasteless gluttony or asceticism to those enmeshed within them.[77] The hopes for a new order based on social movements with more than marginal aspirations and a vibrant 'civil society' may have more substance: certainly, the fact that they are the targets of much hegemonic effort in the IFIs and 'development' agencies would indicate that they have radical potential.[78]

It might be more *à propos* to call the next phase – or transitional moment – one of pseudo-eclecticism. In it, theoretical and political jostling over such issues as sustainable development, state and/or market-led economic policies, and participation (or 'democratic governance'[79]) will take up much of the public stage. The World Bank, the IMF and their lesser kin will appear to take pragmatic and consensual approaches to their hearts, much like in the 1970s, but will rest assured that their real neo-liberal agenda remains intact (perhaps because the challenges to it are not as strong as they were in 1960s and 1970s, when, among other things, the socialist bloc always loomed). Although some of their analyses will point to the state-led development strategies of the Asian 'tigers' as worthy of cross-national consideration, they will pursue what Colin Stoneman has called 'a world-wide market totalitarianism' which at best incorporates fifty per cent of the third world's population (in any case, the NIC answer is highly authoritarian and probably unreplicable).[80] As for more far-reaching challenges, Bjorn Beckman has put it right: the upholders of orthodoxy will reach for hegemonic consensus by drawing on 'radical populist positions, incorporating metaphors of the indigenous, the grassroots, and ... development from below'[81] blending them into the techno-speak of 'sustainable development' and its cousin in the political sphere, 'good governance.'[82]

A multitude of excerpts from the World Bank's *Sub-Saharan Africa: From Crisis to Sustainable Growth* illustrates such linguistic tight-rope walking. Sustainability, equity, and participation are all tied to the imperatives of accumulation and order. *Growth* strategies must be made *sustainable* through sound environmental policies to 'protect the productive capacity of Africa's natural resources.'[83] *Equity* is necessary 'because long-term political stability is impossible without this,' and growth is impossible without a stable social order. However, equity is not to be confused with state or socially-regulated distribution – rather, it can be encouraged by 'improving the access of the poor to productive assets' and moving 'to release the energies of ordinary people by enabling them to take charge of their lives.'[84] The 'focus here is on access to assets and poverty alleviation, not on the distribution of wealth,'[85] the report elaborates, because the latter is tantamount to 'rent-seeking' – the ultimate World Bank sin – instead of the creation of wealth. But how can such access be granted without (re)distribution? The World Bank ideologists insist that dilemma can be overcome: 'by giving the poor access to assets and promoting their productivity, a higher level of growth can be ensured.'

Giving access to productive resources and the means of poverty placation? Surely such a word is not amenable to the cut-and-thrust world of the free market, made up of entrepreneurs who, if one translates from the French, 'enter' and 'take.' If 'giving' mandates a distributional mode, it might also be wise to remember that it also indicates control. It seems that the World Bank and the other international agencies are encouraged to follow its lead (by shifting 'their assistance from . . . projects to financing a 'time-slice' of sectoral or subsectoral programmes'[86]) can *give* popular admission to the means of production and reproduction only by *taking it away* from the state. The populist aspect of this prospect is tied up to the linkage of the state to a vaguely defined 'elite' which has appropriated the 'machinery of government . . . to serve their [*sic*] own interests.'[87] Popular *participation* is implied here: 'ordinary people' the study goes, 'should participate more in designing and implementing development programmes.'[88] However, the World Bank is not about to give the state to these people even though it contends that the state has taken the resources from them. Rather than have the state controlled by the common people, the World Bank would control the local state's withdrawal from the economy. Resources must be taken away from the state and placed in the 'market,' where all citizens will supposedly have equal access to them.

If the 'market' is not there, however, the IFIs will create it. Their intellectuals know that 'in every country the number of people who are inherently entrepreneurial is limited. Market incentives, not innate instincts, are the primary motivations for most entrepreneurs.'[89] To forestall the possibility that 'rent-seeking,' is innate (perhaps only in the third world?) 'capacity-building' in the state has been advocated because Africa needs 'not just less government but better government – government that concentrates its efforts less on direct interventions and more on enabling others to be productive':[90] in other words, a government that can institutionalize market incentives – a state that is the educator. Because local states cannot do this job, the *international* state – i.e. the IFIs – must fill the void. This process is nothing less than re-colonization.

It is hard not to see the ever-pervading influence of modernization theology here: 'development' is still in the hands of a state elite, but this elite must be constantly disciplined in the realities of global capitalism: if the 'market' and 'democracy' do not do the trick, the western development agencies will, by striving to 'channel resources more selectively to the governments that are already implementing reform and making good use of the external assistance they receive,'[91] regardless, one assumes, of the demands of the popular classes, who were supposed to be freed from the state's chains by structural adjustment programmes.

The silences in this discourse are deafening: where are the transnational corporations, which have so much access to productive capacity? Where are the domestic class forces in these social formations? Are the only dominant groups the 'state elite?'[92] Where are local capitalists?[93] Are the 'informal sector' entrepreneurs and small-commodity producing peasants the only dominated classes? How can the working class be ignored when the World Bank examines labour markets – which governments are, of course, encouraged to ignore because 'if left alone, they work well.'[94] Did the state 'interfere' with them by setting minimum wages of its own volition? How can one account for all these vacuums and the resultant contradictions?

Ideological attacks on states are easy, but reforming them to better match the will of capital is a harder task and requires much more delicacy. Ammunition for targeting the state can be easily drawn from the arsenals of neo-classical economics *and* anarcho-populist ideologies.[95] Besides, the very visibility of the state makes it easier to find 'corruption' there than in the 'private' realm of invisible hands hiding the inevitable links between criminality and primitive accumulation of *any* sort. Making the state serve capital better requires a precarious balancing act of opening elite political competition to better keep its members 'honest,' yet keeping the *demos* out so their demands on the state will not crowd out private investment; of slowing down state spending on 'rent-seeking' activity while simultaneously bolstering capacity and thus giving the elite *more* opportunity for self-aggrandizement; and of encouraging the growth of civil society while fearing that such development will lead to popular ideologies seeing the state/capital link and seeking to replace it with one building new bonds between the state and a 'popular' civil society.[96]

It is this last scenario which, of course, is most feared. If the World Bank's advice on *giving* productive access to the 'people' were really taken seriously, the state would be made much more accessible to them than it is now. Indeed, the productive assets of transnational capital would be made available to the people. The fact that the principal on African international debt has been handsomely repaid, while the continent is paying more interest every year than it receives in aid and investment, would be recognised and reversed.[97] The persistently diminishing terms of commodity trade would be faced up to and altered.[98] And, if productive assets were *given* to citizens, they would have to construct an organizational apparatus for their management: they would have to build a *new state*, and it would have to be accountable to them instead of local and international 'elites.'

Even relatively benign versions of liberal democracy leave room for such possibilities, so the econocrats have to fear them. For at least part of democracy's history, the state has been considered as a 'buffer protecting the national economy from disruptive external forces'[99] and as the focal point for the organization and maintenance of domestic employment and welfare. It seems that this is no longer the state's job, so those tasks must be delegitimized. Of course the state will remain, but its job will be that of tailoring discrete geographical and social spaces to the whims of the world economic czars and fashioning a 'civil society' made up of those with interests congruent with 'the global marketplace:'[100] the state will be revamped in global capitalism's image.[101] This renovation will not be an easy task, so international capital would prefer to control it.

'Ordinary people,' then, are to be encouraged to 'participate' but discouraged from congealing into 'radical-populist' social movements considering making alliances coalescing around and permeating the state – especially a state that just might not be strong enough (i.e. have the 'capacity') to absorb any hegemonic challenges posed by such movements. Thus a new emphasis has been broached, combining 'good governance' (better administrative management in the state) with 'participation' in civil society.

As the World Bank is formally restricted to a hands-off approach to politics (at least, 'public (P)olitics') such considerations are left to the bilateral agencies, such as the USAID. According to a paper feeding into the USAID 'Africa Bureau Democracy and Governance Program,' the notion of 'democratic governance' is one way to maintain the balance between popular democracy and prudent capitalist pragmatism.[102] The concept is a remarkable effort to link truly empowering notions of democracy with the fundamental pre-requisite of capitalist growth and the 'order and stability' that the World Bank believes goes along with the accumulation process.[103] According to the consultant's report, the US Foreign Assistance Act requires that all aid activities of the Development Fund for Africa (DFA) be linked to 'producing long-term, sustainable economic development in Africa,' but Congress has included 'qualitative norms, such as social equity and civic participation, as *modifiers* to the DFA's quantitative economic development activities' (emphasis mine). Thus, support for democracy must be 'logically and empirically linked to long-term economic development.'[104] However, the Senior Governance Expert who sold his intellectual labour to USAID is well aware that 'the notions of predictability and effectiveness' which pervade the language of governance and its master-discourse of growth 'do not form an integral part of democratization.'[105] The latter process has much more to do with the 'underlying normative issues involved in the relationship between governors and the governed.'[106]

In order to get around this dilemma, he suggests that strengthening civil society and the many Weberian 'publics' within it will assist in the spreading and legitimization of the 'rules' and values necessary for regime creation and maintenance:[107] in other words, helping a hundred flowers bloom will gain hegemony for the disciplines of the new capitalism. This will occur because the groups benefitting most from the liberalization of civil society will be 'local-level actors, and productive economic actors, such as business associations and farmer groups [which] have frequently been excluded from the policy process in the past.' Their assistance 'will not only strengthen governance, but would likely open up opportunities for better economic decisions.'[108]

In case these public groups will lobby for consumption instead of 'investment, savings and sound fiscal management,' we should remember that preferences for

> government spending, such as expenditures for education, health care, clean water and . . . housing and food subsidies . . . stem from structures of authoritarian, often illegitimate, states which have excluded most societal interests from participation in public policy making, rather than from excessively participatory states.[109]

According to this view, small and medium farmers and 'much of the private sector business community' were excluded from such 'government as patron' mentalities. These groups are likely to be involved in a democratization process, so 'interests representing productive forces in society seem more likely to be able to both [*sic*] demand policy consistent with their interests.' There thus should be no 'fear of the consequences of broadening involvement in policy-making':[110] the unsteady balance has been maintained. Admittedly, this proposition is only a hypothesis, but it is 'worthy of promotion' and can be made self-fulfilling by 'strengthening the advocacy and analytic capabilities of non-governmental organizations, particulary those . . . associated with production.' USAID could also assist such efforts in other sectors of society. In the media, for example, it could 'support training for journalists in covering economic policy issues with greater comprehension and clarity, so that readers can fully understand not only the sacrifices which reform policies entail, but the potential benefits to particular groups in society, particularly to productive groups.'[111] In other words, such training would assist the promulgation of the idea that a short, sharp shock – or maybe even long-term pain – will be (potentially) worth it.

This document takes a small hop of faith, hoping that the flowers of incipient capitalism will crowd out the weeds of rent-seeking. Other USAID documents are even more wary. One cable to missions asking for comments on a background paper on democratization is so bold as to pose this query:

[the paper] also discusses the relationship between political liberalization and economic reform. It argues that the historical evidence on this relationship is mixed, with some cases suggesting that democratization helps economic reform, and others suggesting that it hurts. If your country were to move to a more open political order, do you think it would help or hurt economic reform?[112]

For some members of the World Bank, the answer to that question in the case of Ghana – considered one of their main success stories[113] – is unequivocal:

The military character of the Government made it possible to implement unpopular measures while depressing [sic] dissent. Policy issues have not been openly debated, and freedom of information and publishing rights are restricted. However, Ghana's military leaders have given considerable decision making latitude on economic matters to the highly qualified technical team which was charged with managing the economic reform.[114]

There are few of the self-doubts here which characterise the more political orientation of the USAID reports. To understand the difference between these agencies, one has to go back to an historical investigation of their discursive formation. As Henry Bernstein has mused, much of the USAID work 'attempting to systematise, codify *and* empirically "operationalise" participation in terms of "development management"' was carried out by 'organic intellectual types' in the USAID in the 1970s and 1980s. They could be seen as 'former Peace Corps-niks of the 1960s' going to work with third world peasants while imbued with a 'diffuse student radicalism.' Their 'subsequent writing as development professionals is marked by a kind of sanitised and depoliticized version of Maoism.'[115]

One is forced to return to the original question posed by this chapter. How did development discourse get to this eclectic state? A longer look at the periods of development discourse and its transitional moment is thus warranted. However, to close this section on the current impasse, in which 'diversity' is celebrated while simultaneously being flattened by a politically enforced market, we could consider the possibility that Gustavo Esteva's 'marginals' should be elevated to a majoritarian status, to assume the task of taking over their states rather than simply asking them for due space.[116] That would herald a true post-development era, and it would not be much different from what socialists have always aspired to.

EQUITY, DEMOCRACY, AND SUSTAINABILITY THROUGH THE AGE OF DEVELOPMENT: PHASE I – SETTING THE STAGE

'Planning for the international market' might well have been the slogan for the first phase of the age of development. In the wake of the Marshall Plan, the Soviet-Stalinist model of industrialization, the Cold War, the Chinese revolution, and the emergence of the politically independent 'third world,' western policy-makers – led by the United States – had quite a number of problems facing them as they considered how to deal with the former colonial subjects. The word 'development' was the perfect hegemonic catch-all for capturing the goals and aspirations of all parties to the situation. Its basic elements were constructed in the years between 1945 and 1955.[117] In these years, the whole weight of the emerging development apparatuses was oriented to the creation of the basis for industrialization and the conditions for 'takeoff.'[118] Economics was the 'master science' of such efforts, and in a fundamental sense all the rest of the development enterprise followed from it. If sustainability meant anything it was 'sustained growth.' If 'equity' was thought about at all it was assumed that welfare concerns would be eliminated when the trickles coming down from planned industrial development turned into floods of prosperity. Democracy – meaning liberal institutions of representation – would follow the waves of social modernization incumbent on growth, urbanization, incorporation into the world market, education, geographic mobility, and all the modern values which evolved from capitalist diffusion.[119] It was a hasty evolutionist's dream which would be enabled by

a development plan commonly aimed at a forced take-off and high-speed development, with a large amount of public investment and deliberate industrialization at its core, and [which] supplanted the market mechanism with physical planning that involved the government in numerous decisions of a direct, specific character.[120]

Although seemingly benevolent, such a vision also harboured a socially darwinist edge. This became visible as supposedly 'non-economic barriers' to development emerged.[121] The border between social planning and control was broached within a few years, whereby democracy and 'participation' became a concern. When the promises of kick-started growth began to fade, and the counter-examples of Cuba and Vietnam emerged on the horizon, development analysts began to look more carefully for political and institutional ways of implementing their hopes for sustained growth. When the self-interested yet puritanical *homo economicus* assumed by the economists did not automatically appear, sociologists and psychologists began to analyze the *cultural* preconditions for this ideal type.[122] The search began for 'target groups' amenable to the cultivation of appropriate mores and values. The elites and intellectuals selected for such acculturation were to be isolated from – yet intended to lead – the larger population. Thus even though the ideologies of participation purportedly encouraged democratic processes, its articulators were actually aiming for a form of participation that was restricted to an elite. Therein lies the dilemma of democratic participation and capitalist development: the former is to be encouraged in as much as it facilitates the emergence of capitalists oriented to producing for the world market. If other sorts of people participated, though, the conditions for sustained growth were thought to be imperilled, and 'order' was to be preferred.[123]

In Gramscian terms, the economists' hopes that a bit of economic tinkering would unleash an otherwise spontaneous capitalist 'common-sense' were beginning to be frayed.[124] Sociologists, psychologists, political scientists and even anthropologists were called in to *organize* hegemony – to further institutionalize the naturalization of the capitalist mode of production. With this expansion of the developmental vocation, the academy more firmly joined the World Bank's quickly proliferating missions. With the merging of the disciplines came a congruence of hopes for the economists' plans and the 'softer' social scientists' fears of disorder. An acceptance of authoritarian states was the result, as long as they were oriented toward the sort of liberty inherent in 'the market.'

José Nun's retrospective on 'democracy and modernization' contends that in the post-World War II era, the rise of the Communist bloc and the movement to decolonization led to this great confidence in the state's capacity to programme and lead processes of modernization: in Joel Migdal's phrase, the state was to be the 'tool in the hands of the sculptors.'[125] Nun claims that the third world state was never strong enough for the impatient artists' wishes to be realized. Now they have turned to the market in its purity, hoping that liberal democracy is the best possible shell for it.

Nun's argument may be correct, but it needs a subtle adjustment. The theorists of political and social order needed a strong state for different reasons than did the economists: the former needed to repress dissent while the latter needed an efficient administrative state. The authoritarian state may have been too weak to usher in the market and to keep corrupt rent-seekers at bay, but it also threatened to be too strong. If it had combined with the anti-capitalist social and political forces emerging in the 1960s and 1970s its possible strengths could have been arrayed against the market *and* the compradorian groups in the state. The state was potentially emerging as a force poised against capital. From guerrilla movements in southern Africa to the prospects of OPEC and a New International Economic Order led by the likes of Julius Nyerere, by the mid-1970s the state forces of the third world did not look weak.

It must be remembered, too, that development discourse does not only derive from conditions in the third world. The global guardians of order feared western anti-free market propensities too: the Trilateral Commission's *The Crisis of Democracy*, written by famed third world analyst / Vietnam strategist Samuel Huntington and two other conservative political scientists, warned that an 'excess' of democracy in the advanced capitalist countries had 'increased demands on government for services' while simultaneously challenging and weakening government authority. These inflationary demands 'overloaded' the state, and could only be abated by 'a degree of political demobilization of those 'marginal' groups that were pressing new demands.'[126] The ideological nature of such prognoses can be seen if one turns the notion of 'overload' on its head: in actuality, the state and the 'marginal' groups pressuring it (and were students – the vanguard of middle-class society – really marginal?) were gaining power over capital. The state was becoming *transformed* rather than 'overloaded.' It was *overloaded* only if one believed it should have solely the powers of Adam Smith's (very male) night-watchman. It was in the process, however, of being recast into a much more economically powerful apparatus. It was being remade into something exceeding the post-war Keynesian compromise. The state may have been losing the authority to say no to the demands made on it, but that simply meant that it was being more accountable to citizens than in the past. In the process the people and their state were gaining power over the market. This is what concerned the Trilateral Commission's rapporteurs. The students, who stood to gain the state within a decade or so, were poised on the verge of an alliance with 'marginal groups' in the west and in the third world. A new historic bloc was in the offing, and the preservers of the old had to put a stop to it – in all the regions of the world. Their solution marked the end of the first phase of development discourse.

CRISIS AND TRANSITION: DEPENDENCY AND BASIC NEEDS

The crisis in development discourse that came out of the 1960s was more complicated than the Huntington report indicated. Its roots were in the profound alteration in the global political economy based in the shift from 'Fordist' to 'post-Fordist' production, the decoupling of finance from industrial capital, the relative decline of the US economy, and the more immediate ramifications of the increases in the price of oil in 1974 and again in the late 1970s.[127] Added to those worries were the increasing number of third world countries who were able to utilize the low interest rates and aggressive marketing of loans afforded by private banks to finance their own state-capitalist projects and programmes,[128] and the increasingly threatening prospect of revolutions in the third world. From Iran to Nicaragua to Zimbabwe, it looked like the dominoes were falling away from the free-market model and towards the other side of the Cold War dichotomy.[129]

In the realm of academic development discourse, dependency theory imparted a sense of the changes occurring in the emerging challenges in post-war social and political practice. Its radicalization and popularization of Raùl Prebisch's ECLA critique emphasizing the secular trend of deteriorating terms of trade between the developed and the underdeveloped worlds – itself a sort of logical extension of the international Keynesianism which grew out of the post-war compromise and the emphasis on state-aided accumulation which grew out of it – could have led to a far-reaching rethinking of how to use the state more effectively. Instead, its odd combination of the determinacy of global exchange relations and the voluntarist alternatives it implied left little room for the sort of real activity which had allowed it the space to emerge: the poles it implied left little leeway for manoeuvring in the middle spaces.[130] It was ironic that dependency's radical pessimism came onto the scene just as concerted action on the periphery was changing the global order. Perhaps its theoretical closure hindered the furtherance of such change: as it was, the World Bank's meagre efforts to co-opt 'basic-needs' ideas and the later impositions of neo-liberalism met little real resistance. Theories of 'dependent development,' which reflected more actual activity in the periphery and thus might have led to its deepening, were wiped out in the clash of polar opposites.[131]

Coincidentally, the major radical critiques of dependency theory also shared a debilitating determinism. Modes of production analysis and Warrenite 'free-market socialism' shared with dependency a mirror-image of reactionary 'futility, perversity and jeopardy' arguments against reformist or progressive change.[132] As with much western leftist theory, these theories' lack of ability to conceptualize what might now be called 'structural reform' allowed the monetarist critique to enter and fill the vacuum.[133]

Yet it must be remembered that what seems like determinism today was radical voluntarism in the sixties. If the structures of capitalism were seen as immutable to reform, they were also perceived to be amenable to complete, and necessary, transformation. At the same time as radical theory was unintentionally contributing to the erasure of radical praxis, it was growing out of that sort of activity occurring on the ground. The discursive practice of participation and sustainability was a key part of the social movement which culminated in Paris's May 1968. As noted before, the likes of Che Guevera, Ho Chi Minh and Nelson Mandela from the third world had great influence on these western events – their personalities, along with Daniel Cohn-Bendit, Abbie Hoffman, and Rudi Dutschke, seemed to symbolize a *longue durée* of liberation.[134] The efforts of capital's hegemonic organizers to bring these transformations into its orbit varied from American Community Action Programmes, started in 1964 at home[135] to the Peace Corps abroad, and to the 1972 UN Conference on the Environment at Stockholm.[136] The World Bank's linguistic conversion to the philosophy of 'basic needs' was also part of the recognition of the threat of these practices.

It was not inevitable that basic needs projects at the World Bank were turned into 'an international welfare programme to be carried out as far as possible by the poor themselves' so they would not rely on the state and capital to recompense their marginalization.[137] Nor was it foreordained that the discourse of 'participation' and sustainability would be rhetorically neutered.[138] The combination of the proliferation of development agencies[139] and liberatory social movements could well have maintained a far-reaching institutional restructuring process. What stopped it was not liberal co-optation alone, but a radical and reactionary reversal symbolized by the ideologies of Reaganism and Thatcherism, and legitimized by what James Ferguson has called the 'scientific capitalism' of the international financial institutions.[140] The guardians of political order and financial freedom feared that the soft liberal techniques of hegemonic absorption were not enough: if the liberals were going to replace the ten troops-per-guerrilla of the old counter-insurgency formula with ten anthropologists, the neo-liberals planned on a dozen economists – with the military in the very visible backgrounds of Grenada and the Gulf area.[141] For them, co-optation looked like appeasement and even surrender, in spite of the fact that for many radicals it looked like defeat.

There was no precise linear logic to this shift away from the sixties and early seventies. Its hegemonic origins may have emerged in the academy – as well as in the apparatuses of state and influence[142] situated 'above' the development agencies – rather than within the circles of development agency discourse themselves. As Cammack points out, US policy-making circles got around to committing to political participation just '*after* the analysts of democracy had adopted *en masse* a strongly revisionist account which saw it as the greatest danger to stability and US influence abroad.'[143] This was not simply a co-optive reaction, but, given the laggardness of government responses to social movements, more likely a delayed reflection and refraction of these societal forces. It was these indications of democracy's strengthened institutionalization which the apostles of order felt led to the undermining of authority and the ungovernability of society.

Alongside the 'loose-living' of participatory democrats so worrisome to the old guard was the 'loose-lending' which threatened the finances of the global system.[144] That the latter was instigated by the transnational rulers rather than the former's international insurgency made it no less critical. It is only ironic that the hegemonic organizers used real conservatism on the democrats while only appearing to shackle global financial laxity: such is, one supposes, the essence of the compatibility of neo-conservative politics and neo-liberal economics. In any case, the impact of radical ideologies within the official development apparatuses was soon removed: as Lehman has put it, by the early 1980s the people who pursued 'the idle talk about income distribution and 'basic needs' which MacNamara and Chenery had tolerated, if not at one stage actually encouraged' were turfed out of the World Bank's research wing'[145] while senior policy planners promulgating the 'liquidation of the privileged groups and vested interests' resigned.[146]

As with the discourse of participation, it is hard to discern whether the post-1960s origins of neo-liberal development economics came first from the academy or the agency. If the example of one very influential intellectual is anything to go by, the roots are in many soils: Elliot Berg, the author of the foundational *Accelerated Development in Sub-Saharan Africa: An Agenda for Action*, was an academic just before taking on the World Bank job to write the report that now carries his name, so it is fair to say that the ideas for the vast programmes of structural adjustment he has instigated percolated in the university, amidst the stalemating of *dependencia* alternatives and the steadfastness of the long-established traditions of the P.T. Bauers and Harry Johnsons – while, of course, the wider ideologies of the new global economy permeated the walls of the ivory towers more than ever before.[147]

The discourse of sustainability never did seem to establish clear academic beachheads,[148] so the battles over its hegemonic articulation have been waged more on the ships of Greenpeace, in Mobil Oil's glossy advertisements, in environmental hearings,[149] and within state agencies than in the university. The World Bank has maintained the same sort of contradictions in this realm as it has on democracy and equity: it is clear that its agenda closely matches the concerns presciently, if cumbersomely, articulated by the 1979 meeting of the Woodlands Conference group, which decided that 'the quest for the sustainable society is finding ways to make complex decisions that do not require government to handle all aspects of governance for a necessarily pluralistic society in an increasingly interdependent world.'[150]

PHASE II: NEO-LIBERALISM, ECLECTICISM, AND TOWARDS A CONCLUSION

No radical who takes a cool look at the tenacity and pervasiveness of dominant ideologies could possibly feel sanguine about what would be necessary to loosen their lethal hold. But there is one place above all where such forms of consciousness may be transformed almost literally overnight, and that is in active political struggle. This is not a Left piety but an empirical fact. When men and women engaged in quite modest, local forms of political resistance find themselves brought by the inner momentum of such conflicts into direct confrontation with the powers of the state, it is possible that their political consciousness may be definitely, irreversibly altered . . . such death-dealing beliefs may be practically affected.[151]

This essay has already considered the current phase of development discourse in some detail. One must conclude that – if one is concerned to construct a future in which the capabilities[152] of all the world's citizens are enhanced – it is still at an impasse.[153] The advertised goals of modernization have not been reached, be the means for them state or market led. When state-led methods threatened to turn the whole project on its head, they were abandoned. Yet the legacies of the turned heads live on, resulting in widespread critical recognition of the intricate, if complicated, realities involved in the linkages between the 'local and the global.' The task is to widen that recognition so that it can threaten the hegemony of the status-quo, to further the realization for the oppressed groups and classes making up so much of the 'new world order' that 'without grasping something of their own material location within a wider system, they will never be effectively able to realize their highly specific interest in emancipation.'[154]

Contrary to James Manor's post-modernist claims about the contributors to *Rethinking Third World Politics*, we *are* 'interested here in influencing the countries [and institutions and people] we are studying.'[155] The onus is thus upon us to pull out the radical tensions within the buzzwords of development discourse in such a way that they cannot be re-incorporated into the hegemony of the status-quo. If Terry Eagleton's above words are anything to go by, we must push the discourse of 'participation' to its extreme.[156] If this responsibility can be met, the corpse-producing ways in which the abstractions of equity and sustainability have been misrepresented can be reversed too.

Advocating participation means using the state's (i.e. the agencies and institutions working within its international and national ambits) still intact capacity as 'educator' to further popular struggles for equity, democracy and sustainability.[157] This is particularly the case when the 'state' posited by Eagleton is becoming increasingly fragmented. As it splinters into international and local fragments that make Jean-François Bayart's portrayal of the African state look universal,[158] we have to use what is still left of it to pull its internationalization away from capital and to (the admittedly 'populist' notion of) 'the people.' During this process we can only hope that it will be strengthened, to meet their demands of accountable accumulation,[159] to facilitate the true opening of the hegemonic quest,[160] and to put a halt to a process which is making us all live in the 'third world.'[161]

Most of the readers of this book are residents of that uncomfortable social space best defined by a combination of Miliband's and Gramsci's analysis. We are 'bourgeois organic intellectuals' – albeit in the subordinate and ever-slipping ranks – try as we might to conceptualize ourselves out of that social category. But no social analysis can proscribe ideological and political choice.[162] Thus, we can facilitate movement towards the greater flowering of the liberal political dream promised by socialism. If we do not, and yet continue to espouse the values of democracy, we risk falling into Timothy Findley's vicious trap: we will be 'lying . . . lying and afraid we'll be found out. So afraid, in fact, that most of our days [will be] taken up compounding the lies we told the day before.'[163]

Notes

1. Karl Marx and Friedrich Engels, 'The Communist Manifesto,' in Robert Tucker (ed.), *The Marx–Engels Reader*, 2nd Ed. (New York: W.W. Norton, 1978), p. 477. I have chosen to mark the beginning of the modern age of development with 1945 because it was after the close of World War II that the United States began to seriously consider the third world and its relationship to the new hegemon's desire for an international capitalist order. See Robert Wood, *From Marshall Plan to Debt Crisis: Foreign Aid and Development Choices in the World Economy* (Berkeley: University of California Press, 1986) pp. 34–60 and *passim*. Of course, there was much 'development discourse' during the colonial age, too.

2. To avoid a long discussion of the meaning of 'discourse' I will subsume it under the phrase 'practice and theory' – material activity which transforms nature and society and the modes of thought that inform this action at the same time as they arise out of it – simply to indicate that one does not transpire without the other and that a 'base and superstructure' metaphor is too simple. In earlier days the word might have been 'praxis.' See Terry Eagleton, *Ideology: An Introduction* (London: Verso, 1991) p. 73.

    In this essay the weight of analysis will rest on the ways in which the practice of development (meaning both the 'development' that goes on as a particular activity of those transforming the 'third world,' especially those who work in agencies and institutions constructed specifically for this task, *and* the more depersonalized and systematized way in which the process of capitalist 'development' more or less spontaneously occurs, albeit with emphasis on the former) has been reflected upon, synthesized, and systematized. In this sense, the way in which the chapter precedes is closer to an ideological analysis than an examination of practice, but the 'discourse' referred to is much closer to the particularities of the development apparatuses than the much wider concept of ideology ever could be. Discourse remains much closer to the practices of discrete institutions, the struggles within them, and their 'micro-power' than is ideology. This elaboration of the term is still very tentative and preliminary. For some assistance with it I thank Henry Bernstein (written communication, 7 January 1992).

3. The term 'hegemony' and its descriptors come from Antonio Gramsci, *Selections from the Prison Notebooks* (ed. and trans. Quinton Hoare and Geoffrey Nowell-Smith) (New York: International Publishers, 1971). For Robert W. Cox, one of the first and most influential theorists to work with this notion in international relations, 'this is the meaning of hegemony: the temporary universalization of a particular power structure conceived not as domination but as the necessary order of nature' (from 'Production and Hegemony: Toward a Political Economy of World Order,' in Harold K. Jacobson and Dusan Sidjanski (eds), *The Emerging International Economic Order: Dynamic Processes, Constraints, and Opportunities* (Beverly Hills: Sage, 1982), p. 38). To suggest that a social order appears to be 'natural' does not mean that it is universally liked or admired, but that it seems to be immutable and serves to '*frame* all competing definitions of the world within *its* range', J. Clarke *et. al.*, 'Subcultures, cultures, and class,' in Stuart Hall and T. Jefferson (eds), *Resistance through Rituals* (London: Hutchinson,

1976), p. 39; also, importantly, Stuart Hall, *The Hard Road to Renewal: The Challenge of Thatcherism* (London: Verso, 1988).
4. For attempts to conceptualize the notion of hegemony on a global scale, see Robert W. Cox, *Production, Power, and World Order: Social Forces in the Making of History* (New York: Columbia University Press, 1987); Stephen Gill and David Law, *Global Political Economy: Perspectives, Problems, and Policies* (Baltimore: Johns Hopkins University Press, 1989); Stephen Gill (ed.), *Gramsci, Historical Materialism and International Relations* (Cambridge: Cambridge University Press, 1993). Many essays in Richard Stubbs and Geoffrey R. D. Underhill (eds), *Political Economy and the Changing Global Order* (Toronto and London: McClelland and Stewart and Macmillan, 1994) also share this perspective.

One can offer several indicators of the increasing dominance of global capital in the world economy: William Drozdiak, 'Uncertainty Greets Signing of Trade Treaty,' *Manchester Guardian Weekly* (April 24, 1994), p. 19, writing of the signing-off in Marrakesh of the Uruguay Round of the General Agreement on Tariffs and Trade (GATT) discussions, notes that in 1947, when the GATT was established, world trade was worth $25 billion – and the United States controlled half of it. Now, world commercial exchanges total over $3,600 billion (or $3.6 trillion) and the USA is involved in less than 15 per cent of them. Harry Magdoff, 'Globalisation: To What End?' *New World Order? Socialist Register 1992* (London: Merlin Press, 1992), pp. 47, 59, notes the increasing dominance of global finance capital by recounting that 'the London Eurodollar market, in which the world's financial institutions borrow and lend to each other, turns over $300 billion each working day, or $75 trillion a year, a volume at least 25 times that of world trade' and that 'foreign exchange transactions . . . in which one currency is traded against another . . . run around $150 billion a day, or about $35 trillion a year, 12 times the worldwide trade in goods and services . . . Capital movements unconnected to trade – and indeed largely independent of it – greatly exceed trade finance.' Tom Athanasiou, 'After the Summit,' *Socialist Review*, 22, 4 (October–December 1992), pp. 66–7, summarizes the current status of transnational corporations (TNCs):

> TNC activities involve a quarter of the world's productive assets, 70 per cent of the assets in world trade, the majority of international financial transactions, and the lion's share of the world's advanced technology . . . in the early 1980s, internal transfers within the 350 largest corporations already accounted for about 40 per cent of total world trade, and . . . 70 per cent of all trade was controlled by only 500 corporations . . . TNCs control 80 per cent of the land that globally is given to large-scale export agriculture, land that has often been taken over from local food production . . .

During the 1980s, 'foreign direct investment throughout the world increased at three times the rate of growth for world trade and four times that of world output.' Mel Watkins, 'Foreign Ownership '94 – Buy, Bye Canada,' *This Magazine*, 27, 8 (April–May 1994), p. 30.

5. One cannot fail to notice how Frans Schuurman (ed.), *Beyond the Impasse: New Directions in Development Theory* (London: Zed Press, 1993) seems – in spite of its welcome updating of the discipline – but a belated effort within development studies to recognize the impact of the theory and practice of post-modernism and new social movements in the social sciences: must development studies remain a depository of academic trickle-down? Perhaps ironically, some of the contributors' celebrations of 'diversity' in the field seem to have replicated post-modernism's tendency to forget capital's own tendencies to afford 'no alternatives,' while caricaturing those who insist on accounting for the unidimensional reality of global capital's streamrolling structural adjustment programmes as 'essentialist and economically reductionist.' (See David Booth, 'Development Research: From Impasse to New Directions,' p. 55, criticizing Henry Bernstein, 'Agricultural "Modernisation" and the Era of Structural Adjustment: Observations on Sub-Saharan Africa,' *Journal of Peasant Studies*, 18, 1 (October 1990), pp. 3–35.) Yet the contributor who is the strongest advocate of 'bottom-up' analysis and local action explicitly recognises that the 'essentialist' theoretical proposition asking 'who owns the means of production' is valid (Michael Edwards, 'How Relevant is Development Studies?' pp. 84–5). A general question for the advocates of the 'actor' approach in this sort of analysis might be: why not analysis based on 'struggle'? For one interesting work based on this perspective, see Patrick Bond and Mwazinele Mayekiso, 'South African Civic Associations and International Urban Social Movements,' Report to Einstein Institute, Project on Civil Society, May 1994.

6. For some efforts of Canadian political economists to disentangle this era and map a post-Fordist political economy, see Jane Jenson, Rianne Mahon, and Manfred Bienefeld (eds), *Production, Space, Identity: Political Economy Faces the 21st Century* (Toronto: Canadian Scholars' Press, 1993), and Daniel Drache and Meric Gertler (eds), *The New Era of Global Competition: State Policy and Market Power* (Montreal and Kingston: McGill-Queen's Press, 1991). On aid regimes in the global political economy, see the excellent Robert E. Wood, *From Marshall Plan to Debt Crisis: Foreign Aid and Development Choices in the World Economy* (Berkeley: University of California Press, 1986). A more wide-ranging analysis of post-Fordism and postmodernity is David Harvey, *The Condition of Postmodernity: An Inquiry into the Origins of Cultural Change* (Oxford: Basil Blackwell, 1989).

7. So much so that E.A. Brett can say that 'in the 1950s we were all (or almost all) socialists' (except for the Americans). E.A. Brett, 'States, Markets and Private Power: Problems and Possibilities,' in Paul Kirk and Colin Kirkpatrick (eds), *Privatization in Less Developed Countries* (New York: St. Martin's Press, 1988), p. 49.

8. The term 'third world' is placed in quotation marks here to indicate that it is very much a socially and politically constructed notion, marked by as much heterogeneity as homogeneity. Nevertheless, it may be possible to say that a fundamental similarity among 'third world' countries rests in the fact that most of their citizens lack the basic essentials of health and longevity most people in the 'first world' take for granted as 'basic needs.' There will be no consistent marking of the phrase throughout the chapter. For a 'history' of the notion of the Third World in social science, see Carl E. Pletsch,

'The Three Worlds, or the Division of Social Scientific Labour, circa 1950–1975,' *Comparative Studies in Society and History*, 23 (October 1981), pp. 565–90.

9. Those who contend (because Bill Clinton is president of the United States, perhaps) that we are now in a post-neo-liberal phase have only to turn to Roger Douglas, *Unfinished Business* (Auckland: Random House, 1993) to see what the future income tax and welfare-state-less world will look like if the ex-finance minister of New Zealand and current globe-trotting World Bank consultant has his way.

10. David R. Marples, 'Money, Muscle and the Mafia – driving forces of the Russian economy,' *Edmonton Journal* (May 14, 1994), p. A8; Seymour Hersch, 'The Wild East,' *Atlantic Monthly* (June 1994), pp. 61–86, on the consequences of unleashing a free market before constructing the social and political conditions in which it can safely operate (paraphrasing Stephen Handelman in *Foreign Affairs*, March–April 1994). One of these repercussions is the entry of a loosely-guarded nuclear stockpile into the 'global market.'

11. Cranford Pratt is one of the more persuasive chroniclers of the demise of the humanitarian motivation in foreign aid in Canada. See his edited *Canadian International Development Assistance: An Appraisal* (Montreal and Kingston: McGill-Queen's University Press, 1994).

12. Stephen A. Marglin and Juliet B. Schor (eds), *The Golden Age of Capitalism: Reinterpreting the Postwar Experience* (Oxford: Clarendon Press, 1990).

13. The words have been attributed to Margaret Thatcher.

14. See Jonathan Barker, 'Solidarity in a New Key: The Reflections of a Bespectacled Solidarity Supporter,' *Southern African Report*, 7, 4 (March 1992), pp. 3–8; Judith Marshall, 'Keeping Pace: Solidarity Work and the New Globalism,' *Southern African Report*, 9, 4 (March 1994), pp. 9–13, for some thoughtful approaches to Western NGO work in the present era.

15. This chapter began as an investigation of the words 'sustainable growth, equity and participation' in the International Development Research Centre's (IDRC – Ottawa) *Programme and Policy Review: VIII. 1987–88 – 1990–1* (Ottawa: IDRC, 1986), but the terms are widespread. The World Bank's *Sub-Saharan Africa: From Crisis to Sustainable Growth. A Long-Term Perspective Study* (Washington: The World Bank, 1989) emphasises the term sustainable growth with equity, supplemented by the participatory aim 'to release the energies of ordinary people by enabling them to take charge of their lives' (p. 4). This report's words on states' capacities to implement structural adjustment programmes also initiated the current concern with 'governance.' The World Council of Churches – perhaps an institution with more moral authority, but less power, than the World Bank – also envisages an economic order that is 'just, participatory, and sustainable' (Herman E. Daly and John B. Cobb, Jr., with contributions by Clifford W. Cobb, *For the Common Good: Redirecting the Economy toward Community, Environment and a Sustainable Future* (Boston: Beacon Press, 1989, p. 20). The IDRC's guiding words from 1991 until the time it was anointed the Canadian government's implementing agency for the United Nation's Conference on the Environment and Development's post-Rio 'Agenda 21' were 'Empowerment Through Knowledge.' See James Petras,

'The Metamorphosis of Latin America's Intellectuals,' *Latin American Perspectives*, 17, 2 (Spring 1990), pp. 102–12, for some thoughts on 'knowledge for whom?'

16. In noting the potential of significant reform within prevailing notions of development, I contend that variations within development discourse's 'system of meanings' are worthy of note: the social-democratic hues of the first half of development's short history are preferable to the contemporary neo-liberal orthodoxy on their own terms, and also because they leave much more room for the social and political projects which portend their expansion. This approach is in some, but not total, contradistinction to that of Arturo Escobar, whose system of post-war development discourse – including Marxism and neo-Marxism at times – is a practically seamless fragment of modernism. It is simply to say that neo-liberalism allows less room for the construction of progressive 'post-modernist' spaces than does social democracy. See Arturo Escobar, 'Discourse and Power in Development: Michel Foucault and the Relevance of His Work to the Third World,' *Alternatives*, 10 (Winter 1984–85), his doctoral thesis, 'Power and Visibility: The Invention and Management of the Third World,' University of California at Berkeley, 1987, and his 'Imagining a Post-Development Era? Critical Thought, Development and Social Movements,' *Social Text*, 31/32 (1992), pp. 20–56. For a sensitive discussion of the variances between 'reform' in the interests of preserving a crisis-ridden capitalism versus 'structural reform' which advances the prospects of radical social transformation, while recognizing the fact that social democratic reforms are too easily co-opted and also that in these times a revolutionary overthrow of capitalism is a pipe-dream, see John. S. Saul, 'South Africa: Between "Barbarism" and "Structural Reform",' and 'Structural Reform: A Model for the Revolutionary Transformation of South Africa?', in *Recolonization And Resistance In Southern Africa In The 1990s* (Toronto and Trenton, New Jersey: Between the Lines Press and Africa World Press, 1993), pp. 89–169. Also published in *New Left Review*, 188 (July–August 1991) and *Transformation*, 20 (1992).

17. David Slater, 'The Political Meanings of Development: In Search of New Horizons,' in Frans Schuurman (ed.), op. cit., pp. 94, 98.

18. World Bank, *Accelerated Development in Sub-Saharan Africa: An Agenda for Action* (Washington: World Bank, 1981) – commonly named after its author, Dr. Elliot Berg. See Henry Bernstein, op. cit., p. 5, for an indication of how the data in Africa (and the case may well be so for other third world social formations) can support a myriad of ideological positions, and thus feed into notions of 'crisis' at the author's will.

19. Robert Cox, 'Ideologies and the New International Economic Order: Reflections on Some Recent Literature,' *International Organization*, 33, 2 (Spring 1979), p. 271 and *passim*.

20. Samuel Huntington, *Political Order in Changing Societies* (New Haven: Yale University Press, 1968). See the classic critique of Huntington and company, Donal Cruise O'Brien, 'Modernization, Order, and the Erosion of a Democratic Ideal,' *Journal of Development Studies*, 7 (1971), pp. 141–60, as well as Mark Kesselman, 'Order or Movement? The Literature of Political Development as Ideology,' *World Politics*, 26 (1973), pp. 139–54; Colin Leys, 'Samuel Huntington and the End of Classical Modernization Theory,'

in Hamza Alavi and Teodor Shanin (eds), *Introduction to the Sociology of 'Developing Societies'* (New York: Monthly Review Press, 1982), pp. 332–349. Noam Chomsky, 'The Struggle for Democracy in the New World Order,' in Barry Gills, Joel Rocamora and Richard Wilson (eds), *Low Intensity Democracy: Political Power in the New World Order* (London: Pluto Press, 1993), pp. 80–83, unravels what the advocates of liberal democracy in the West have meant all along. Leonard Binder, 'The Natural History of Development Theory,' *Comparative Studies in Society and History*, 28, 1 (January 1986), pp. 3–33, offers a somewhat apologetic survey. The first post-1960s fears about ungovernability in the west and Japan were raised in Michel J. Crozier, Samuel P. Huntington, Joji Watanuki, *The Crisis of Democracy: Report to the Trilateral Commission* (New York: New York University Press, 1975).

21. See Gerald J. Schmitz 'Democratization and Demystification', Chapter 2 in this volume.
22. See Manfred Bienefeld, Chapter 3 in this book.
23. Michael Redclift, *Sustainable Development: Exploring the Contradictions* (London: Methuen, 1987). Timothy O'Riordan, 'The Politics of Sustainability,' in R. Kerry Turner (ed.), *Sustainable Environmental Management: Principles and Practice* (London: Belhaven Press, 1988), pp. 29–50.
24. S. N. Eisenstadt, 'Modernization and Conditions of Sustained Growth,' *World Politics*, 16, 4 (July 1964), pp. 576–94.
25. Such is the language of the World Commission on Environment and Development, *Our Common Future* (Oxford: Oxford University Press, 1987), commonly called the 'Brundtland Report,' after its chair, Gro Brundtland. For an update on activities inspired by the Commission, see Linda Starke, *Signs of Hope: Working Towards our Common Future* (Oxford: Oxford University Press, 1990). See Tom Athanasiou 'After the Summit', *Socialist Review*, 22, 4 (October–December 1992), pp. 57–92 for a pithy account of corporate activity at the United Nations Conference on Environment and Development (UNCED) in Rio de Janeiro in June 1992.
26. E. A. Brett, op. cit., p. 47, notes that a close look at the 1960s reveals that rather than a 'period of freedom and irresponsibility when the radical challenge to the dominance of capitalist structures was at its most extreme' these years 'introduced a much more significant shift in attitude, and one which was, in fact, to reaffirm rather than undermine the logic of the capitalist order.' Perhaps the 'irresponsibility' Brett alleges also bolstered the logic of the 'free market,' wherein one has only responsibility for one's self. Socialism surely can not abide by such dereliction of obligation to and trust in others.
27. Graham Hancock's scathing but unmoored *Lords of Poverty* (London: Mandarin, 1989), pp. 42–5, puts the monetary impact of Official Development Assistance (ODA) in a comparative perspective. Using disparate sources of data, he estimates that between $45 and $60 billion per annum go into the coffers of official aid bureaucracies (i.e. multi- and bi-lateral organizations that, in the words of the UN Charter, assist the Third World's quest to 'create social progress and better standards of life in larger freedom . . .' with loans and grants of a concessional nature, and not including non-governmental organizations). This ranks the development business higher than IBM or Unilever, but is about one-twelfth the amount of money spent

by the USA and the USSR on arms per annum in the 1980s. If all the annual
incomes of the USA's millionaires in the early 1980s were added up – and
it was assumed their annual incomes were only $1 million – their net worth
would be approximately eighteen times more than global ODA. (And that
statistic is culled from data compiled before Reaganite policies led to creation of many more American millionaires.)

28. Gramsci, op. cit., p. 57.

29. For Gramsci, op. cit., the key actors involved in the organization of hegemony are the 'intellectuals:' the 'entire social stratum which exercises an
organizational function in the wide sense – whether in the field of production,
or in that of culture, or in that of political administration' (p. 97) and which
comes into existence simultaneously with the fundamental classes, giving
them

> homogeneity and an awareness of [their] own function not only in the
> economic but also in the social and political fields. The capitalist entre-
> preneur creates alongside himself the industrial technician, the specialist
> in political economy, the organisers of a new culture, of a new legal
> system, etc. . . . If not all [members of the fundamental class], at least an
> elite among them must have the capacity to be an organizer of society
> in general, including all its complex of services, right up to the state
> organism (p. 5).

Section iii below will elaborate on the notion of 'intellectuals', paying heed
to the complication that now many intellectuals are 'middle class' rather
than unambiguously bourgeois or working class.

30. For some sobering statistics, see Martin Walker, 'American dream that
became a nightmare,' *Manchester Guardian Weekly*, 148, 1 (January 3,
1993), p. 1. For theoretical explanations, see Stephen A. Marglin and Juliet
B. Schor, op. cit. Aside from the question of whether capitalism could
produce a first-world style of life for all people, Vittorio Hösle reminds us
that if all the world's people 'consumed as much energy as the average
European and North American, numerous eco-systems would have already
collapsed,' Vittorio Hösle, 'The Third World as a Philosophical Problem,'
Social Research, 59, 2 (Summer 1992), p. 247.

31. I make the geographical distinction regarding California because Los Angeles and much of southern California cannot be taken to represent the American dream any more, in spite of the fact that most of the images of that
fantasy are manufactured there. According to many northern Californians,
the myth may still have a basis in reality there. For Los Angeles, see Mike
Davis, 'Who Killed LA? A Political Autopsy,' *New Left Review*, 197 (Janu-
ary/February 1993), pp. 3–28; 'Who Killed Los Angeles? Part Two: The
Verdict is Given,' *New Left Review*, 199 (May–June 1993), pp. 29–54; *City
of Quartz: Excavating the Future in Los Angeles* (London: Verso, 1990).

32. See David Harvey, *The Condition of Postmodernity* (Oxford: Basil Blackwell,
1989) for a vindication of Marx's validity in the contemporary world. For
an example of how these notions can be applied to one area of the 'Third
World,' see Patrick Bond, *Commanding Heights and Community Control*

(Johannesburg: Ravan Press, 1992). A vigorous Marxist critique of post-modernism can be found in Alex Callinicos, *Against Postmodernism* (Oxford: Polity Press, 1990).

33. Alain Lipietz, 'Towards Global Fordism?' and 'Marx or Rostow?,' *New Left Review*, 132 (March–April 1982), pp. 33–58. Walter W. Rostow *The Stages of Economic Growth: A Non-Communist Manifesto* (Cambridge: Cambridge University Press, 1960). See also Paul Cammack, 'Dependency and the Politics of Development,' in P. F. Leeson and M. M. Minogue (eds), *Perspectives on Development: Cross-disciplinary Themes in Development Studies* (Manchester: Manchester University Press, 1988), pp. 89–125, wherein he notes that the classical Marxist works on European countries other than England and France are 'a long way from the notion that the process of capitalist development will be reproduced in identical circumstances in case after case . . .' (p. 95).

34. Giovanni Arrighi, 'World Income Inequalities and the Future of Socialism,' *New Left Review*, 189 (September/October 1991), pp. 39–66. See also Arthur MacEwan, 'What's "New" About the "New International Economy",' *Socialist Review*, 1, 3–4 (July–December 1991), esp. pp. 115–19. Athanasiou, op. cit., pp. 75–6, presents further substantiating data:

> the global polarization of wealth *doubled* between 1960 and 1989, by which time the richest fifth of the world's population received 82.7 per cent of the world's total income, while the poorest fifth received only 1.4 percent. In 1960, the top fifth of the world's population (a group that, significantly, includes most of the northern poor) made 30 times more than the bottom fifth; by 1989 the spread had increased to 60 times. Even these figures conceal the true scale of the injustice, for they are based on average per capital income within countries. If we instead compare the richest and poorest fifths of the world's people, the income differential rises to at least 150 to 1.

35. As Henry Bernstein writes, 'the term "actually existing capitalism" . . . distinguishes the materialist method of historical investigation and its theoretical conditions from various essentialist and ideal-typical conceptions of capitalism which fail to recognize, let alone analyze, phenomenal forms of capitalism that "deviate" from the ideal types proposed.' ('Agricultural Modernisation . . . ,' op. cit., note 1, p. 28.) It could be added that many of the deviations from an ideal type depend on the level of opposition to capitalism within these social formations, and how it has been incorporated into the ruling class's hegemony.

36. André Gunder Frank, 'Marketing Democracy in an Undemocratic Market,' in Gills, Rocamora, Wilson (eds), *Low Intensity Democracy* (London: Pluto Press, 1993), p. 35.

37. Michael Edwards, 'The Irrelevance of Development Studies,' *Third World Quarterly*, 11, 1 (January 1989), pp. 116–35, for an example of an approach which sees most development work as only benefitting expatriate development workers, of whom he notes there were 80,000 in Africa in 1985, costing some $4 billion.

38. Wolfgang Sachs, 'Development: A Guide to the Ruins,' special issue, *New Internationalist* (June 1992); and Sachs (ed.), *The Development Dictionary: A Guide to Knowledge as Power* (London: Pluto Press, 1992).

39. James Ferguson, *The Anti-Politics Machine: 'Development,' Depoliticization and Bureaucratic State Power in Lesotho* (Cambridge and Cape Town: Cambridge University Press and David Philip, 1990), p. xiv. Ferguson spends some time denying that the *intent* of development apparatuses is to expand capitalist relations of production, but suggests that this may be what is happening behind peoples' backs (pp. 11, 18–19).

40. For interpretations of the 'impasse' in left-leaning academic development discourse, see David Booth, 'Marxism and Development Sociology: Interpreting the Impasse,' *World Development*, 13, 7 (July 1985), pp. 761–87 and Nicos Mouzelis, 'Sociology of Development: Reflections on the Present Crisis,' *Sociology*, 22, 1 (February 1988), pp. 23–44, which indicate the crisis in development theory and practice, as does Stuart Corbridge, 'Post-Marxism and Development Studies: Beyond the Impasse,' *World Development*, 8, 5 (May 1990), pp. 623–40, who also notes the convergence of postmodernism with the beginnings of post-development. See also Tariq Banuri, 'Development and the Politics of Knowledge: A Critical Interpretation of the Social Role of Modernization Theories in the Development of the Third World,' and 'Modernization and its Discontents: A Cultural Perspective on the Theories of Development,' in Frédérique Marglin and Stephen Marglin (eds), *Dominating Knowledge: Development, Culture, and Resistance* (Oxford: Clarendon Press, 1990), pp. 29–72, 73–101. Schuurman (ed.), op. cit., is a nearly convincing attempt to persuade us that the leftist impasse is over. The contributions realizing the increased vigour of global capitalism carry more weight than those ignoring this fact, but that argument goes against the thrust of the book's title.

41. Escobar (1992), op. cit., pursues the notion of post-development, as do the contributors to W. Sachs (ed.), *The Development Dictionary* (London: Pluto Press, 1992).

42. Ferguson, *The Anti-Politics Machine*, pp. xiv, 256, 267–77. Ferguson invokes the image of the 'anti-gravity machine' of nineteenth century science fiction to make his point: the development apparatuses can perform a similar trick by suspending politics from 'even the most sensitive political operations' (p. 256). The questions Ferguson poses on the relationship between development discourse and bureaucratic state power would have to be expanded, in the case of this chapter, to the relationship between these two ensembles and the larger one of 'capitalism.'

43. It might even be possible to consider those fighting for developmental reform from within the ideological framework of capitalism in the same light as did Marx of the factory inspectors of early industrial England – provided they 'improve' capitalism in its own terms *and* materially benefit the subordinate classes. See his 'Preface to the First German Edition [of *Capital*],' in Robert C. Tucker, op. cit., p. 296.

44. Gramsci never hesitated to say that the basis of hegemony was an expanding and widening material base – the development of the forces of production and the realization of that development by a critical mass of the population. When that begins to falter, concerted hegemonic reform becomes necessary.

Thus, as Frank op. cit., noted, when it becomes apparent to even capitalists that they can no longer 'deliver' as they once did, they must start to change their promises. It is unlikely, however, that those to whom capitalism has promised great material benefits will soon forget the promise of 'development' with that of much less tangible ones like 'democracy.'

45. 'Passive revolution' can be seen as the absorption and co-option of oppositional forces, but also as the contradictory terrain of molecular and potentially transformational change contributing to gains in the long 'war of position' for socialism. See Gramsci, op. cit., p. 108 ff., and Kees Van Der Pijl, 'Soviet Socialism and Passive Revolution,' in Stephen Gill (ed.), *Gramsci, Historical Materialism and International Relations*, pp. 237–41, and again John. S. Saul, 'South Africa: Between "Barbarism" . . . ,' op. cit.

46. Erik Olin Wright's early notion of the 'contradictory class location' of this group was indicative of the difficulties in labelling it. See his *Class, Crisis and the State* (London: Verso, 1979).

47. Ralph Miliband, 'Class Analysis,' in Anthony Giddens and Jonathan H. Turner (eds), *Social Theory Today* (Cambridge: Polity Press, 1987), pp. 325–46.

48. Gramsci, op. cit., p. 97.

49. Miliband, op. cit., p. 330.

50. Peter Meiksins, for example, asserts that 'all types of wage-labour [including many traditionally 'privileged' workers such as teachers or public sector employees – and other members of the so-called middle classes] share a common interest,' and that 'only an approach that bases itself on the essential unity of the working class is able to take seriously its real segmentation and heterogeneity.' ('Beyond the Boundary Question,' *New Left Review*, 157 (May–June 1986), pp. 120, 116.)

51. Miliband, op. cit., p. 332.

52. For a classic exposition of unequal representation in the administrative structures of the state, see Rianne Mahon, 'Canadian Public Policy: the Unequal Structure of Representation,' in Leo Panitch (ed.), *The Canadian State: Political Economy and Political Power* (Toronto: University of Toronto Press, 1977), pp. 165–98, and substitute 'international development' for her 'labour.'

53. Robert W. Cox, *Production, Power and World Power* (New York: Columbia University Press, 1987), pp. 359–60, 367–8. See also Stephen Gill, 'Intellectuals and Transnational Capital,' in Ralph Miliband and Leo Panitch (eds), *Socialist Register 1990* (London: 1990), along with Craig N. Murphy and Enrico Augelli, 'International Institutions, Decolonization, and Development,' *International Political Science Review*, 14, 1 (January 1993), pp. 71–85, whose notion of 'international civil society' (p. 76) may be too state- and institution-centric.

54. See Arturo Escobar (1992), op. cit., and for the shift to South-South-North linkages (meaning linkages among third world NGOs, with northern NGOs acting as bases of support rather than as agenda-setting institutions among non-government organizations, see the special issues of *Southern Africa Report*, 7, 4 (March 1992) and 9, 1 (July 1993).

55. But see Jorge Nef, 'The Political Economy of Inter-American Relations: A Structural and Historical Overview,' in Stubbs and Underhill, *Political*

Economy and the Changing Global Order (Toronto and London: McClelland and Stewart and Macmillan), pp. 412, 417, note 24, noting that ECLA's 1990 *Changing Production Patterns with Social Equity* is 'non-critical' about neo-liberal prescriptions. Elliot Berg's reactions to the ECA's *African Alternative Framework to Structural Adjustment Programmes for Socio-Economic Recovery and Transformation* (Addis Ababa: UN Economic Commission for Africa, 1989) suggest that the ECA is still opposed to structural adjustment programmes. See Berg's 'Reappraising Export Prospects and Regional Trading Arrangements,' in Douglas Rimmer (ed.), *Action in Africa: The Experience of People Involved in Government, Business and Aid* (London: The Royal African Society and James Currey, 1993), pp. 58–71.

56. Perhaps third world leaders and intellectuals could be considered the 'subordinate ranks' of an emerging global ruling class. Thus Radhika Desai's 'Second-Hand Dealers in Ideas: Think-Tanks and Thatcherite Hegemony,' *New Left Review*, 203 (January–February 1994) in which he notes that a very important part of the hegemonic process is 'to subject the subordinate ranks of the *ruling classes*, and secure the congruence of *their* practices to the requirements of any hegemony' (p. 39), makes essential reading. Such a notion is close to Joseph Femia's idea of 'minimal hegemony,' in which a dominant group is united in aims and purpose, whether or not the subaltern groups are following suit. Joseph Femia, *Gramsci's Political Thought: Hegemony, Consciousness and the Revolutionary Process* (Oxford: Clarendon Press, 1981), p. 47. Those third world leaders who are genuinely attempting to keep an anti-imperialist agenda alive while entering the institutions of development discourse arrive on the terrain of passive revolution and war of position. Of relevance here is also the literature of postcoloniality, on which see Arif Dirlik, 'The Postcolonial Aura: Third World Criticism in the Age of Global Capitalism,' *Critical Inquiry*, 20 (Winter 1994), p. 328, deliberately misanswering the question 'when . . . does the "post-colonial" begin?' with 'when Third World intellectuals have arrived in First World academe.' More substantially, Dirlik notes the ambiguity of postcoloniality discourse on the question of global capitalism – often rejected as a legitimate subject of inquiry because it implies a foundational 'master-narrative' of modernity (p. 335) – and the possibility that 'postcolonial discourse is an expression not so much of agony over identity . . . but of newfound power' (p. 339). Could this discourse be part of Desai's hegemonic project? Dirlik's serious answer to the initial question is: 'with the emergence of global capitalism' (p. 352).

57. According to Don Babai's incisive entry in Joel Krieger (ed.), *The Oxford Companion to Politics of the World* (Oxford: Oxford University Press, 1993), pp. 981–6, John Maynard Keynes vociferously opposed the decision to locate the Bank's headquarters in Washington, preferring New York. As Babai says, 'the outcome was a foregone conclusion,' and the present location ensures continuous political scrutiny and predominant American influence (p. 981). As Robert Wood has noted, many officials in the World Bank and the International Monetary Fund (across the street) have serious doubts that third world debt should and can be repaid, but US dominance keeps these ideas off the agenda. (See 'The International Monetary Fund and the World Bank in a Changing World Economy,' in Arthur MacEwan and William K.

Tabb (eds), *Instability and Change in the World Economy* (New York: Monthly Review Press, 1989), p. 304). One wonders if a different physical location would have any effect on such ideological closure.

58. Erik Olin Wright, 'Class and Politics,' in Joel Krieger (ed.), op. cit., p. 149.

59. Irene L. Gendzier, *Managing Political Change: Social Scientists and the Third World* (Boulder: Westview, 1985), must surely be recognized as the classic work on the relationship between the academics of 'political development' and American foreign policy and 'aid.' Escobar, op. cit. (1984–5, 1987) is very instructive on the many academic economists in the development business. On anthropologists see his 'Anthropology and the Development Encounter: The Making and Marketing of Development Anthropology,' *American Ethnologist*, 18, 4 (1991), pp. 658–82.

60. Patrick Bond, 'From the Boardrooms to the Townships,' *BankCheck* (January 1994).

61. See Vandana Shiva, *Staying Alive: Women, Ecology and Development* (London: Zed Press, 1989) for a synthesis of social movement and academic study: for an example of the entry of such concerns to the World Bank, see Herman Daly *et al.*, op. cit. For an analysis of how the World Bank absorbs such efforts, see David Korten, 'Sustainable Development,' *World Policy Journal*, 9, 1 (Winter 1991–92). Apparently Daly has returned to a university post after his time with the World Bank.

62. Robert Cox's classic, 'Ideologies and the New International Economic Order: Reflections on Some Recent Literature,' *International Organization*, 33, 2 (Spring 1979) is essential reading on this point.

63. David Harvey, 'The Geographical and Geopolitical Consequences of the Transition from Fordist to Flexible Accumulation,' in George Sternlieb and James W. Hughes (eds), *America's New Market Geography: Nation, Region, and Metropolis* (New Brunswick: Rutgers University Press, 1988), pp. 110 ff; Bob Jessop, 'Regulation Theories in Retrospect and Prospect, *Economy and Society*, 19, 2 (May 1990), pp. 153–216.

64. Kees Van der Pijl, *The Making of an Atlantic Ruling Class* (London: Verso, 1984).

65. To borrow from Joseph Hanlon's illustrative work, *Mozambique: Who Calls the Shots?* (London: James Currey, 1991).

66. Adrian Leftwich, 'Governance, Democracy and Development in the Third World,' *Third World Quarterly*, 14, 3 (October 1993), p. 608 and *passim*.

67. Much of the 'impasse' literature cited above (Booth *et al.*) can be interpreted as a delayed academic coming to terms with the imperatives of neoliberalism. The fact that Bill Warren's work matched – and perhaps even foresaw – the new ideological 'reality' so quickly may account for its devastating impact on much Marxist and neo-Marxist work on underdevelopment. As Bruce Berman notes, students repeatedly ask 'why so much of Warren sounds exactly like liberal development economics,' ('African Capitalism and the Paradigm of Modernity: Culture, Technology, and the State,' in Bruce J. Berman and Colin Leys (eds), *African Capitalists in African Development* (Boulder: Lynne Reinner, 1994), note 2, p. 256). Could Bill Warren's 'Imperialism and Capitalist Industrialization,' *New Left Review*, 81 (September–October 1973), have influenced Elliot Berg's report (1979–80)?

68. This brief analysis of 'intellectuals' has stopped short of considering the notion that they create their own discourse and as such have played the historical role of bringing capital and capitalists into existence, as advanced by Nancy Armstrong and Leonard Tennenhouse, *The Imaginary Puritan: Literature, Intellectual Labor and the Origins of Personal Life* (Berkeley: University of California Press, 1992). They contend that 'the activity called intellectual labour represents itself as secondary and derivative – dependent on the world to which it refers – just when it acquires the power to revise the very nature of things,' (p. 19) that it dominates 'other social and economic practices in the most blatant and undeniable way,' (p. 119) and that 'the capitalist (is) a later sub-species of the intellectual' (p. 139). On reading Manfred Bienefeld's analysis of World Bank discourse in this book, such words begin to make some sense: the econocrats *are* creating a world out of their own discourse, whether or not it has much connection to a 'real world' outside of their own ideologies. However, I still prefer to believe that such a world is being created more or less at the behest of larger powers, as indicated by Desai, op. cit. and Van der Pijl, op. cit. Let us not give Milton Friedman more power than he deserves.

69. This complication has been noted by Henry Bernstein (written communication, 7 January 1992). Such analysis requires 'a "sociology of ideas" that is very rigorous in analyzing both shifts in ideas and the conditions and agents that produce, reproduce, defend, adapt (etc.) them . . .' and necessitates examination of 'how systems of ideas or ideologies are "driven" by the intrinsic "logic" of their discursive practices (the discourse theory position) as well as by changing conditions that affect their coherence or "fit" with reality.'

70. Escobar, 'Discourse and Power in Development,' *Alternatives*, 10 (Winter 1984–85).

71. As Robert Wood makes clear in his *From Marshall Plan to Debt Crisis* (Berkeley: University of California Press), p. 191:

> Despite the proliferation and diversification of aid sources, changes in fashion in development thinking, and significant shifts in the international balance of power, the bulk of economic assistance from the days of the Marshall Plan to the present has been structured to oppose the development both of national capitalism and of more radical, socialist departures from multilateral capitalism; to promote the expansion of the private sector, both domestic and foreign, and the dominance of market principles of exchange; and to encourage 'outward-looking,' export oriented types of development.

> Nevertheless, I contend that the first phase threatened to turn into something contrary to the intentions of the architects of the aid regimes, and thus had to be altered.

72. Henry Bernstein, 'Agricultural "Modernisation" . . . ,' op. cit., p. 4, notes that the 'brave new world' of neo-liberalism and structural adjustment 'incorporates the same kinds of assumptions about . . . modernization' as the previous era, but these are prescribed 'exclusively for the private sector rather than shared with the public sector.' Yet in spite of structural adjustment's moral unilateralism, it relies on the state to implement its imperatives – not least to repress those people who rise up against it (p. 28).

73. Gender, too, made its first discursive appearance during this moment. The fact that I do not pay enough attention to this realm is simply because it has not appeared at the 'first level' of agency discourse. It can be said, however, that the language of gender politics is pulled into the same hegemonic directions as its counterparts of equity, participation and sustainability. See, for fears on the discourse of 'Women in Development,' Barbara Spronk, 'Wearing the WID Label: A Case of Unease,' in Penny and John Van Esterik (eds) *Gender and Development in Southeast Asia* (Montreal: Canadian Asian Studies Association, 1992). Also see Patricia Stamp, *Technology, Gender, and Power in Africa* (Ottawa: International Development Research Centre, 1990).

74. Of course, for post-modernist sticklers, Marxism does not represent a challenge to the dominant order either, because it is 'Western.'

75. For examples, see Wolfgang Sachs (ed.) *Development Dictionary . . .*', Arturo Escobar, 'Imagining . . .' (n. 16); Stuart Corbridge, 'Post-Marxism . . .' (n. 40).

76. Gustavo Esteva, 'Development,' in W. Sachs (ed.), *The Development Dictionary* (London: Pluto Press, 1992), p. 22.

77. Ivan Illich, *Tools for Conviviality* (New York: Harper and Row, 1973).

78. See the essays in this volume by Laura Macdonald, Patrick Bond, and to a lesser extent, Lloyd Sachikonye and Michael Gismondi, Joan Sherman and Mary Richardson for illustrations of this trend.

79. Gerald J. Schmitz and David Gillies, *The Challenge of Democratic Development: Sustaining Democratization in Developing Societies* (Ottawa: The North–South Institute, 1992), and Leftwich, op. cit.

80. Colin Stoneman, 'The World Bank: Some Lessons for South Africa,' *Review of African Political Economy,* 58 (November 1993), pp. 87, 91–3. Among the scores of writings on the 'Asian Tigers,' Bruce Cumings' remain the best: 'The Origins and Development of the Northeast Asian Political Economy: industrial sectors, product cycles, and political consequences,' *International Organization,* 38, 1 (Winter 1984), pp. 1–40, and 'The Abortive Abertura: South Korea in the Light of the Latin American Experience,' *New Left Review,* 173 (January–February 1989), pp. 11–32.

81. Bjorn Beckman, 'The Liberation of Civil Society: Neo-Liberal Ideology and Political Theory,' *Review of African Political Economy,* 58 (November 1993), p. 21.

82. See Gerald Schmitz in this volume.

83. World Bank, *Sub-Saharan Africa: From Crisis to Sustainable Growth* (Washington: The World Bank, 1989), p. 4.

84. Loc. cit.

85. Ibid., p. 38.

86. Ibid., p. 193.

87. Ibid., p. 192.

88. Ibid., p. 1.

89. Ibid., p. 135.

90. Ibid., p. 5

91. Ibid., p. 193.

92. For some thought-provoking analyses of local bourgeoisies in Africa, see Bruce J. Berman and Colin Leys (eds), *African Capitalists in African*

Development (Boulder: Lynne Rienner, 1994), and David Himbara, *Kenyan Capitalists: the State, and Development* (Boulder: Lynne Rienner, 1994).

93. For some answers to this question, see the essays in Berman and Leys, ibid., and for *how* to look for African capitalists, see Leys, 'African Capitalists and Development: Theoretical Questions,' esp. pp. 28–32. For some compelling advice on what to do until this class finds itself and is discovered, see his 'Confronting the African Tragedy,' *New Left Review*, 204 (March/April 1994), p. 46.

94. World Bank, *Sub-Saharan Africa: From Crisis to . . .* , op. cit., p. 42.

95. Henry Bernstein, 'Taking the Part of the Peasants?' in Henry Bernstein, Ben Crow, Maureen Mackintosh, Charlotte Martin (eds), *The Food Question: Profits versus People?* (New York: Monthly Review Press, 1990), pp. 67–79. For required reading on the African post-colonial state, see C. L. R. James, *Nkrumah and the Ghana Revolution* (London: Alison & Busby, 1977 [with letters and essays from 1962, 1964, 1969 and 1977]).

96. For an example of what happens when World Bank officials meet with groups in civil society with just such ideas, see Patrick Bond, 'From the Boardrooms to the Townships, *BankCheck* (January 1994).

97. John Stackhouse, 'Africa Inc., Where the Bottom Line is Starvation,' *Toronto Globe and Mail*, 14 September 1992.

98. Michael Barratt Brown and Pauline Tiffen, *Short Changed: Africa and World Trade* (London: Pluto Press, 1992); Michael Barratt Brown, *Fair Trade: Reform and Realities in the International Trading System* (London: Zed Books, 1993).

99. Robert W. Cox, 'The Global Political Economy and Social Choice,' in Daniel Drache and Meric Gertler (eds), *The New Era of Global Competition* (Montreal and Kingston: McGill-Queen's Press, 1991), p. 337.

100. Part of that marketplace is made up of environmental images, into which a proliferation of southern 'civil society' and NGO activists can insert themselves. See Ian Cherrett, Phil O'Keefe, and Anne Hendenreich, 'Non-Government Organizations – The Demise of A Panacea?' (North Shields, UK: ETC Foundation, August 1992), who address the question raised by many social-democratic northern NGOs 'that NGO activity is little more than welfare payment to Third World professionals who milk the Northern aid agenda for their own ends' (p. 1).

101. Bjorn Beckman, 'The Liberation of Civil Society', *Review of Africa Political Economy*, 58 (November 1993), p. 30; also Peter Gibbon, ' "Civil Society" and Political Change, with Special Reference to "Developmentalist" States,' paper presented to Nordic Conference on 'Social Movements in the Third World,' University of Lund, Sweden, 18–21 August 1993, p. 34.

102. Robert Charlick, PhD, Senior Governance Expert, 'The Concept of Governance and its Implications for AID's Development Assistance Program in Africa,' prepared for the AID Africa Bureau under the Africa Bureau Democracy and Governance Program (Washington: Associates in Rural Development, Inc., June 1992). I also refer to this paper's draft version, 'Governance Working Paper,' (January 1992).

103. Mark Kesselman, 'Order or Movement? The Literature of Political Development as Ideology?,' *World Politics*, 26 (1973), pp. 139–54, remains a powerful analysis of the way in which the American political development

literature has made 'order' the logical, functional and chronological predecessor of liberty. The international financial institutions have simply replaced liberty with 'economic growth' and whatever elements are inside that ideological envelope.

104. Charlick, 'Governance Working Paper,' op. cit., p. 1.
105. 'The Concept . . . ,' op. cit., p. 7.
106. 'Governance Working Paper . . . ,' p. 5.
107. Ibid., pp. 8–9.
108. 'The Concept . . . ,' p. 16–17.
109. Ibid., p. 12.
110. Loc. cit.
111. Ibid., p. 16.
112. 'Draft Cable to All Missions. Subject: AFR Strategy on Democratization and Governance,' 428A, October 1990. The background paper, 'Democracy and Governance in Africa,' 4297A notes that 'in the long term' the assumption that political and economic liberalization go hand in hand *may* (emphasis mine) be correct, but 'in the short term, most political scientists believe that there is little positive correlation, and may even be a negative correlation, between how democratic a government is and its willingness and ability to pursue market-oriented reforms' (p. 7). It goes on to tentatively modify that view, however, in a manner similar to Robert Charlick's report. The background paper also notes that 'there is no inherent link between improved governance and democracy. Democratic governments can perform quite poorly on dimensions of governmental effectiveness and administrative efficiency' (p. 6).
113. But see John Loxley, 'Structural Adjustment Programmes in Africa: Ghana and Zambia,' *Review of African Political Economy*, 47 (Spring 1990), pp. 8–28, and more generally, Manfred Bienefeld's chapter in this volume.
114. Robert H. Nooter and Roy A. Stacy, 'Progress on Adjustment in Sub-Saharan Africa: Implications for Future Lending Strategies,' October 15, 1990, p. 3. One assumes that the 'highly qualified team' was a World Bank team, of course. This seems to be all the democracy required.
115. Henry Bernstein (written communication, 2 April 1992). Bernstein goes on to compare this 'American muscularity and energy' with the 'dry as dust' British 'administration' approach, and notes that socialists should try to reformulate the work on popular participation – 'part of the reformulation being to confront, rather than sidestep, 'contradictions among the people.' One could add that the American 'muscularity and energy' is not lacking in the World Bank literature, but seems more attuned to an imperial mission than to populist empathy with 'the people.' On the anthropologists' implication in the discourse on participation, see Arturo Escobar, 'Anthropology and the Development Encounter: The Making and Marketing of Development Anthropology,' *American Ethnologist*, 18, 4 (1991), pp. 658–82.
116. Gustavo Esteva, 'Development,' in Sachs (ed.), op. cit., p. 22.
117. Arturo Escobar's 'Discourse and Power . . . ' and his doctoral thesis, op. cit., *passim*. remains essential for an understanding of this period, as do the essays in Gerald M. Meier and Dudley Seers (eds), *Pioneers in Development* (New York: Oxford University Press for the World Bank, 1984), wherein a *pre*-1945 intervention on 'development' is noted, namely Paul N.

46   *Development Discourse as Hegemony*

Resenstein-Rodan, 'The International Development of Economically Backward Areas,' *International Affairs* (April 1944).

118. Walter W. Rostow's *The Stages of Economic Growth: A Non-Communist Manifesto* (Cambridge: Cambridge University Press, 1960), is famous for coining this term. However, the book is really only a schematization of the thinking that was going on in development circles in the late 1940s and the 1950s.

119. José Nun, 'Democracy and Modernization, Thirty Years Later,' *Latin American Perspectives*, 20, 4 (Fall 1993), p. 9.

120. Gerald M. Meier, 'The Formative Period,' in Meier and Seers, op. cit., p. 18. It should be noted, too, that many of these 'pioneers' had hopes that an International Trade Organization would stabilize the prices of international primary commodities, so domestic planning would not be dependent on the vagaries of unregulated trade. The United States forced the shelving of this idea. It was revived in the 1970s with UNCTAD. See Hans Singer, 'The Terms of Trade Controversy and the Evolution of Soft Financing: Early Years in the UN,' ibid., p. 279 ff.

121. Bert F. Hoselitz, 'Non-Economic Barriers to Economic Development,' *Economic Development and Cultural Change* (March 1952), as cited in ibid., p. 6.

122. See, for example David McClelland, *The Achieving Society* (Princeton: Van Nostrand, 1961), and Edward Shils, 'The Intellectuals in the Political Development of the New States,' *World Politics*, 12, 3 (April 1960), pp. 329–68. For a critique of McClelland, see Henry Bernstein, 'Modernization Theory and the Sociological Study of Development,' *Journal of Development Studies*, 7, 2 (1971), p. 148 ff, and for a retrospective on the career of his 'science of success,' see Nicholas Lemann, 'Is There a Science of Success?', *The Atlantic Monthly* (February 1994), pp. 83–98.

123. S. N. Eisenstadt, 'Modernisation and Sustained Conditions of Sustained Growth', *World Politics*, 16, 4 (July 1964), pp. 567–94, which precedes the much more notorious work of Samuel Huntington, *Political Order in Changing Societies* (New Haven: Yale University Press, 1968).

124. Arturo Escobar, 'Planning,' in Sachs (ed.), *The Development Dictionary* (London: The Pluto Press, 1992), p. 136, suggests that the World Bank's report on its first mission to Colombia in 1949, remarking that the 'natural order' of things would not lead to economic development, indicates a disposition to eliminate local culture. Without disagreeing with that, one could also note that such phraseology also points to a distrust of the 'free market' and the necessity for Keynesian engineering, at least.

125. Nun, op. cit., p. 11, quoting Joel Migdal, *Strong Societies and Weak States* (Princeton: Princeton University Press, 1988), p. 4.

126. Michel J. Crozier *et al.*, *The Crisis of Democracy* (New York: New York University Press, 1975), quoted in Robert W. Cox, 'Global Restructuring: Making Sense of the Changing International Political Economy,' in Richard Stubbs and Geoffrey R. D. Underhill (eds), op. cit., p. 51. For a comprehensive and theoretically sophisticated understanding of the Trilateral Commission, see Stephen Gill, *American Hegemony and the Trilateral Commission* (Cambridge: Cambridge University Press, 1990).

127. Stuart Corbridge's many writings cover these issues well, especially indicating

how they lead up to the debt crisis: 'The Debt Crisis and the Crisis of
Global Regulation,' *Geoforum*, 19, 1 (1988), pp. 109–30; 'The Asymmetry
of Interdependence: The United States and the Geopolitics of International
Financial Relations,' *Studies in Comparative International Development*,
23, 1 (Spring 1988), pp. 3–30; 'Ethics in Development Studies: The Example of Debt,' in Frans Schuurman (ed.), *Beyond the Impasse* (London: Zed
Press, 1993), pp. 123–39; *Debt and Development* (Oxford: Basil Blackwell,
1992).

128. Robert Wood, op. cit., Chapter 6. Jeffrey Frieden, 'Third World Indebted
Industrialization: International Finance and State Capitalism in Mexico, Brazil
Algeria and South Korea,' *International Organization*, 35, 1 (1981).

129. Fred Halliday, *The Making of the Second Cold War* (London: Verso, 1983),
p. 79.

130. Henry Bernstein and Howard Nicholas, 'Pessimism of the Intellect, Pessimism of the Will? A Response to Gunder Frank,' *Development and Change*,
14, 3 (1983), pp. 609–24. As Colin Leys, 'Confronting the African Tragedy',
New Left Review, 204 (March/April 1994) p. 41, note 20, notes in his discussion of the lack of 'historicity' shared by all theories of post-colonial
development in Africa: 'It is easy to caricature schools of thought, and to
exaggerate their characteristic weaknesses. By no means all dependency
theorists, nor all Marxists, nor even all modernizers, exhibited all the failings attributed to them by contemporary critics. But it is equally mistaken
to pretend that these schools of thought did not have a tendency to give rise
to such failings.' It should be noted that Leys is somewhat uncomfortable
with Jean-François Bayart's use of the word historicity, and indeed with his
book, *The State in Africa: The Politics of the Belly* (London: Longman,
1992), on which, with Basil Davidson's *The Black Man's Burden: Africa
and the Curse of the Nation-State* (London: James Currey, 1992), 'Confronting the African Tragedy' is a wide-ranging review.

131. Fernando H. Cardoso and Enzo Faletto, *Dependency and Development in
Latin America* (Berkeley: University of California Press, 1979), and Paul
Cammack, op. cit., pp. 101–8, for an appreciation of this work. Cardoso's
1994 election to Brazil's presidency, and the policies he has been implementing, may affirm the links between theories of 'associated dependent
development' and neo-liberalism.

132. See Bill Warren, 'Imperialism and Capitalist Industrialization,' *New Left
Review*, 81 (September–October 1973), and his *Imperialism: Pioneer of
Capitalism* (ed. John Sender) (London: Verso, 1980), compiled after his
death in 1978, for the view that capitalism in the Third World is ably
serving the task of preparing the road to socialism. See Alain Lipietz (n. 33)
for criticism of Warren. Also see Ernesto Laclau, 'Feudalism and Capitalism
in Latin America,' *Politics and Ideology in Marxist Theory* (London: Verso,
1977), pp. 15–50 – originally published in *New Left Review*, 67 (1971) – for
one of the original critiques of dependency from the modes of production
perspective, emphasizing the manner in which various non-capitalist structures
of production and reproduction were joined onto the encroaching capitalist
system, providing cheap labour to the capitalism and thus remaining un-
transformed. For an excellent summary and critique, see Aidan Foster-Carter,
'The Modes of Production Controversy,' *New Left Review*, 107 (January–

February 1978), pp. 47–77. Robert Brenner, 'The Origins of Capitalist Development: a Critique of Neo-Smithian Marxism,' *New Left Review*, 104 (July–August 1977), pp. 25–93, has also offered a critique of the circulationist perspective of the dependency school, but it is not clear whether his alternative of class struggle as the motor of social change is tantamount to a Warrenite critique or not.

The notion of perversity and its correlates is advanced by Albert Hirschman in *The Rhetoric of Reaction: Perversity, Futility, Jeopardy* (Cambridge: Harvard University Press, 1991). Along with his critique of the right, he criticizes James O'Connors' *The Fiscal Crisis of the State* (New York: St. Martin's Press, 1972), for putting a premature closure on liberal/welfare reform and playing into the hands of the right, noting how Huntington's essay in the Trilateral Commission's *The Crisis of Democracy . . .* , op. cit., utilizes O'Connors' work, changing his thesis about the incompatibility of the welfare state with capitalism to the assertion that the welfare state leads to a crisis in 'democracy' (pp. 115–19). Interestingly, Hirschman surmises that Huntington's analysis of 'political decay' in the USA may well have emerged from his work on the south: we may have an example here of development discourse from the third world having impact upon ideological movements in the advanced capitalist countries. Just as interesting is Hirschman's grudging acceptance of the Huntington thesis' 'partial confirmation' in the south, but not in the north, where 'the evidence . . . is at best ambiguous' (pp. 120–1): is there a stark difference between 'partial confirmation' and 'ambiguous evidence?' For a critique closer to a Marxist position, but also reliant to a great degree on Karl Polanyi: *The Great Transformation* (Boston: Beacon Press, 1957) see Fred Block, 'Political Choice and the Multiple "Logics" of Capital,' *Revising State Theory: Essays in Politics and Postindustrialism* (Philadelphia: Temple University Press, 1987), pp. 171–85.

133. John. S. Saul, 'Structural Reform: A Model for the Revolutionary Transformation of South Africa?', in *Recolonization and Resistance in Southern Africa in the 1990s* (Toronto and Trenton, NJ: Between the Lines Press and Africa World Press, 1993), pp. 89–169, and 'Globalism, Socialism and Democracy in the South African Transition,' in Ralph Miliband and Leo Panitch (eds), *Socialist Register 1994* (London: Merlin Press, 1994), for some promising efforts to work on this notion. Mouzelis, 'Sociology of Development', *Sociology*, 22, 1 (February 1988), offers promising analysis of the many forces involved in accumulation strategies.

134. See David Caute, *Sixty-Eight: The Year of the Barricades* (London: Paladin, 1988) for an excellent international survey of 1968.

135. C. B. Macpherson, *The Life and Times of Liberal Democracy* (New York: Oxford University Press, 1977), p. 93.

136. Edward B. Barbier, 'The Concept of Sustainable Economic Development,' *Environmental Conservation*, 14, 2 (Summer 1987), p. 102, suggests that the 1968 meetings in Paris of the 'Biosphere Conference,' and in Washington DC on the Ecological Aspects of International Development, are responsible for the origins of the term 'sustainable development.' However, the Stockholm conference had wider media impact, at least.

137. Robert Cox, 'Ideologies and the New International Economic Order: Reflections on Some Recent Literature,' *International Organization*, 33, 2 (Spring 1979), pp. 279, 271.

138. Majid Rahnema, 'Participatory Action Research: The "Last Temptation of Saint" Development,' *Alternatives*, 15, 2 (Spring 1990), p. 201, states that the World Bank assimilated the concept of participatory research and development as early as the 1970s and drained it of its 'subversive connotation.'

139. See Robert W. Cox, *Education For Development* (Geneva: International Institute for Labour Studies, Reprint No. 14 [from *International Organization*, 22, 1, 1968], 1968), for a fascinating contemporary study of how international development agencies proliferate.

140. See his and Manfred Bienefeld's essays in this volume.

141. Henry Bernstein, 'Modernization Theory . . . ,' *Journal of Development Studies*, 7, 2 (1971), p. 148, quotes a specialist working in 'Project Agile' in the Thai–American Military Research and Development Centre at Bangkok in the 1960s: 'the old formula for successful counter-insurgency used to be ten troops for each guerrilla . . . Now the formula is ten anthropologists for each guerrilla.'

142. By these apparatuses I mean those such as the Mount Pélèrin Club, the Trilateral Commission, and the Institute for Economic Affairs. See Simon Gunn, *Revolution of the Right: Europe's New Conservatives* (London: Pluto Press, 1989) and Desai, 'Second-Hand Dealers in Ideas,' *New Left Review*, 203 (January–February 1994). D. Lal's *The Poverty of 'Development Economics,'* a neo-liberal tract on the literature of the first development era, was published by the IEA in 1983.

143. Cammack, 'Dependency and the Politics of Development,' in Leeson and Minogue (eds), *Perspectives on Development* (Manchester: Manchester University Press, 1988), p. 111. The emphasis is mine.

144. See Harry Magdoff, 'Globalisation: To What End?' *New World Order? Socialist Register 1992* (London: Merlin Press, 1992), pp. 65–7, notes that in the 1960s, all combined international loans equalled approximately one percent of the world's gross product (the sum of all capitalist countries' gross domestic products). By the mid-1980s that figure was 20 per cent. In trade terms, in the mid-1960s international loans stood at around 10 per cent of the volume of international trade, but by the mid-1980s these cross-border loans surpassed the value of global trade. Magdoff's charts show well the fact that by now the Third World as a whole would actually have a positive balance of payments but for the interest and debt payments it is forced to make every year. His explanation of the vicious spiral forced by this bondage is well worth reading. Patricia Adams, *Odious Debts: Loose Lending, Corruption and the Third World's Environmental Legacy* (London: Earthscan, 1991) credits the debt crisis with slowing environmentally disastrous aid: 'with a government's capacity to borrow curtailed, so too is its capacity to do environmental harm' (p. 50). So, too, unfortunately, would be its capacity to do social good: this book's suspicion of all government leaves it politically unmoored. Adams's vision contrasts with that of Robert Wood, *From Marshall Plan to Debt Crisis* (Berkeley: University of California Press, 1986), p. 233, 269, and *passim*, whose analysis of 'loose-lending'

sees that moment as a significant disjuncture within 'aid regime norms' which gave power to some state capitalist projects in the Third World – power which had to be clawed back by the international financial institutions. Wood does not pay much heed to the environment, however. Both works, by failing to tackle the question of 'what kind of state' serve to avoid analysis of the state, so it turns out to be either all corrupt or relatively benevolent. See also my polemical version of the debt crisis, offered in Unit 7 of Athabasca University's course package, *Power, Production and Global Order: International Political Economy 483* (Athabasca: Athabasca University, 1994), where I consider the possibility that much of the intensity of the structural adjustment programmes around the third world derives from the fact that they are experiments, later to be applied to the west.

145. David Lehman, 'Dependencia: an Ideological History,' Institute of Development Studies, IDS Discussion Paper, DP 219 (Sussex: IDS, July 1986), p. 26.

146. Mahbub ul Haq, *The Poverty Curtain: Choices for the Third World* (New York: New York University Press, 1976), p. 41, quoted in Cox, 'Ideologies and . . . ,' op. cit., p. 262. Cox asks of this: 'How is one to interpret this talk of revolution coming from a high official of the World Bank?' According to Robert Wood, op. cit., p. 226, ul Haq resigned in 1982, citing major policy differences with the World Bank's new president A. W. Clausen. Wood states that Clausen advocated the virtues of the private sector more insistently than did his predecessor, but 'no more insistently than pre-McNamara Bank presidents.' Ul Haq later became director of the United Nations Development Programme, an agency which subsequently saw its role as modifying and offering alternatives to structural adjustment programmes, but whose policies appear to be supplementing the SAPs. See Sheila Smith and Georges Chapelier, 'UNDP and Policy Reform,' Policy Division/BPPE, June 1990. Also see the UNDP *Human Development Report 1990* (New York: Oxford University Press, 1990), much of which was drafted by Amartya Sen, according to David Crocker, 'Functioning and Capability: The Foundations of Sen's and Nussbaum's Development Ethic,' *Political Theory*, 20, 4 (November 1992), p. 587.

147. World Bank, *Accelerated Development . . .* , op. cit. Dr. Berg is listed as the vice-president of Development Alternatives Incorporated in Douglas Rimmer (ed.), *Action in Africa* (London: The Royal African Society and James Currey, 1993). For some of the forces influencing such an ideology, see Eric Helleiner, 'From Bretton Woods to Global Finance: A World Turned Upside Down,' in Stubbs and Underhill, *Political Economy and the Changing Global Order* (Toronto and London: McClelland and Stewart and Macmillan), pp. 163–75 – a concise explanation of the post-war shifts in state and finance relations which have led to the present neo-liberal financial order, and a chilling commentary on the ramifications for the Keynesian welfare state.

148. This is an admittedly impressionistic view, but it seems that the proliferation of university degrees, departments and institutes in environmental studies is a more recent phenomenon than that of development studies. This may be because development studies has more direct antecedents in the traditional disciplines. However, as the notion of 'sustainable development' gains institutional power so will its entrenchment in the university.

149. See the chapter by Gismondi, Sherman and Richardson in this volume on how substantive participation threatened to alter the dominant version of 'sustainable development.'

150. James C. Cooper, 'Introduction,' *Quest for a Sustainable Society* (New York: Pergamon, 1981), p. xi. One can only wonder how Herman Daly, whose work advocates a communitarian approach to sustainable development, managed to stay within the research wing of the World Bank for so long. See David Korten, 'Sustainable Development,' op. cit., for how such views are deflected and absorbed, and David Lehman, op. cit., for the similar fate of the *dependentistas* in the World Bank.

151. Terry Eagleton, *Ideology: An Introduction* (London: Verso, 1991), pp. 223–4. I thank Jeremy Mouat for bringing these words to my attention.

152. David Crocker, op. cit., pp. 607, 588, and *passim* on Amartya Sen's and Martha Nussbaum's extension of basic needs perspectives through the notion of 'cooperative critical discourse,' by which such needs could be determined. This perspective does not seem far off a socialist one, encapsulated by Terry Eagleton, op. cit., p. 175: 'the "interest" of a radical is just to bring about the kind of social conditions in which all men and women could genuinely participate in the formulation of meanings and values, without exclusion or domination.'

153. To be sure, many of the works in Schuurman (ed.), *Beyond the Impasse . . .* , op. cit., indicate ways out, but if the actors are considered without the structures confining the ways in which they make history, they will come to the dead-ends described so well by Laura Macdonald in this volume.

154. Eagleton, op. cit., p. 175. Notably, the more modest aspirations of Dietrich Rueschemeyer, Evelyn Huber Stephens, and John D. Stephens, *Capitalist Development and Democracy* (Chicago: University of Chicago Press, 1992), are advanced by the same sort of cause as Eageton's: their widely drawn comparative study concludes that 'democracy – even in its modest and largely formal contemporary realizations . . . ' is highly dependent on a powerful and articulate working class, the 'most consistently pro-democratic force' (pp. 11, 8).

155. James Manor, 'Introduction,' in his edited *Rethinking Third World Politics* (London: Longman, 1991), p. 2.

156. Note Orlando Fals-Borda's discussion of participatory action research, 'The Application of Participatory Action Research in Latin America,' *International Sociology*, 2, 4 (December 1987), p. 330, which he states can enable 'the capacity of grass-roots groups, which are exploited both socially and economically, to articulate and systematize knowledge (both their own and that which comes from outside) in such a way that they can become protagonists in the advancement of their own class and group interests.' But also be cautioned by Rahnema, for a warning *and* his fears about the 'vanguardist' presumptions of the left. However, his image of 'pure' participatory democracy, wherein the 'participants see and listen, unencumbered by any corrective device, any conditioning, any preconceived image of one another, or any fear or design of any kind' (op. cit., p. 206), seems naïve and rather like the 'pragmatic pluralist' ideology of liberal American political science discussed in Binder, op. cit., p. 12. Richard Sandbrook, *The Politics of Africa's Economic Recovery* (Cambridge: Cambridge University Press, 1993), Chapter

5, presents a sober assessment of the possibilities for 'people-centred development' in Africa, arguable only for its admittedly qualified support of structural adjustment programmes.

157.   In this regard, Gregory Albo, David Languile, and Leo Panitch (eds), *A Different Kind of State? Popular Power and Democratic Administration* (Toronto: Oxford University Press, 1993), might make good course material for the World Bank's proliferating 'capacity building' seminars, indications of which can be seen in Alexander A. Kwapong and Barry Lesser (eds), *Meeting the Challenge: The African Capacity Building Initiative* (Halifax: Report on a Roundtable Conference Convened by the Lester Pearson Institute for International Development and the African Capacity Building Initiative, Harare, 1992).

158.   Jean-François Bayart, *The State in Africa: The Politics of the Belly* (London: Longmans, 1992), p. 210 and *passim*. See also René Lemarchand, 'Uncivil States and Civil Societies: How Illusion Became Reality,' *Journal of Modern African Studies*, 30, 2 (1992), pp. 177–91.

159.   Peter Gibbon, 'Structural Adjustment and Multipartyism,' in the indispensable volume, Gibbon, Yusuf Bangura and Arve Ofstad (eds), *Authoritarianism, Democracy, and Adjustment: The Politics of Economic Reform in Africa* (Uppsala: The Scandinavian Institute of African Studies, 1992), p. 168, indicates the link between participation and accumulation by noting that 'the emergence of people's organizations outside of the parliamentary arena must be encouraged if "accumulation from above" is to be replaced by something more progressive and dynamic' (p. 168). See also Leys, 'Confronting the African Tragedy', *New Left Review*, 204 (March/April 1994), pp. 45–6, for an historical explanation of the lack of accumulation in Africa and a qualified defense of the state as a suitable starting point for a remedy – along with some credible suggestions for international assistance. Nzongola-Ntalaja, 'Presidential Address. African Crisis: The Way Out,' *African Studies Review*, 32, 1 (April 1989), p. 121, also notes the fact that if participation is to be practicable, the people expected to participate must have the material means to do so.

160.   Bayart is fond of chiding socialists for theoretical closure, at one time quoting John S. Saul to the effect that there can be no 'linear or finalist conception of the quest for hegemony' and that the production of the state is equivalent to the unpredictable unfolding of social struggles (op. cit., p. 210). One should respond to this that in spite of its multi-coloured consumerist palettes, the hegemony of capital is closed. The socialist alternative, however, is open: as Eagleton puts it, once the issue of class domination and power is resolved, the meanings and values resulting from genuine participation are indeterminate: 'As to what meanings and values might result from this comradely encounter of differences, the radical has absolutely nothing to say, since his or her whole political commitment is exhausted in the effort to bring about its historical conditions of possibility' (op. cit., p. 175).

161.   As Colin Leys quotes Marx, in a world where the life expectancy for blacks in Harlem is now lower than Bangladesh's average 'the story [of the 'third world'] is about you', 'Confronting . . . ,' op. cit., p. 47.

162.   Sue Golding, *Gramsci's Democratic Theory: Contributions to a Post-Liberal Democracy* (Toronto: University of Toronto Press, 1992), contends with

Gramsci's efforts to resolve the contradictions of contingency, choice and condition.

163. Timothy Findley, *Headhunter* (Toronto: Harper Collins, 1993) p. 203. In as much as this novel brings Conrad's *Heart of Darkness* home to bourgeois Toronto, it may be fitting to include it an essay on development discourse.

2 Democratization and Demystification: Deconstructing 'Governance' as Development Paradigm

Gerald J. Schmitz

> As in every crisis, the present situation has elements of both despair and hope, of destruction and reconstruction. As Gramsci said, 'the old order is dead, but the new order cannot yet be born.'[1]

INTRODUCTION

On the threshold of the third millennium, there is a pervasive sense that fundamental forces are at work reshaping the world system as we know it. Yet there is much less confidence, on the part of either governments (despite their slogans of 'managing change') or the governed (still more herded than heeded), that matters can be controlled (effectively and democratically?) to achieve the public purposes ritually promised by political rhetoric.

A few years ago, as many in the West extolled the Cold War's declared death as some sort of vindication, a former US State Department official Francis Fukuyama went so far as to proclaim the arrival of the 'end of history' in a universal apotheosis of capitalist liberal democracy. But that was then, this is now. Looking ahead – post-Gulf War; post-Yugoslavia and Somalia; soon perhaps post-Yeltsin – the mood had turned markedly more sombre notwithstanding the energetic fresh face of the quickly embattled Clinton presidency. The season's trend-setting book, historian Paul Kennedy's *Preparing for the 21st Century*, resonated with near-Malthusian melancholy about global prospects. Fukuyama's pseudo-Hegelian rapture already seemed an ironically historical footnote.

54

This overriding emotional predicament reflects a failure of present structures and institutions to come to grips with profound problems confronting humanity. It also reflects an intellectual failure to understand that the 'old order' cannot be the basis on which a new 'sustainable' one is constructed. The task of radical deconstruction must therefore not be avoided any longer.

What follows aims to make a modest contribution in beginning to apply that task to the problematics of 'democracy' and 'development,' for which 'governance' has emerged as an old-order solution in the guise of new insight. I argue that the elaboration of a 'governance and development' paradigm is driven primarily as an exercise of elite institutional self-preservation responding to the threat posed by systemic breakdown. It is itself a symptom of the world crisis, not a true diagnosis much less a cure. As such, it offers no way forward to the expansion of democratic freedom and social creativity. At a time when millions still lack even minimal conditions for human dignity, that struggle must be located elsewhere.

DEMYSTIFYING THE DISCOURSES

'The question is,' said Alice, 'whether you can make words mean so many different things.'
'The question is,' said Humpty Dumpty, 'which is to be master – that's all.'

(Lewis Carroll, *Alice in Wonderland*[2])

The ideology of developmentalism is in trouble, and at least some of its proponents know it. Without denying the improvements that can be pointed to in various indices of human progress for various countries at various times, development as 'modernization in a hurry' (typically justifying elitist, coercive patterns of growth) has visited enough horrors upon peoples that it has become much harder to celebrate *per se* as a self-evidently 'good thing.' Increasingly, therefore, pro-development discourses are seeking to be associated with attractively qualitative processes, and with their derived humanistic, politically and environmentally 'correct' vocabularies – e.g., those of 'sustainability', 'equity', 'participation', etc.[3] Even classical terms such as 'democracy' and 'rights' have been enlisted on the side of development. Yet, as the authors of *The Development Dictionary* expose, the professional manipulation of seemingly benign words and concepts belies the deepening contradiction of a modern development paradigm which remains essentially driven by techno-scientific and economistic variables, and which rests on a prevailing global power structure that is grossly *in*equitable and *un*democratic.[4]

Disciplinary self-criticism is in order, since professional elites have often been complicit in rationalizing or attempting to legitimize repressive forms of development. This holds particularly for practitioners of the 'queen' of the development sciences, since as Cristovam Buarque argues, 'economists have managed to make their language look legitimate by putting over the idea that the concepts they use are neutral,' when clearly they are not. More generally, academic circles remain 'aloof from the population. The prevailing paradigm ensnares thought in the prison of its language.'[5] It is precisely the *denial* of ideological captivities that needs to be confronted, and in those terms, connecting the problematics of knowledge to the realities of power.

In a penetrating critique of the compromises of the Brundtland Report, William Graf cites Robert Cox that: 'Ideological analysis is . . . a critic's weapon and one used most effectively against the prevailing orthodoxies which, when stripped of their putative universality, become seen as special pleading for historically transient but presently entrenched interests.'[6] As Graf shows, the Brundtland Commission avoided as much as possible historical-political analyses which might have interfered with its consensus-building functions around 'technocratized' solutions. Despite rhetorical references to popular participation, it is apparent that the primary source of the 'political will' required to implement the 'environment and development' bargain will be among Southern elites collaborating with those of the North – a 'multilateral' approach which accepts the hegemony of the existing ruling structures and institutions of the world system. As will be examined later, there are strong similarities with the governance paradigm currently being promoted by these same powers. The emperor's new wardrobe camouflages what ought to be contested.

Indeed what is remarkable about much of the fashionable discourses on 'participatory development' are the extent to which they evade the actual relations of power which keep people poor and dis-empowered. For example, why is it that the much-proclaimed globalization of markets (usually assumed to be inexorable if not always desirable) corresponds to what Mabub Ul-Haq of the UN Development Programme has termed the 'globalization of poverty'? One is unlikely to find much in the way of historical-political explanation in the official literature. While the UNDP at least calls for 'radical reforms' to these pervasive market structures to benefit poor countries and people, the ideological premise persists that competitive capitalist development is inherently empowering (notwithstanding what democratic political inquiry might conclude).[7]

In fact, the word 'empowerment' has been virtually co-opted to promote the ideological linkage of popular participation to economic liberalization. This means that planning development projects to make them appear more participatory, 'pro-poor,' 'people-oriented,' and so on, is fine, as long as it takes place within the parameters of the 'structural adjustment of politics' – that is, the limited state which dutifully pursues 'responsible' policies ('market-friendly' and meeting the approval of Northern powers) and accordingly is relatively insulated from 'rent-seeking' demands from the body politic.[8] To the extent that democratic development is accepted, it is in a privatized form which celebrates the freedom of supposedly voluntary exchange within a state-less 'civil society.' In effect, this arena for the participatory enterprise is completely delinked from any societal project of democratization – via historical-political struggles – at the level of the state and who ought to determine public policies.

The results can be ironic: the World Bank's rhetoric of participation has led some critics to accuse it of being too enamoured of NGOs and 'empowering society' at the expense of strengthening the developmental capacity of states;[9] while other critics see this as a smokescreen behind which client governments are still enjoined to implement the prescribed neoliberal policies, if necessary by repressing their domestic sources of popular opposition.[10]

Another telling contradiction to note is *who controls* the construction of the established discourses. Even in the area of participation and em-powerment, it is quickly obvious that it is not poor peoples' organizations themselves (who may more likely be expected to be consumers of others' expert 'help'). A recent survey of the literature prepared for World Bank deliberations on the subject of participatory development, paradoxically entitled 'Demystifying Popular Participation,' begins by revealing to us that:

Fostering popular participation is a deeply serious matter, but it is not rocket science. When the reams of paper on the subject are put aside, **we development professionals** sense intuitively that participation is a good thing, and **we know how to foster it**.

(emphasis added)[11]

The author lightly passes over the extraordinary (and often violent) history of peoples' struggles for democracy:

The debates and conflicts about popular participation [are] really quite few when compared to other issues. . . . there is mildly ideological debate over whether popular participation is good in itself (representing the goal of empowerment of the poor and, in the larger political sense, the goal of democracy) or as a means to an end – project sustainability.[12]

The latter is of course the true key, since it makes participation World Bank-friendly and neutralizes its historical-political content. In contrast to *self*-empowerment and grassroots democratic action, it is 'we professionals,' with access to our reams of paper, who know best how others should do participatory development. Extending the paradox, more 'participation' ends up reinforcing the Bank's role, even though more real democracy in developing countries would quite likely reduce it!

Another revealing example are the remarks by the co-director of CIDA's Montreal-based Centre of Excellence on Development and Structural Adjustment Policies that: '. . . in sharing North American concepts of efficiency and equity and in particular the language used by the World Bank and the International Monetary Fund, we are helping the decision-makers of these countries [in the South] to negotiate better, to keep their autonomy and their right to their own decisions.'[13] As I have commented elsewhere: 'The "autonomy" of those to whom "development" is done is circumscribed within a language which is not their own and within an international set of rules over which they have little or no say.'[14] In fact, the Northern experts are themselves trapped within the comforting conceits and fertile mystifications of the hegemonic paradigm – which remains, cosmetics aside, profoundly *undemocratic*: patriarchal as well as elitist, and 'functional' mostly in its capacity to reproduce structural relations of unequal power within societies and between North and South.

GLOBAL DILEMMAS OF DEMOCRATIZATION

What, then, to make of the much-celebrated trend in recent years of the spread of democracy around the globe? At a fairly superficial level, there has indeed been a large increase in the number of nominally democratic multiparty elections being held. Many more countries are at least going through the motions. In a number of cases (Latin America, the Philippines), too, these electoral transitions predate the so-called Cold War victory of Western democratic ideals in 1989–90. At the same time, as even conservative democracy boosters such as Larry Diamond acknowledge, there is also the evidence of reversal (Haiti), critical erosion (Sri Lanka, India), brutal suppression (China, Burma), fundamentalist challenge (North Africa, Sudan); not to mention the extraordinary tasks of institutionalizing democracy in the former Soviet empire, and the systemic crises afflicting some rich established democracies (Italy). In a 'tour d'horizon', Diamond concludes that 'democracy is likely to continue to expand and to manifest itself as a global phenomenon; nevertheless, in most of the world throughout the 1990s, democracy will remain insecure and embattled. During this period there will be new democratic breakdowns as well as many badly functioning, illiberal, and unstable democratic regimes.'[15]

The neo-liberal explanation of democracy's growth, albeit uneven and uncertain, appeals to Western good intentions. But it rests on some doubtful and inadequate premises, as well as being open to vigorous challenge from radical popular perspectives. First, unlike more self-critical, qualitative approaches to democracy,[16] it tends to regard advanced capitalist Western (especially Anglo-American) liberal democracy as a defining high point, from which movement is either towards or away. Democratization is associated, in general and over the long term, with liberal economic development and the growth of a large middle class.[17] In short, since capitalism is seen overall as philosophically and empirically allied with 'democracy,' there is typically little or no inquiry into contradictions arising from structurally unequal relations of market power, or the invasive global reach of markets and transnational corporations versus the preservation of nation-state or popular sovereignties.

A second premise is that democracy needs the West's 'help.' The 'white man's burden' has been replaced by a new democratic one. For example, Diamond takes pride that, 'despite an unprecedented budget crisis . . . current US spending for democracy promotion is probably about $200 million (or twice that if the relevant programs of the US Information Agency are included).' Sandinista Nicaragua is included with Poland and Chile as a 'dictatorship' that US support helped to bring down. He also agrees with Huntington that El Salvador and Guatemala are among countries in which 'US support was critical to democratization . . .'[18] Ironically, he trips himself up later by stating that 'it is difficult to assert that "democracy" has diffused to . . . Guatemala and El Salvador (at least until the 1992 settlement) where the military virtually define the extent of civilian authority and influence most aspects of government policy'.[19] One of the results of that settlement was the United Nations Truth Commission report released March 15, 1993, laying bare the massive human rights violations committed with impunity by the Salvadoran army and security forces, and the clear US complicity in financing operations and covering up.

Diamond's ingenuous message boils down to trusting in Western benevolence and superior knowledge. Then, *and only then*, can one make allowances for adaptations appropriate to local conditions. After listing at length things to which other countries 'must' aspire, with our help, if they are to become more 'democratic' (including foremost, 'self-sustaining growth, based on open, market-oriented economic structures'), Diamond observes with unintended irony: 'the West must be careful to assist the organic development of these institutions in the particular "soil" of each country, without imposing its own particular vision of *how* democracy should work.'[20] But the main point is in fact that democratic 'conditionality' *is* a one-way street. In return for mandatory Western assistance and advice, weak dependent democracies 'must show that they can function politically,' with leaderships able 'to choose the right policies and to build political constituencies around them, and to conduct the business of government and politics with probity, respect, and restraint.'[21]

Such exigencies and constraints have seldom applied when it comes to governing the actions of Western governments! As Chomsky extensively documents, an unvarnished reading of post-war history leads to the conclusion that Western powers have done rather a better job of *deterring* than promoting democracy.[22] Among more positive assessments of Western donors' democratic mission, the most useful also tend to be reserved and to carry important qualifications.[23] Moreover, the North's own historical experience confirms that authentic democratization and human rights progress almost always arises from popular struggles against elite domination. It is in vain, therefore (if not a delusory conceit), to conceive democratic development as a gift to be bestowed by rich-country elites upon a waiting world.[24]

There are nonetheless crucial reasons why this 'necessary illusion,' as Chomsky might call it, gets promoted – namely, its continued strategic utility. Reaganesque 'democracy crusades' are no longer needed to 'win' the Cold War. But at a time when millions are protesting the effects of capitalist economic 'globalization,' free-trade 'rationalization,' and the harsh 'medicine' of structural adjustment – which have coincided with growing poverty and disparities within and between North and South[25] – to ally democracy with economic liberalization, on terms favourable to Western capitalist 'competitiveness,' is tremendously important. As Gills and Rocamora state, '*democratisation is considered the necessary and natural product of submission to the rationality of the worldwide market.*'[26]

Instead of the authentic *deepening* of democratization processes (both within government *and* civil society) being perceived as a continuous challenge for all societies,[27] what is more powerfully at stake is the effective extension of elite market interests through a global 'democratic' sphere of influence. The appeal is to an international regime of 'low intensity democracy' capable of managing conflicts (including those engendered by neoliberal policies) without threatening the system itself or its major powerholders. The main difference now is that the reactionary version, which favoured a civilianized facade of 'democracy' to carry out conservative policies, has been replaced by the more reformist interventionism of the Clintonesque version outlined in February 1992:

> Our leadership is especially important for the world's new and emerging democracies. To grow and deepen their legitimacy, to foster a middle class and a civic culture, they need the ability to tap into a growing global economy. . . . If we could make a garden of democracy and prosperity and free enterprise in every part of this globe, the world would be a safer and a better and a more prosperous place for the United States . . .
>
> Democracy's prospects are dimmed, especially in the developing world, by trade barriers and slow economic growth. . . . Trade, of course, cannot ensure the survival of new democracies. . . . But . . . if we believe in the bonds of democracy, we must resolve to strengthen the bonds of commerce.[28]

What this ignores, of course, are the realities of domestic and international economic *bondage*, and the actual class biases underlying the power politics of commerce-driven policymaking – for example, in the case of North American free trade. Governing elites' worries about debt and demography may have had something to do with Mexico's success in seeking the NAFTA negotiations; certainly it was not any impulse towards democracy. A brash survey in *The Economist* bluntly observed that, although Mexico is now 'poised for the spotlight' ('the club of rich nations hails it as the perfect student of economics'): 'Mexico is in no sense a democracy. Government is conducted by an unelected bureaucratic elite accountable only to the president.'[29] NAFTA's critics are concerned that it will reinforce the concentration of wealth and market power in the hands of ruling elites, and further remove areas of policy from domestic debate to technocratic decision by appointed expert panels.[30]

Perhaps trade liberalization and economic integration can be linked to democratic social reforms benefiting popular majorities.[31] But the search for alternatives and transnational democratic alliances will have to contend with the apathy, cynicism and weariness induced by the establishment version of 'democracy' in many populations. A Mexico City-based journalist describes the loss of faith in her region:

> Only a minority bother to vote and elect governments. The majority are tired of unkept promises, political machines, useless congresses and

corrupt leaders. The gap between the rich and the poor in virtually every Latin American country continues to widen. Free trade, that new trend depicted as the international economic arm of democracy, has so far made the rich richer and the poor poorer.[32]

Small wonder that we are revisiting the déjà vu of a crisis of 'governability', but in a context which more intensely interrelates the domestic malaise with the dynamics of the global system. All regions, increasingly integrated within the capitalist world economy, face new challenges to their governance institutions. What are the chances for democratic responses? As David Held observes,

> the globalization of economic relationships has altered the possibility of deploying whole ranges of economic policy. . . . As the boundaries of domestic politics become blurred, the politics of economic policy, and of many other domains of policy as well, becomes more complex. In this context, the meaning and place of democracy has to be rethought in relation to a series of overlapping local, regional, and global structures and processes.[33]

Argue Gills and Rocamora:

> There is a 'crisis of democracy' in the world today as much as an opportunity for democracy. All states . . . face increasing economic competition at the international level, and are beset by mounting social tensions with which they are less and less able to deal effectively with the traditional national policy tools at their disposal.[34]

In the North, such pressures are provoking sober re-evaluations of the alienation of citizens from the formally democratic machinery, and as well in the case of Western Europe, of the supranational 'democratic deficit' threatening the integrationist project.[35] In the South and East, the democratic struggle is being waged at a more basic level. But the nature of globalizing phenomena (either welcomed or feared) increasingly forces interconnections. The question is whether these can be contained, and popular demands appeased, within an elite-managed 'governance' regime, or whether the current crisis will spark a more fundamental transformation of inequitable global structures 'through a global democratization from below.'[36]

Radical democrats envisage that 'there must be a new global participatory politics aimed at the hitherto unaccountable and unrepresentative governing institutions of the international system.'[37] They emphasize the role of citizens' social movements and popular organizations in the deepening of democratization within civil society, extending to the struggle – through engagement in transnational networks and alliances – for a 'global civil society' corresponding to the global problematic.[38] This means confronting the dominant paradigm of world development, and thereby turning back from the 'manufactured consent' of its elite-constructed governance solutions, towards opening up once again the basic social questions of democracy – in a new cosmopolitan key.

THE DEVELOPMENT OF CRISIS AND CRISIS OF DEVELOPMENT

Before examining the governance 'solutions' more closely, it is worth reviewing briefly why they have become so necessary to the self-preservation of established developmentalist ideology. The end of the long period of post-war economic expansion in the 1970s, and deconstruction of the Keynesian compromise of 'embedded liberalism' (whereby welfare states compensated for cyclical market failures), exacerbated the underlying contradictions of North–South development: namely, the extraction of large financial surpluses side by side the creation of poverty. The 'monetarist' reversion to neoclassical orthodoxy decreed that it was the patient itself that was the problem. *Too much* social demand led to excessive inefficient government intervention, to public failure that was worse than market failure, and so on. Yet the prescribed anti-inflationary 'cure' and interest rate shocks of the early 1980s produced a crisis 'which was the most serious world economic setback since the Depression of the 1930s, [and which] spread through the Third World by a variety of channels.'[39]

The crisis, of which unserviceable debt burdens were a severe manifestation, was managed, after a fashion, by a succession of 'stabilization' and 'structural adjustment' programmes to restore economies to external 'balance' and 'sustainable growth.' But in the leaner, meaner 1980s, there was to be no returning to the indulgences of the interventionist state. Government, after all, was the problem. So the watchwords became instead austerity, restraint, discipline, privatization and marketization wherever possible. As Thomas Callaghy remarks: 'The compromise of embedded liberalism has not been extended by the major powers to the Third World since the onslaught of the debt crisis in 1982;' adding: 'Nor has it been extended now, with the collapse of communism, to what used to be the Second World.'[40]

Much of the job of enforcing these new dictums was left to the principal lenders of last resort, the international financial institutions (IFIs) of the

International Monetary Fund (IMF) and the World Bank. As more of their lending became policy-based, subject to stringent economic 'conditionality' based on the above prescriptions, deliverance would come from roving teams of international economic experts with 'a justification for a much more active intervention in the local politics of developing countries.'[41] At its most extreme, using dependence on aid as an instrument of power, the neoliberal orthodoxy required the virtual dismantling of what had been built up under now taboo economic nationalism, the abandonment of social policy roles, and the exclusion of interest-group politics (much less populist democracy) from decision-making processes. Theories of 'rent-seeking,' drawn from neoclassical economics and the public choice and rational expectations schools of the so-called 'new political economy,' were employed to show that, *given any choice*, developing-country governments would only serve themselves and their (mostly urban) supporters. Only freely-operating markets could actually benefit the rural poor. The implicit conclusion was that the only acceptable governance regime was one which functioned as much as possible *without* governments and politicians (unless perhaps they had repented and learned to apply the 'right' policies) in order to maintain openness to international market forces.[42]

Unfortunately for this scenario, the story of the 1980s did not produce a very happy equilibrium. As already noted, poverty and income disparities worsened during the decade, and with the erosion of state power and social safety nets, became less politically sustainable. The social agenda had virtually to be relaunched, not without a struggle, by UNICEF and others calling for 'structural adjustment with a human face.'[43] The political agenda of a positive (if 'market friendly') role for governments and pluralistic politics was rediscovered by the World Bank itself a few years later.[44] But this relaxation and modification of the orthodoxy has not, into the 1990s, been able to overcome the contradictions of the 'lost decade.'

This is apparent from even the most cursory survey. North–South financial flows have become massively negative, with the perverse result of an overall net export of capital *from* poorer *to* richer countries. Although structural adjustment theory originated with the monetarist revival in the North, the South (and now the East) became a virtual laboratory for draconian 'shock therapies' decreed from the top down, which western political systems would have great difficulty withstanding.[45] More generally, governments, unable to meet even their macro-financial targets, have become discredited and lost confidence, chilling the climate for alternative public policies, and contributing to a crisis of legitimation that, as we will see, is unlikely to be remedied by forced marriages of economic and political liberalization or the invocation of 'good governance' mantras.

At the level of production and consumption in the 'real economy,' too, the 'Fordist' compromise of embedded liberalism within the dominant development/modernization paradigm is in crisis. The appeal of 'post-Fordist,' 'post-modern' politics, based on as yet rather unformed ideals of ecological ethics and decentralized democracy, is most evident in the North where the decline of standardized mass production is most advanced. But increasingly the conventional economic growth model is also being resisted in the South.[46] Brazilian Cristovam Buarque contends that: 'Development should not be criticized – as most economists believe – merely because of the way production is distributed but because of the nature of production itself.'[47] The very pattern of elite-engineered and economy-driven development has come under fire as entrapping and harming people, rather than supporting their progress towards democracy and human rights.[48]

Buarque argues that: 'Each poor country became underdeveloped the moment it imported the idea of development without analyzing it, contesting it, adapting it or making it match indigenous values and resources.' In formulating the idea of dependent underdevelopment, even 'the dependency theorists likewise bowed down to cultural dependence . . . the thinking elites of a people acquiesced in being labelled "barbarous".'[49] (Another writer, repudiating the notion that 'democracy cannot work here in Africa,' laments that the 'worst type of crippling is when the mind loses faith in itself and thinks itself inferior *a priori*.'[50])

The economic parameters of the debate have reinforced an impoverished and skewed conception of development. So that, in the case of Brazil, economic 'miracles' coincided with social immiseration; many indicators of a large modern economy were achieved, yet in qualitative areas of civilized life, environmental health, and conserving other societal assets, there has been no great progress or even regression. For the most part, the governing classes have gone along with this fetishism of modern economic competition. The result: 'Degradation of the machinery of the state, which, after efficiently serving the purposes of organization and repression in prompting an elitist, dependent scheme, then founders in financial, political and administrative terms.'[51] Buarque concludes: 'The only solution is to change the way the social process is viewed in Brazil and the Third World, bringing economic interests to heel instead of subjugating social concerns to the economic imperative.'[52]

This appeal is echoed in Gustavo Esteva's call for a renewal of politics at the grassroots level in order to put 'political controls on the economic sphere, while re-embedding economic activities in the social fabric;' recognizing that: 'Such political controls can be implemented only after public awareness of the limits of development has become firmly rooted in society. Even those still convinced that development goals are pertinent ideals for the so-called underdeveloped should honestly recognize the present structural impossibilities for the universal materialization of such goals.'[53] The distorted hegemony of economy in relation to community is manifest within the 'developed' societies of the North as well – for example, in the creation of a 'generation X' of jobless or underemployed youth with lower expectations than their parents; and in what Robert Reich has termed the 'politics of secession' in which the highly skilled (and therefore well-off and politically articulate) members of the community increasingly enclose themselves within islands of prosperity, while the public health and safety of society as a whole erodes.[54]

The problem is that the deepening crisis of the conventional economic paradigm seems paradoxically to have reinforced the tyranny of economy-driven solutions. Reich, for example, accepting the increasingly global and mobile character of capital and skills, advocates interventionist public strategies designed to raise the general 'competitiveness' of American society within the integrated world marketplace. A positive role for governments and governance is thereby affirmed. Social policy initiatives, too, are seen as instrumental to restoring the competitive position of the American workforce. But all of this remains governed by, indeed it is subjugated to, the exigencies, imperatives and 'rules' of the international economy. It is a matter of economic necessity and the politics of globalization, *not* of democracy and a search for socially-governed alternatives. We see this tyranny operating as well in the notion that the primary test of government budgets is whether they appease nervous markets and fickle investors, especially footloose international ones, not whether governments tax and spend so as to meet long-term social needs.

The development of the economic crisis therefore has served mostly to intensify the crisis of economic development. Solutions which seek to build public policy consensus around approaches governed by economic globalization are themselves trapped within this logic. At best, their social dimension is confined to mitigation of the worst (i.e., clearly dysfunctional) effects of the class and power divisions which are *exacerbated* by the extension and global integration of the dominant development paradigm. Where the social and political processes are not marginalized, they are in effect captured by the overriding dynamic of the economic world process which creates and perpetuates poverty and inequality. As Buarque contends:

The outcome is a trend towards transnational apartheid: an internationalism with those integrated into modernity and all the excluded remainder (including poor youths in rich countries) being separated into opposing camps. In 'rich countries', the majority will vote democratically to pre-serve privileges keeping the foreign poor at bay. In 'poor countries', the rich minority will find new forms of 'democracy' to keep the majority from impossible mass consumption.[55]

Instead of promoting a democratic ethics of global responsibility and equality, and fostering a spirit of critical solidarity among peoples, 'governance' ultimately puts the onus on *existing* governments – North and South, East as well as West – 'successfully' to manage the *prevailing* capitalist political economy of globalization, and notably to manage the resulting social tensions in such a way that the lid does not blow off and threaten the entire elite development regime of accumulation and legitimation. The question is: will it work?

'GOOD GOVERNANCE' TO THE RESCUE?

> Humpty Dumpty sat on a wall
> Humpty Dumpty had a great fall
> All the king's horses and all the king's men
> Could not put Humpty together again.
> *(nursery rhyme)*

Given nervous global outlooks for the 1990s and the grim legacy of the 1980s for much of the South, the historic toppling of the Berlin Wall acutely contrasted with less transitory 'walls' built on poverty, illiteracy, and discrimination based on gender, race, ethnic origin, religion and na-tionality.[56] A yearly Human Development Report instituted by the UN Development Programme in 1990 also brought renewed attention to broader measures of comparative societal development than an economically or-thodox preoccupation with 'getting prices right' had seemed to allow. Going a step further, its authors suggested at least a strong correlation (even if no clear causal linkage) between achieving high levels of eco-nomic welfare and high levels of 'political freedom.' Notwithstanding the controversies provoked by such measures and methodologies, the more important subtext was to renew faith that history did not have to leave developing countries behind: a liberal reformist political economy of de-velopment could work for them too. Under the right conditions and with the right policies, all countries could make progress up the ladder of the 'human development index,' the top rung of which, not incidentally, was occupied exclusively by advanced capitalist countries.[57]

Yet the perceived need for the UNDP's accounting was itself a telling indication that all was not well in the world of development. The incandescence of revolutionary upheaval in the Second World seemed to put in shadow the depressing familiarity of most news from the Third, and to augur a marginalization of the South's development concerns. Once again development was on trial, and the development community put on the defensive. Why, despite billions spent on foreign assistance over decades, did the promises of development still appear to be so distant to growing numbers of absolute poor? And then if Communism could collapse in the official enemy Russia and its former satellites, why could poor countries receiving Western aid not get themselves out of the poverty trap (a less difficult task, one might have thought)? Something more was required. Two separate but interlinked sets of responses have been constructed within the mainstream development discourse. Both identify 'governance,' *in developing countries* (not globally or in the North), as the primary source of the problem (explaining the lack of success of past benevolence), and as the basis for solution (justifying new conditions and limitations on this benevolence).

The first set of responses constitute the World Bank view (although there is considerable diversity *within* the Bank), and while both stimulated and complicated by events since 1989, their origin goes deeper to the crisis in the internal logic of development, particularly the relative failure of Sub-Saharan Africa to achieve economic success in the Bank's terms. Despite the ministrations of donors, African countries had not turned the corner and remained highly dependent on concessional flows (and therefore susceptible to still more intrusive forms of donor influence). Convinced that its neoliberal economic policy prescriptions (i.e., the existing economic conditionality of structural adjustment loans) were correct, that integration into world markets was desirable, and unable or unwilling directly to attack governments on political grounds, the Bank's search for what was wrong required a more subtle strategy. This was outlined in the seminal *Long-Term Perspective Study* released in 1989 which spoke for the first time of a 'crisis of governance' and which declared that 'the root cause of weak economic performance in the past has been the failure of public institutions.'[58]

In other words, the problem was not adverse conditions, unfair markets, or inappropriate economic reforms, but lack of proper institutional capacity to manage necessary processes of adjustment. The view which has gained the widest acceptance in the Bank sees 'governance' as really only a logical extension of previous economic conditionality. President Lewis Preston's foreword to an April 1992 discussion booklet begins: 'Good governance is an essential complement to sound economic policies.' Defining governance as 'the manner in which power is exercised in the management of a country's economic and social resources for development,' the booklet declares it to be 'synonymous with sound development management.'[59] Such management includes the 'good public administration' menu of information, transparency, accountability, adequate legal norms, predictability, trust, responsiveness, professionalism, anti-corruption measures, and so on. None of this is very revolutionary. In fact an earlier draft of the discussion document had argued that 'there is no need for additional criteria to reflect concerns with governance: merely the effective and consistent application of existing criteria based on a greater awareness of the importance of issues of governance for development performance.'[60]

The key thing to ask of developing countries was **not** whether they were democracies or autocracies (judgments as to 'form of political regime' were explicitly ruled to be outside the Bank's mandate[61]), but whether they had the governing will and wherewithal to create the 'appropriate policy framework' required to achieve efficient markets and the successful implementation of donor and creditor-mandated economic liberalization programs. This has not meant exactly a 'see no politics' approach. In some analyses, a preference emerges for Western liberal (or more precisely, Anglo-American) modes of governance, selectively involving elements of participation and political pluralism, though always carefully tied instrumentally to economic development performance objectives.[62] In several cases, the Bank has benefitted from less-than-deserved public associations with bilateral donors' explicit calls for political and human rights reforms.[63] As well, there has been scope for bolder staff positions to surface on the margins, and this in turn has provided an opening for some to see the Bank as a potential positive agent of political liberalization.[64] For example, Landell-Mills and Serageldin, by enlarging the definition of governance to include normative bases of legitimacy in 'the use of political authority . . . and the nature of the relationship between the rulers and the ruled,' are led to conclude:

> Economic and social progress are not the only objectives of good governance. Civil liberty and the ability to participate in the political system can also be viewed as elements of a full and meaningful life that should contribute to the well being of individuals and the development of societies.[65]

And although the term 'human rights' never appears in the *Governance and Development* booklet, the Bank's inter-divisional governance thematic team included a 'human rights subgroup' whose work program terms of reference stated: 'The use of the word 'governance' gives explicit recognition to the political dimension of the issue.'[66]

Clearly the Bank has been affected by the post-Cold War rhetoric of its major OECD shareholders, but perhaps even more by the risks to itself from the escalating demands of growing democracy movements in client countries calling for real regime change. It must therefore find a way to contain these pressures for political reform within the boundaries of 'good governance,' or suffer the unpalatable results. This presents a large unresolved dilemma for future Bank policy and a challenge to its own crisis management skills. For example, numerous African critics see the IFIs as having collaborated with discredited authoritarian governments in resorting to coercive imposition of unpopular adjustment policies. They see the demands of external creditors as having contributed mostly in a negative way to anti-government, pro-democracy protests, which could also destabilize newer elected or transitional governments, and not as reflecting the development of democratic expressions of popular will.[67] If governments with domestic democratic legitimacy were to begin to repudiate, rather than enforce, the Bank's development model, the unintended consequences of the 'crisis of governance' would indeed hit home!

The second set of responses, which derive from the policies of the bilateral aid donors, has so far been driven more by the shifting external politics of the development crisis than by the threatened internal logic of the dominant neoliberal paradigm. This is particularly true in the case of the United States, where foreign aid is tough to sell at the best of times (and increasingly so in areas of decreasing strategic foreign policy interest – as is the case with Africa), and where a new post-Cold War rationale must be found. Moreover, US policymakers need face few qualms about exporting American values.[68] Britain and France do not have the same superpower concern about promoting stable congenial governance abroad, but are still considerably affected by ties to former colonies. Among the donors generally, there is a mixture of contextual and ideological motives: their publics increasingly expect aid to be linked to human rights and other standards of good behaviour; 'friendly' but dictatorial or corrupt regimes have become embarrassments, and worse, less reliable and useful; slower growth (or actual declines) in aid flows coupled with new demands from the post-Communist East encourage a broader application of more demanding policy conditionalities; and not least, a focus on correcting the governance flaws of others may deflect more dangerous questions about Western authority in these matters.

Unlike the tortuous equivocations and restrictions circumscribing the World Bank view of 'good governance,' the bilateral donors' view candidly promotes a liberal political ideology of 'participatory development' based on the (OECD) consensus that 'human rights and democracy are valuable in themselves and constitute legitimate goals for aid.'[69] Some of its exponents have expressed dissatisfaction with the Bank's cautious instrumentalism, arguing that the pursuit of even narrower governance goals cannot credibly be held to be independent of the concrete form of political system and its degree of democracy and respect for human rights.[70] Others have stretched the concept into virtual public-policy wish lists. For example, in an official Canadian definition, good governance is said to go much beyond human rights and democracy to include 'sufficient priority given to basic social programs, defence spending that is not excessive, and the pursuit of sensible market-based economies.'[71] In practice, however, the advertised normative framework often does not determine aid allocations; much less is there a transparent, consistent or coherent application of such catch-all conditionalities.[72] Moreover, since Western governments would have trouble with close scrutiny of many of their own domestic policies on these grounds, and given that precise operational benchmark criteria of good governance have not been developed, it is difficult to take much of this thrust too seriously.

What is clearly serious, and wherein lies the critical interlinkage of World Bank and OECD consensus views, is the anchoring of political conditionalities within the good-governance regime to orthodox economic conditionality and the fundamentals of 'market-friendly' development. Frequently, it is asserted or implied that political liberalization will serve to advance the latter agenda of economic liberalization. As one commentator rather innocently observes: 'After more than ten years of structural adjustment efforts in the Third World there is a growing consensus that economic reforms cannot succeed without political reforms based on the respect for human rights and participation of the population.'[73] But in fact, it cannot be assumed that, based on such a respectful democratic public process, policymakers in developing countries would choose the 'right policies' already selected for them by the donor community. The linkage of economic 'good governance' to Western ideas of liberal democracy rests more on ideological conviction than empirical evidence.

As one examination concludes:

> While there are some encouraging signs, developing country experience in the 1980s does not give a firm assurance that greater democracy will result in better economic management, effective adjustment policies or faster economic growth. *Ultimately, democracy's case may stand better on its own.*[74]

The contrast between democracy's appeal and its unreliability (for elite-approved purposes) spells looming trouble for the notion that 'good governance' – on terms decided *by* governing elites in the North *for* their counterparts in the South – is just the rescue operation that is needed to sustain the dominant economic development model and the 'orderly' integration of developing economies into the global capitalist political economy.[75] At best, this governance regime can attempt to manage the deepening contradictions of an inequitable and undemocratic system of North–South relations. But its recent emergence is a symptom of, not a remedy for, the internal and external crises of development and development policy. If more democracy and popular participation are really the goal, then a fixation on governance and 'governability' is exactly the wrong response.[76] This central point deserves further elaboration.

GOVERNANCE AS DEVELOPMENT PARADIGM?

History tells us that in politics there must be visions.[77]

A striking thing about this new, or actually reborn, vision is how apolitical it is. It is a vision propelled by the competition of autonomous economic markets and rational, autonomous citizens working their will on minimalist state structures that are now democratic, as both economic and political arrangements adjust to changing conditions. Does this transcendent vision collide with the political realities of everyday life? Are vision and politics at odds?[78]

Sheldon Wolin, author of a classic political theory text *Politics and Vision*, declared in an editorial 'Why Democracy?' in the inaugural 1981 issue of the American journal *Democracy*: 'We have been hypnotized so long by the ideology of economic and technological progress that we have scarcely noticed that, politically, we have become a retrogressive society, evolving from a more to a less democratic polity and from a less to a more authoritarian society.'[79] Unfortunately, as the Reagan era began, Wolin's call for a radical democratic renewal fell on deaf ears, at least in elite circles. More than a decade later, it has become more pertinent than ever to ask 'why governance?' and 'why not democracy?'

Applied to the development debate, the clues lie in the interests of historically governing classes in managing necessary economic and political 'reform' processes so that the fundamental stability (and power inequity) of the North–South regime is not challenged. At first, it seemed that democratic development could be bypassed to achieve this 'adjustment.' The purpose of neoliberal economic conditionality was, after all, to reduce political intervention in markets and to shrink the public sector not encourage its democratic expansion. Mosley *et al.* describe these tendencies of the new economic theory of politics as representing 'a dramatic shift away from a pluralist, participatory ideal of politics and towards an authoritarian and technocratic ideal based not on big government but on small and highly efficient government. In the longer perspective, they signal the return in the 1980s to dominance of the non-participatory strand of western political theory.'[80] And since governing elites in developing countries could not be trusted, they had to be helped to do the job by international economic experts.

The problem was that not only did this fail to generate any domestic political 'ownership' of the neo-liberal economic agenda, but it also engendered dangerous mass protests against it linked to pressures for democratic reform. The eventual resort to 'governance' was driven by a recognition that something had to be done to forestall this impending crisis of the development model, not by a sudden desire to welcome democratic change. In the elite vision of reform politics, the burgeoning demands for democratic development had somehow to be contained within a controlled and superordinate 'good governance' regime which could then be counted on to deliver 'political sustainability' for neoliberal policies. The result was an alliance of political to economic conditionality, of political to economic liberalization, and at its most ideological, of 'democracy' to the quest for free markets. Callaghy, however, is sceptical of how much has actually been achieved in this regard.

> Some learning about economic reform and the necessity of macroeconomic restraint has taken place, but the question becomes *who* has learned – technocrats, rulers, military officers, government officials, politicians, leaders of groups in 'civil society,' or the mass electorate? Thus far the learning has been mostly at the technocratic level. . . . 'informed constituencies of restraint' are not likely to emerge in very many places.[81]

Put another way, manufacturing 'democratic consent' is (fortunately, I believe) proving to be much more difficult at the mass than at the elite level!

The 'vision' of governance tries to evade the implications of this because at bottom, even when it speaks of popular participation and 'empowerment' of the poor, it is really not a democratic approach which respects peoples' rights freely to choose their own modes of development and to decide their own public policies. Participation – which has obvious appeal for the purposes of fund-raising and building public support for development – is seen more restrictively as instrumentally valuable to the success of development projects, as mobilizing private sector resources for development, and as promoting self-reliant entrepreneurship.[82] For example, a recent World Bank study urges it to see the poor as its 'principal customers,' with the goal of creating an 'enabling environment in which . . . the poor cease to be beneficiaries, passively receiving largesse from government, but more like customers in good standing who must be enabled to pay the costs for what they see will bring about their own betterment with their time, labour and capital.'[83]

Helping the poor in this way sounds attractive. But it implies an idealized 'self-reliant' society in which Bank professionals act as understanding managers interacting with their clients on the basis of 'voluntary' market exchanges. An alternative view of social development would be to see it as bringing to participants not only direct material benefits from particular economic projects, but also 'a transformation of consciousness and self-perception which would enable them to understand their social situation and to see it as something that they can, with others, struggle to change.'[84] Once again, the Bank's vision rests on an ideological construction which is strikingly apolitical, without any sense of the real organization of political power within societies, of hierarchical class structures, or therefore of the democratization of the state in order to make it serve community needs. In this vision, NGOs working with the poor are simply useful as agents of project participation, private service delivery, and local 'civic culture,' not as agents for wider democratic change. As Laura Macdonald astutely observes, the neoliberal representation of 'civil society'

> in fact attempts to restrict the political sphere by ensuring that all the relevant decisions are made by national and international elites, while the popular sector is caught up in income-generating activities and organizational activity at the margins of the political system. What is promoted then is the privatization of both development and democracy. The failure to address the legitimate role of the state may ultimately lead to strengthening mechanisms which enforce the political submissiveness in civil society, rather than those which empower the poor or incorporate their demands into the public sphere.[85]

At one point the Bank's *Governance and Development* booklet contains the statement: 'Citizens need to demand better governance.'[86] Exactly. Yet, since discussion of democracy is off limits, what this seems to mean is that people, if they know what is good for them, should support the kind of rational-legal, technocratic (however 'participatory') governance regime which its professional analysis determines to be the most development-friendly. In this discourse, 'accountability' is circumscribed within systems of abstract rules, and the 'power to manage' is treated as an objectively neutral resource, similar to the ahistorical concept of market exchange in neoclassical economics. Missed completely is any concrete contextualization of actual power relationships. As Buarque remarks, citing Mark Blaug: 'In reviewing Smith or any other economist, we should always remember that brilliance in handling purely analytical concepts is very different from a firm grasp of the essential logic of economic relations. This comment could well apply to the technocracy schooled and groomed during the last decades to administer the capitalist state. ... They cannot detach themselves from the premises that legitimize the prevailing framework and have grown incapable of criticizing the essence of the process.'[87]

The same critique needs to be brought to bear on political science approaches to governance, especially since, as Mick Moore points out – 'Now that good government is on the development policy agenda, political scientists are being commissioned to work on the practical implications.' While this seems like an innovation, 'good government' issues have long been familiar to political scientists and theorists, ... few sudden break-throughs in knowledge are likely.' Much of what is known, moreover, proves troublesome to facile neoliberal syntheses of democratic and capitalist development.[88] Turning to the comparative politics literature, much of which has been devoted to problems of modernization, political development, development administration and the politics of public policy in developing countries, the work of Goran Hyden on Africa is noteworthy for illustrating some of the problems with conceptualizing reform of the state on the basis of liberal developmentalism.[89]

In a recent seminal essay, Hyden attempts to reorient the discourse on developing-country politics – *away* from classical concepts such as 'democracy' and towards a new development paradigm based on 'governance'.[90] Some of his reasons for doing so have a certain validity: the danger of ethnocentrism in equating democracy with Western-style multiparty systems; the need for other criteria to assess the viability of democratic transitions; the problems facing governments within established democracies. But overall his rationale is as dubious as his contention that the World Bank's governance perspective at least implicitly favours 'democratization' because of the belief that: 'Development will take place only if political leaders abandon their authoritarian practices.'[91] In fact, what the tethering of politics to governance does is to marginalize questions about authentic degrees of democratization within both government **and** society, in favour of issues of functional utility related to development performance. The effect, ultimately, is to de-politicize policy debates while still casting them within a normative framework which subordinates democracy to development.

Drawing from structural-functionalist discourse, Hyden goes further to elaborate a definition of governance as 'the conscious management of regime structures with a view to enhancing the legitimacy of the public realm.'[92] A regime 'determines who has access to political power, and how those who are in power deal with those who are not.' However, it 'is not a set of political actors . . . but rather a set of fundamental rules about the organization of the public realm [which] provides the structural framework within which resources are authoritatively allocated.'[93] Moreover:

> What is of interest here is the extent to which there is a civic public realm and how it is being managed and sustained by political actors, some in the state, others in civil society. Do civic institutions, like government departments, political parties, or the media, all of which participate in the public realm, enjoy respect and legitimacy? Such questions point to the significance of respect for rules that protect the public realm.[94]

The key goal becomes in fact regime maintenance – conducted according to the properties of a well-regulated serviceable system of 'good politics' (not unlike the instrumentalist criteria in *Governance and Development*). The concentration is on an enabling environment for efficient action to preserve and enhance regime performance. Indeed, Hyden explicitly distinguishes political development in this governance sense from democratic development in its own right, arguing that

> . . . the study of governance is performance-oriented. It examines how well a polity is capable of mobilizing and managing social capital – both fixed and movable – so as to strengthen the civic public realm. In this respect, it comes closer to the literature on business management. In the same way as business management theory treats the organization as crucial to business success, the governance approach treats regime – the organization of political relations – as essential for social and economic progress.[95]

It is one thing to suggest, as Hyden does, that 'it is time to abandon the idea of stages in political development – with regimes placed in ladderlike fashion, with Western democracies on top'; quite another to go from that to suggest that what is really important is not whether societies are more, or less, democratic, but whether their governance institutions 'work' better in the sense of promoting development that generates 'social capital.' Hyden claims that 'no regime is necessarily superior to the others. Governance crises are integral parts of all.' Yet this supposed pragmatism carries within it a semi-concealed ideological frame of reference, as when he concludes: 'The question of how regimes can be altered to strengthen the contribution that politics makes to development is of special significance in the post-cold war period when the Leninist-Stalinist mastodon has been largely abandoned and societies are looking for alternative governance structures.'[96]

Suffice it to say, following the World Bank view, that neoliberalism promoting a more politically 'sustainable' integration of the domestic into the global market economy is the essential characteristic of these 'alternatives,' not democracy. Effectively, democratization *as a value in itself* ceases to be of much interest, because what matters in the governance agenda is to get the politics of development policy right. As one analyst poses the question: 'How likely is it that policy makers in the Third World can be influenced to choose the right economic development policies, assuming that we know what those policies are?'[97] The 'we' in question is of course *not* the people in developing countries exercising democratic free choice as to the content of public policy! And without our external supervision, their governments, *especially* democratic ones, cannot be trusted to 'do the right thing' in putting 'prudence before populism.'[98] They must be 'accountable,' but first of all to us, not we to them for our interventions, much less to their citizens. So, paradoxically, as Manfred Bienefeld asserts, it may, after all, be 'no great threat to give people the democratic right to elect governments that have no effective power to determine social or economic policy. It may also be a hollow victory for the people to win that right.'[99]

Governance to the contrary, the struggle for better and more democratic societies must be about fundamentals more than functions, politics more than management – in short, about democracy not just in its form but more importantly, its substance. In contrast to the governance paradigms's nearly exclusive focus on developing countries' policy failures, this struggle must also extend to democratizing global governance: to democratic challenges to transnational actors, public and private, and to the undemocratic transnational regimes of the international political economy. Liberal internationalist perspectives have tended to see the solution as embedding liberal-democratic values within these regimes, as if the spread of 'good governance' entails increasing global convergences around liberalized policies.[100] More radical approaches see the regimes themselves, and the development model which they promote, as fundamentally flawed. Their *de*construction must therefore precede democratic efforts at practical *re*construction based on renewed forms of domestic public participation in policy deliberation and new forms of transnational democracy through solidarity among citizens' movements and other institutional means.[101]

This means putting democratic politics back into 'governance,' and not pretending that the contemporary problematic of development can be safely contained by neat neoliberal governance regimes, in which an emphasis on 'participation' (combined with the usual elite professional fixes of 'capacity-building,' informational, technical and managerial proficiencies, and 'performance') masks the real state of ideological conformity. Furthermore, as Ignatieff correctly observes in another context, 'ideological conviction, the shared belief in a vision of a decent society and how to get there, is the chief link between the ruler and the ruled.' Without ideological discourse, there is no real holding to account. 'When ideologies wane, voters drift away from public debate and leaders feel free to turn politics into administration.'[102]

Far from rescuing the dominant development paradigm, the governance approach, unless it undergoes a far more substantial democratic conversion, will lead to another dead end. A recent appeal for 'putting democratic politics back into development' states the issue well:

> The development crisis calls for solutions that ordinary administration cannot address. Politics should be the building of cooperation based on consensus of what are basic values. The people's lack of involvement in the political process even in the world's advanced democracies means that we are working with a false consensus. The people can be seduced by an image of freedom, cooperation and participation through the mass media, opinion polls, and costly electoral campaigns. . . . An effective political process would be a broader more inclusive process challenging the fundamental inequities not discussing the administrative trimmings.[103]

To conclude, new governance orthodoxies emanating from high places are not the answer to current North–South problems of democracy and development. On the contrary, hope lies in the emergence – through growing movements world-wide for democratic change based on human rights, equality and ecological stewardship – of demystified approaches to development and democratization, and of political actors unwilling to settle for an articulation of 'good governance' that treats the formulation of public policy as akin to 'building a better mousetrap.' These actors will instead insist on the accountability of *all* regimes and their builders. They will be concerned about more than any model's advertised efficiency and price, but also its underlying values, and above all, the political freedom it allows – within an ethic of global responsibility and solidarity – for self-empowerment and for the realization by each society of its own path to the common good. To that end, deconstructing governance as development paradigm constitutes a necessary step in the ultimate construction of a more truly democratic and global praxis.[104]

Notes

1. Barry Gills and Joel Rocamora, 'Low Intensity Democracy,' *Third World Quarterly*, 13, 3 (1992), p. 522.
2. Cited in Schmitz, 'Why Words Matter: Some Thoughts on the "New" Development Agenda,' paper prepared for the annual meeting of the Canadian Association for Studies in International Development, Charlottetown, June 1992.
3. See David Moore, 'The Dynamics of Development Discourse: Sustainability, Equity and Participation,' paper presented to the CASID Annual Meeting, June 1992, and Moore's chapter in this book.
4. Wolfgang Sachs (ed.), *The Development Dictionary: A Guide to Knowledge as Power* (London: Zed Books, 1992). Apologists of modern capitalist development, who lament 'intellectuals' hostility' to it, also thereby acknowledge the ideological power of symbolic construction. As Seymour Martin Lipset comments: 'Perhaps anticipating recent developments in the ranks of the Modern Language Association, Schumpeter even noted that "from the criticism of a text to the criticism of a society, the way is shorter than it seems".' ('Reflections on *Capitalism, Socialism and Democracy*,' *Journal Of Democracy*, 4, 2 (April 1993), p. 45.)
5. Cristovam Buarque, *The End of Economics? Ethics and the Disorder of Progress* (London: Zed Books, 1993), pp. 160–1.
6. William Graf, 'Sustainable Ideologies and Interests: beyond Brundtland,' *Third World Quarterly*, 13, 3 (1992), p. 553.
7. See United Nations Development Programme, *Human Development Report 1992* (New York: Oxford University Press, 1992) esp. pp. 4–7. The leading American theorist of pluralist democracy, Robert Dahl, acknowledging the manifest failures of actually existing socialism and the experiences of the most advanced and successful market economies, nonetheless cautions that: 'Capitalism is persistently at odds with values of equity, fairness, political equality among all citizens, and democracy.' (Cited in Gerald Schmitz and David Gillies, *The Challenge of Democratic Development: Sustaining Democratization in Developing Societies* (Ottawa: The North–South Institute, 1992), p. 28.)
8. This approach lacks an adequate constructive concept of state behaviour to confer benefits. For an apologetic analysis of some shortcomings, cf. Jeffrey

Herbst, 'The Structural Adjustment of Politics in Africa,' *World Development*, 18, 7 (July 1990), pp. 949–58. See also Richard Sandbrook, 'Taming the African Leviathan,' *World Policy Journal*, 7, 4 (Fall 1990), pp. 673–99.

9. Mick Moore, 'Declining to Learn from the East? The World Bank on "Governance and Development",' *IDS Bulletin*, Issue on 'Good Government?, 24, 1 (January 1993), pp. 47–9. It is interesting to note that John Clark, formerly of Oxfam UK and author of *Democratizing Development: The Role of Voluntary Organizations*, has joined the Bank's International Economic Relations Division and is a core team member of the 'Bank-wide Learning Group on Popular Participation.' (See also note 11 below.)

10. Claude Ake, 'Rethinking African Democracy,' *Journal of Democracy*, 2, 1 (Winter 1991), pp. 32–44; Bjorn Beckman, 'Empowerment or Repression? The World Bank and the Politics of African Adjustment,' in Peter Gibbon, Yusuf Bangura and Arve Ofstad (eds), *Authoritarianism, Democracy and Adjustment: The Politics of Economic Reform in Africa* (Uppsala: The Scandinavian Institute of African Studies, 1992).

11. Thomas Dichter, 'Demystifying Popular Participation: Institutional Mechanisms for Popular Participation,' in Bhuvan Bhatnagar and Aubrey Williams (eds), *Participatory Development and the World Bank*, Discussion Paper No. 183 (Washington, DC: The World Bank, 1992), p. 89.

12. Ibid. 'Popular participation' as tamed and institutionalized by the established patron-client regime actually disguises the ideological and class character of the power relationship:

> . . . the professionals are on top, not on tap; they have a solution in search of a problem. . . . This in itself, is a reductionist response as the history of participatory development only too well illustrates. . . . Instrumental concepts of participation justify its contribution to realising the pre-determined goals of the project. It also follows within that logic that the need is to encourage participation from amongst those whose willingness and capacity to help implement the goals of the project are greatest. . . . In contrast, . . . the transformative view argues, firstly, that it is essential to seek and stimulate the participation of just those groups who from a cost-effectiveness point of view would rank lowest.

(Ian Cherrett, Phil O'Keefe and Anne Heidenreich, 'Non-Governmental Organizations – The Demise of a Panacea? The Case of Environmental NGOs in Eastern and Southern Africa,' Report by ETC Foundation, Consultants for Development Programmes, North Shields, UK, August 1992, pp. 12–14.)

13. Cited in Schmitz, 'Why Words Matter,' pp. 8–9.

14. Ibid., p. 9.

15. Larry Diamond, 'The Globalization of Democracy,' in Robert O. Slater, Barry M. Schultz and Steven Dorr (eds), *Global Transformation and the Third World* (Boulder: Lynne Rienner Publishers, 1993), p. 61.

16. For example, the Carter Centre's attempt to devise a 'quality of democracy index' which highlights historical inequalities of access among social groups and admits examination of US failings. (See *Africa Demos*, 2, 3, August 1992, pp. 8–9.)

17. Diamond, op. cit., p. 36; and 'Economic Development and Democracy Reconsidered,' *American Behavioral Scientist*, 35, 4–5 (March–June 1992), pp. 450–99.
18. Diamond, 'Globalization of Democracy,' pp. 50–5.
19. Ibid., p. 59.
20. Ibid., p. 61.
21. Ibid. Indeed Diamond would extend this guardianship globally, campaigning for Western, specifically American, initiative as crucial to prospects for achieving democracy and security worldwide ('The Global Imperative: Building a Democratic World Order,' *Current History*, 93, 579, January 1994, pp. 2–7). Contrast this with the more critically democratic perspectives in David Held (ed.), *Prospects for Democracy: North, South, East, West* (London: Polity Press, 1993).
22. Noam Chomsky, *Deterring Democracy* (New York: Hill and Wang, 1992).
23. Cf. Joan Nelson with Stephanie Eglinton, *Encouraging Democracy: What Role for Conditioned Aid?* (Washington, DC: Overseas Development Council, 1992); Bard-Anders Andreassen and Theresa Swinehart, 'Promoting Human Rights in Poor Countries: The New Political Conditionality of Aid Policies,' in Andreassen and Swinehart (eds), *Human Rights in Developing Countries Yearbook 1991* (Oslo: Scandinavian University Press, 1992).
24. See my 'Democratization, Governance and Political Deficits: A South–North Perspective,' *International Insights*, 9, 2 (Fall 1993), pp. 71ff. Benjamin Barber issues a similar warning about treating democracy as a presumptive Western 'export' rather than an indigenous impulse: 'Jihad vs. McWorld,' *The Atlantic Monthly*, 269, 3 (May 1992), p. 63. Moreover, elites in the globally dominant democracies may not actually believe in more democracy at home, no more than they should be looked to as its natural standard bearers abroad. See, for example, the mordant observations of American social hierarchy by Lewis Lapham, *The Wish for Kings: Democracy at Bay* (New York: Grove Press, 1993).
25. See the evidence in Keith Griffin and Azizur Rahman Khan, *Globalization and the Developing World* (Geneva: United Nations Research Institute for Social Development, 1992); and Dharam Ghai, 'Structural Adjustment, Global Integration and Social Democracy,' Discussion Paper (Geneva: UNRISD, October 1992).
26. Gills and Rocamora, 'Low Intensity Democracy', *Third World Quarterly*, 13, 3 (1992), p. 503.
27. This is emphasized in Schmitz and Gillies, *The Challenge of Democratic Development* (Ottawa: The North–South Institute, 1992). Indeed, democracy is arguably the *most* challenging concept in political discourse. See also John Dunn (ed.), *Democracy: The Unfinished Journey, 508 BC to AD 1993* (Oxford: Oxford University Press, 1992).
28. US President Bill Clinton, 'American University Convocation Address,' Washington DC, February 26, 1993 (US Information Service transcript), p. 7.
29. 'Survey of Mexico,' *The Economist* (February 13, 1993), pp. 1–2. This seemed unlikely to change any time soon, even if growing pressures for political liberalization (accelerated to uncertain effect by the Chiapas revolt of 1994) made it in some sense 'inevitable.' See, *inter alia*, Michael Coppedge, 'Mexican Democracy: You Can't Get There From Here,' in

Riordan Roett (ed.), *Political and Economic Liberalization in Mexico: At A Critical Juncture?* (Boulder & London: Lynne Rienner Publishers, 1993).

30. For example, Ricardo Grinspun and Maxwell Cameron, 'Mexico: The Wages of Trade,' *Report on the Americas*, xxvi, 4 (February 1993), pp. 32–7; also Grinspun and Cameron (eds), *The Political Economy of North American Free Trade* (Montreal and Kingston: McGill-Queen's University Press, 1993), which questions the political processes determining the fate of the NAFTA and 'whether economic liberalization contributes to the opening or the closing of possibilities for democratic reform' (pp. 13–15).

31. Ibid. And for more detailed analyses and proposals: Andrew Reding, 'Bolstering Democracy in the Americas,' *World Policy Journal*, 9, 3 (Summer 1992), pp. 401–15; Ian Robinson, 'The NAFTA, Democracy and Continental Economic Integration: Trade Policy as if Democracy Mattered,' in Susan D. Phillips (ed.), *How Ottawa Spends 1993–1994: A More Democratic Canada?* (Ottawa: Carleton University Press, 1993), pp. 333–80.

32. Cecilia Rodriguez, 'Faith and failure: Latin America's ramshackle democracy,' *Toronto Globe and Mail* (September 22, 1992).

33. David Held, 'Democracy and Globalization,' *Alternatives: Social Transformation and Humane Governance*, Special Issue on 'The Global Context of Democratization,' 16, 2 (Spring 1991), p. 203.

34. Gills and Rocamora, op. cit., p. 513.

35. On the unravelling of the Maastricht treaty process in Europe, see Michael Ignatieff, 'The political elites need some shock therapy,' *Ottawa Citizen* (reprinted from *The Observer*, September 9, 1992); and more generally on the problematic of building positive citizen engagement in genuinely deliberative democratic processes, Robert Dahl's reflections on 'The Problem of Civic Competence,' *Journal of Democracy*, 3, 4 (October 1992), pp. 45–59. See also Daniel Yankelovich, *Coming to Public Judgment: Making Democracy Work in a Complex World* (Syracuse: Syracuse University Press, 1991); James Fishkin, *Democracy and Deliberation: New Directions for Democratic Reform* (New Haven: Yale University Press, 1991).

36. Yoshikazu Sakamoto, 'Introduction: The Global Context of Democratization,' *Alternatives* (Spring 1991), pp. 120 ff.

37. Gills and Rocamora, op. cit., p. 521.

38. Ibid., and Sakamoto, op. cit. See also David Korten, *Getting to the 21st Century: Voluntary Action and the Global Agenda* (West Hartford: Kumarian Press, 1990); Paul Elkins (ed.), *A New World Order: Grassroots Movements for Global Change* (London: Routledge, 1992); Leslie Paul Thiele, 'Making Democracy Safe for the World: Social Movements and Global Politics,' *Alternatives*, 18, 3 (Summer 1993), pp. 273–305. The challenge of citizen movements within established Western democracies is explored in Russell Dalton (ed.), 'Citizens, Protest, and Democracy,' *The Annals of the American Academy of Political and Social Science*, 528 (July 1993).

39. Paul Mosley, Jane Harrigan and John Toye, *Aid and Power: The World Bank and Policy-based Lending* (London: Routledge, 1991), vol. 1, chap. 1, 'World Development and International Finance since 1970,' p. 8.

40. Thomas Callaghy, 'Vision and Politics in the Transformation of the Global Political Economy: Lessons from the Second and Third Worlds,' in Robert Slater *et al.*, *Global Transformation and the Third World*, p. 163.

41. Mosley *et al.*, op. cit., p. 20.
42. For sharply critical reviews see ibid.; also Gibbon *et al. Authoritarianism, Democracy, and Adjustment*, and Christopher Colclough and James Manor (eds), *States and Markets: Neo-Liberalism and the Development Policy Debate* (Oxford: Oxford University Press, 1992). More sympathetic liberal reformist interpretations can be found in Callaghy, op. cit., and Thomas J. Biersteker, 'The "triumph" of neoclassical economics in the developing world: policy convergences and bases of governance in the international economic order,' in James N. Rosenau and Ernst-Otto Czempiel (eds), *Governance Without Government: Order and Change in World Politics* (Cambridge: Cambridge University Press, 1992).
43. For some revealing reflections see Richard Jolly and Rolph Van der Hoeven (eds), 'Adjustment with a Human Face – Record and Relevance,' *World Development*, 19, 12 (December 1991), pp. 1801–64.
44. Notably in *Sub-Saharan Africa: From Crisis to Sustainable Growth. A Long-Term Perspective Study* (Washington, DC: The World Bank, 1989).
45. For a devastating democratic critique see Adam Przeworski, 'The Neoliberal Fallacy,' *Journal of Democracy*, 3, 3 (July 1992), pp. 45–59; also Przeworski, *Democracy and the Market: Political and Economic Reforms in Eastern Europe and Latin America* (New York: Cambridge University Press, 1991). And specifically looking East, Peter Gowan, 'Old Medicine, New Bottles: Western Policy Toward East Central Europe,' *World Policy Journal*, 11, 1 (Winter 1991–92), pp. 1–33. Looking South, the basis for cynicism is also apparent in Guillermo O'Donnell's comment that: 'According to prevailing theories, the only way the poor are going to do better is if the rich get richer first' (quoted in Thomas Kamm, 'Shock Therapy: South Americans Find Economic Reform Has Initial Social Costs,' *The Wall Street Journal*, April 16, 1992).
46. For a structuralist analysis of different regional impacts of the changing international division of labour, see Michael Dolan, 'Global Economic Transformation and Less Developed Countries,' in Slater *et al.*, op. cit., pp. 259–82. On the challenge to and in the North, see, for example, Herman Daly and Richard Cobb, *For the Common Good: Redirecting the Economy Toward Community, the Environment, and a Sustainable Future* (Boston: Beacon Press, 1989); Joel Kassiola, *The Death of Industrial Civilization: The Limits to Economic Growth and the Repoliticization of Advanced Industrial Society* (Buffalo: State University of New York Press, 1990); also the review by Robin Murray of Alain Liepitz's manifesto, *Towards a New Economic Order; Postfordism, Ecology and Democracy* (London: Polity Press, 1993) in the *Guardian Weekly* (March 7, 1993), p. 26.
47. Cristovam Buarque, *The End of Economics?*, p. 125.
48. For example: Wolfgang Sachs, 'The Archeology of the Development Idea: Six Essays,' *Interculture*, 23, 4 (Fall 1990); C. Douglas Lummis, 'Development Against Democracy,' *Alternatives*, 16, 1 (Winter 1991), pp. 31–66; Denis Goulet, 'Development: Creator and Destroyer of Values,' *World Development*, 20, 3 (March 1992), pp. 467–75; Gustavo Esteva, 'Development,' in Sachs (ed.), *The Development Dictionary*, pp. 6–25; Clarence J. Dias, 'Development, Democracy and Human Rights: An Asian NGO Perspective,' in Gerald Schmitz (coordinator), *Development, Democracy and*

84   *Democratization and Demystification*

the Global Realization of All Human Rights: Towards Collaborative Forward-Looking Strategies (Ottawa: The North–South Institute, 1993).

49. Buarque, *The End of Economics?*, p. 48.
50. Paul Caspersz, 'African democracy and the mindset of neo-colonialists,' letter to the *Guardian Weekly*, October 4, 1992.
51. Buarque, op. cit., p. 56.
52. Ibid., p. 62.
53. Esteva, 'Development,' p. 22.
54. Robert Reich, *The Work of Nations: Preparing Ourselves for 21st Century Capitalism* (New York: Alfred A. Knopf, 1991), especially Part Four 'The Meaning of Nation'.
55. Buarque, *The End of Economics?*, p. 156.
56. The North–South Institute observed: 'The last months of 1989 have been so full of astounding surprises . . . But, for most people of the South, 1989 was a miserable year' ('The Nervous Nineties: Uncertainties Cloud Decade for the Third World – Review '89 Outlook '90,' (Ottawa: The North–South Institute, 1990), p. 1).
57. UNDP, *Human Development Report* (New York: Oxford University Press, annually). Slight variations in the annual HDI rankings do not alter this apparent close connection between capitalist economic development and political rights. But for a less sanguine view of the politics of development and human rights, see Katarina Tomasevski, 'A Critique of the UNDP Political Freedom Index 1991,' in Andreassen and Swinehart, *Human Rights in Developing Countries Yearbook 1991*, pp. 3–24.
58. *Sub-Saharan Africa: From Crisis to Sustainable Growth*, especially the 'Foreword' by then Bank president Barber Conable and pp. 54–62. The sentence quoted is cited in Stephen P. Riley, 'Political Adjustment or Domestic Pressure: democratic politics and political choice in Africa,' *Third World Quarterly*, 13, 3 (1992), p. 542. On the 'bureaucratic' origins of this explanation of public failure, see also Mick Moore, 'Introduction,' *IDS Bulletin* (January 1993), p. 2.
59. *Governance and Development* (Washington, DC: The World Bank, 1992), pp. v, 1–3.
60. 'Managing Development: The Governance Dimension/A Discussion Paper,' (Washington, DC: The World Bank), Draft of June 26, 1991 (cited in Gerald Schmitz, 'Achieving Good Government: Towards an Assessment of Developing Countries' Needs and Opportunities for Assistance,' report prepared by the North–South Institute for the Canadian International Development Agency, Ottawa, October 1991, p. 5).
61. *Governance and Development*, p. 1 and note 1, p. 58, basing itself on the restrictive parameters set out by the Bank's legal counsel, Ibrahim Shihata (cf. 'The World Bank and Governance Issues in Its Borrowing Members,' in *The World Bank in a Changing World* (Dordrecht: Martinus Nijhoff, 1991)). These proscriptions are summarized for internal Bank staff use in 'The World Bank: Current Questions and Answers,' Washington DC, 1992, Annual Meetings, Information and Public Affairs Division, September 1992, pp. 10–12. While these claims to political neutrality are dubious to say the least, Francisco Sagasti, who was involved in the drafting exercise for the booklet, makes a good point about not trusting the political judgements that

most Bank staff might make given the chance. The results might not please democratic advocates! (Comments to the author at an International Development Research Centre workshop on 'Governance and the Changing Role of the State,' Ottawa, March 30, 1993.)

62. For example, Dunstan Wai, 'Governance, Economic Development and the Role of External Actors,' paper delivered at the Conference on 'Governance and Economic Development in Sub-Saharan Africa', Oxford University, May 1991. See also the critique of this ideological bias in M. Moore, 'Declining to Learn from the East?,' op. cit., pp. 39–50.

63. For example, it was widely reported that the Bank had suspended loans to Malawi in May 1992. In fact, only bilateral donor commitments had been frozen for six months as a warning to the Banda dictatorship. The Bank actually approved (despite US opposition) an environmentally dubious power sector loan in June 1992. (See 'Malawi: Misinformation or Disinformation?' *Focus Africa*, July–October 1992, pp. 8–9.) The Bank's internal rationalization also offered not chastisement but sympathetic support and friendly advice:

> The issue of governance also featured prominently at the Consultative Group Meeting on Malawi in May 1992. The participants commended Malawi's performance in terms of strengthened macroeconomic management and progress in tackling the structural issues of economic liberalization. . . .
>
> While a full participant in these deliberations, the World Bank is prohibited by its charter from interfering in the political affairs of any of its members. In the Bank's view, Malawi has succeeded in meeting economic targets and, as a result, no change for the Bank's lending program is warranted at this time. The Bank's support for Malawi's economic reform program could be jeopardized, however, if donors do not provide anticipated development assistance because of their perception that the government of Malawi has not fundamentally changed the way it views human rights issues.
>
> ('Current Questions and Answers,' September 1992, p. 18)

64. Notably Pierre Landell-Mills and Ismail Serageldin, 'Governance and the External Factor,' paper prepared for the World Bank's Annual Conference on Development Economics, Washington DC, April 1991. For an interpretation making the case for positive advocacy by the Bank, see David Gillies, 'Human Rights, Governance, and Democracy: The World Bank's Problem Frontiers,' *Netherlands Quarterly of Human Rights*, 11, 1 (1993), pp. 3–24. The Bank itself was moved to contribute a position paper 'The World Bank and the Promotion of Human Rights' to the studies prepared for the UN World Human Rights Conference in Vienna (UN doc.A/CONF.157/PC/61/Add.19/10 June 1993). More critically, reviewing actual Bank projects, James Paul finds that the multinational business of 'development' greatly needs to be democratized, so that powerful actors such as the Bank do not just promulgate guidelines but become themselves accountable to the people affected by their activities ('The Human Right to Development: Its Meaning & Importance,' *The John Marshall Law Review*, 25, 2 (Winter 1992), pp. 235–65).

65. Landell-Mills and Serageldin, op. cit., p. 3, and in 'Governance and the Development Process,' *Finance and Development* (September 1991), p. 14. Some see other evidence that, even while defending its own preferred economic turf, the Bank has become more receptive to socio-political human rights concerns. For example, cf. Sigrun Skogly, 'Structural Adjustment and Development: Human Rights – An Agenda for Change,' *Human Rights Quarterly*, 5, 4 (November 1993), pp. 751–78.

66. This also suggests considerable scope for heterodox exploration of issues within the coporate culture of the Bank; however, most of this is confined to obscure staff papers or documents intended only for internal use. The Bank's work on governance does not result from, and is rarely exposed to, an open much less democratic political process of debate. Moreover, guardians of orthodoxy within the Bank still have means to contain the contagion of new ideas. Note, for example, David Korten's observations of attempts to suppress the critical work of senior economists on environment and development issues (Review Essay on 'Sustainable Development,' *World Policy Journal* (Winter 1991–92), p. 166).

67. For a review of African reactions see Gerald Schmitz and Eboe Hutchful, *Democratization and Popular Participation in Africa* (Ottawa: The North–South Institute 1992), pp. 12–15 and 21ff. See also John-Jean Barya, 'The New Political Conditionalities of Aid: An Independent View from Africa,' *IDS Bulletin* (January 1993), pp. 16–23. A good analysis of a particular case is Julius Ihonvbere, 'Economic Crisis, Structural Adjustment and Social Crisis in Nigeria,' *World Development*, 21, 1 (1993), pp. 141–53. His ironic conclusion bears noting:

> Since popular forces have not given up their quest for accountability, democracy, social justice and increased participation in the society, and given that the adjustment program has encouraged the unity of popular forces across ethnic, regional and ideological lines, the adjustment program has created some long-term unintended prodemocratic gains.
>
> (p. 150)

More generally, Thomas Callaghy deftly analyses the failure of the Bank-inspired 'neoclassical political logic of reform' in 'Africa: Falling Off the Map?,' *Current History*, 93, 579 (January 1994), pp. 31–6.

68. This does not mean that US policy is not in somewhat of a muddle on issues of 'democracy promotion.' See the sceptical analysis by Carol Lancaster, 'Governance and Development: The Views from Washington,' *IDS Bulletin* (January 1993), pp. 9–15.

69. Development Assistance Committee, *Development Co-operation Report 1991* (Paris: OECD), 1991, p. 66. This has now evolved into a more detailed and substantive formulation, 'DAC Orientations on Participatory Development and Good Governance,' (Endorsed December 1993) which while earnestly striving to be politically sensitive and 'correct,' gives the impression that Western liberal democracy is the prescriptive ideal-type if not in fact the examplar in practice.

70. See Hans Peter Repnik and Ralf-Matthias Mohs, '"Good Governance", Democracy and Development Paradigms,' *Intereconomics* (January/February 1992), pp. 28–33. Seeing democracy as a human right, they argue that it is

'essential for demands on good governance such as accountability and transparency, but does not guarantee sound economic policies' (p. 32).

71. Hon. Barbara MacDougall, Speech by the Secretary of State for External Affairs to a conference commemorating the Sixtieth anniversary of the Statute of Westminster, Toronto, December 10, 1991.

72. As Mark Robinson analyses, announcing good-conduct principles is one thing, conducting state practice is quite another historically-entangled matter ('Will Political Conditionality Work?', *IDS Bulletin* (January 1993), pp. 58–66). A case in point, when implementing 1993 cuts to the budget of the Canadian International Development Agency, large bilateral programs were maintained to some persistent gross human rights violators (China, Indonesia), whereas bilateral aid was eliminated to some of the poorest African countries that have been making recent strides towards democracy (Tanzania, Uganda, Ethiopia and Eritrea). For a wide-ranging critique, see Cranford Pratt (ed.), *Canadian International Development Assistance: An Appraisal* (Montreal and Kingston: McGill-Queen's University Press, forthcoming 1994).

73. Peter Waller, 'After East–West Detente: Towards a Human Rights Orientation in North–South Development Cooperation?,' *Development*, 1 (1992), p. 25.

74. 'Aid and Political Reform,' Briefing Paper (London: Overseas Development Institute, January 1992), p. 3; also John Healey and Mark Robinson, *Democracy, Governance and Economic Policy: Sub-Saharan Africa in Comparative Perspective* (London: ODI Development Policy Studies, 1992); Healey, Robinson, and Richard Ketley, 'Will Political Reform bring about Improved Economic Management in Sub-Saharan Africa?,' *IDS Bulletin*, January 1993, pp. 31–8. See as well Schmitz and Gillies, *The Challenge of Democratic Development*, pp. 26–34 and 58–60.

75. I have raised the issue of the perverse potential for 'conflictive and unsustainable governance' in an earlier article, 'Human Rights, Democratization, and International Conflict,' in Fenn Osler Hampson and Christopher J. Maule (eds), *Canada Among Nations 1992–93: A New World Order?* (Ottawa: Carleton University Press, 1992), pp. 245–47.

76. There is an instructive parallel to the democratic criticism of the notorious report prepared for the Trilateral Commission (Michael Crozier *et al.*, *The Crisis of Democracy: Report on the Governability of Democracies* (New York: New York University Press, 1975) which blamed growing problems of 'governability' **in the North** on **too much** democracy and 'demand overload' by citizens!

77. Repnik and Mohs, 'Good Governance', p. 33.

78. Callaghy, in Slater *et al.*, op. cit., p. 162.

79. Cited in Schmitz and Gillies, op. cit., p. 7.

80. Mosley *et al.*, *Aid and Power* (London: Routledge, 1991), p. 16.

81. Callaghy (1993), op. cit., p. 244. And applied to Africa, on the failure of the 'new neocolonialism' and its successor 'neoclassical political logic of reform,' Callaghy, 'Africa: Falling Off the Map?,' (1994), pp. 31–6.

82. See Majid Rahnema, 'Participation,' in Sachs, *The Development Dictionary*, pp. 116–31.

83. Lawrence Salmen, *Reducing Poverty: An Institutional Perspective*, Poverty and Social Policy Series, Paper No. 1 (Washington, DC: The World Bank, 1992), p. 23.

84. Cherret *et al.*, 'Non-Governmental Organizations,' p. 14. See also notes 11 and 12, supra.

85. Laura Macdonald, 'Turning to the NGOs: Competing Conceptions of Civil Society in Latin America,' paper presented to the annual meeting of the Latin American Studies Association, Los Angeles, September 1992, pp. 6–7; also Macdonald, this volume. Alan Fowler's research on African NGOs produces similarly critical findings about NGOs as differently-conceived deliverers of 'democratic development.' Cf. 'The Role of NGOs in Changing State–Society Relations: Perspectives from Eastern and Southern Africa,' *Development Policy Review*, 19, 1 (March 1991), pp. 53–84; 'Non-governmental Organizations as Agents of Democratization: An African Perspective,' *Journal of International Development*, 5 (May/June 1993), pp. 325–39.

86. *Governance and Development*, p. 11.

87. *The End of Economics?*, pp. 75–6.

88. Mick Moore, 'Introduction,' *IDS Bulletin*, p. 5. As the 'Summary' of Laurence Whitehead's 'Introduction: Some Insights from Western Social Theory' pointedly states: 'Contrary to some recent triumphalism, most Western social theory has been deeply preoccupied with the fragility and reversibility of economic *cum* political liberalization processes' (*World Development*, Special Issue on 'Economic Liberalization and Democratization: Explorations of the Linkages,' 21, 8, August 1993, p. 1245).

89. Hyden's thesis of the 'culture of affection' prominently diagnoses development failure as having institutional, political-cultural causes. See notably *No Shortcuts to Progress: African Development Management in Perspective* (London: Heinemann, 1983); also 'The role of aid and research in the political restructuring of Africa,' in R. C. Crook and A. Morten Jerve (eds), *Government and Participation: Institutional Development, Decentralisation and Democracy in the Third World* (Bergen: Chr. Michelson Institute) Report 1991:1, pp. 33–58.

90. Hyden, 'Governance and the Study of Politics,' in Hyden and Michael Bratton (eds), *Governance and Politics in Africa* (Boulder: Lynne Rienner, 1992), pp. 1–26.

91. Ibid., p. 5.

92. Ibid., p. 7.

93. Ibid., pp. 6–7. This definition has been influential in work done to specify the concept within the US aid program. For example, one consultant proposes a formula that synthesizes the main elements of Hyden's approach: 'Governance is the impartial, transparent management of public affairs through the generation of a regime (set of rules) accepted as constituting legitimate authority, for the purpose of promoting and enhancing societal values that are sought by individuals and groups.' (Robert Charlick, Draft 'Governance Working Paper,' prepared for the AID Africa Bureau under the Africa Bureau Democracy and Governance Program, January 1992, p. 2.)

94. Hyden, 'Governance and the Study of Politics,' p. 6.

95. Ibid., p. 22.

96. Ibid., pp. 20 and 25.

Gerald J. Schmitz 89

97. R. William Liddle, 'The Politics of Development Policy,' *World Development*, 20, 6 (June 1992), p. 803. Even World Bank-supported research that is implicitly sympathetic to democratization processes remains consistently focused on their problematic utility for instituting neoliberal economic adjustment regimens. Indeed an overview by Stephan Haggard and Steven Webb suggests the underlying parameters framing Liddle's question: 'Prescriptive policy analysis by economists aims to identify measures that are optimal according to such criteria as efficiency, stability, or growth. Positive political analysis, however, is often concerned with why optimal policies are not adopted' ('What Do We Know about the Political Economy of Economic Policy Reform?,' *The World Bank Research Observer*, 8, 2 (July 1993), p. 162). See also Haggard and Webb (eds), *Voting for Reform: The Politics of Adjustment in New Democracies* (New York: Oxford University Press, forthcoming); and for a critical alternative perspective, Adam Przeworski *et al.*, *Economic Reforms in New Democracies: A Social Democratic Approach* (Cambridge and New York: Cambridge University Press, 1993).

98. 'Nigeria in Crisis,' *Financial Times* (London), editorial, April 7, 1993. The *Times* argues that: 'Creditors must grasp what may be a last opportunity to persuade Nigeria's leaders that economic reform makes sense. . . . the principle of an IMF deal as a pre-condition for [debt] relief should remain inviolate. But the IMF should use this month's visit to Nigeria to draw up a 'shadow' reform programme with the reform-minded transitional council. The elected government can then inherit this programme at the August hand-over.' Yet as Ihonvbere has pointed out: 'The opposition to continuing adjustment arises from the grossly unequal distribution of the gains and pains of adjustment and the widening inequalities, corruption, intolerance and repression which have accompanied its implementation' ('Economic Crisis,' op. cit., p. 150). Insistence by external powers on mandatory supervision of orthodox adjustment, without addressing these grievances, may jeopardize any democratic transition even before, or if, it takes place.

99. Manfred Bienefeld, 'Structural Adjustment and Democracy in Southern Africa,' paper presented to the Eighth Annual Conference of the Canadian Association for the Study of International Development, Charlottetown, June 1992, p. 14; see also his chapter in this volume.

100. See the essays in Rosenau and Czempiel, *Governance without Government*, esp. Biersteker, 'The "triumph" of neoclassical economics in the developing world,' pp. 130–1; also Czempiel, 'Governance and Democratization,' pp. 270–1. Mainstream North–South analyses now commonly assume and welcome as globally hegemonic a neoliberal political economy twinning 'democracy' with market economics – presented as a matter of persuasion, realism and mutual benefit. This discourse masks the actually unresolved or growing polarizations, contradictions and power imbalances in the international system.

101. Dahl (see note 35) proposes the idea of 'citizens' assemblies' as one possible way to develop popular capacities to engage in coherent deliberation of complex public policies for the general good ('The Problem of Civic Competence,' pp. 54–6). At the international level, appeals have been made

for more representative democratic institutions such as a 'United Nations parliamentary assembly' as part of comprehensive reforms proposed for the United Nations system. Seeking to renew and extend forms of democratic community, Held defends 'the possibility of a democratic international order,' and of a vision of 'cosmopolitan democracy' that is 'radically at odds with the "liberal market constitutionalism" promulgated by the leading industrial countries and their global organizations' ('Democracy: Past, Present, and Possible Futures,' *Alternatives*, 18, 3, Summer 1993, p. 259).

102.   Ignatieff, 'The political elites' (see note 35 supra). Lacking support from genuinely alternative ideological frameworks, populist political engagement on its own is likely to lead only to dangerous disappointment. As Rajni Kothari argues, this frustration or resigned cynicism and 'erosion of hope under a regime of hegemonism and homogenization . . . which produces growing vacuums in civil society in so many countries, cannot be a matter of comfort to any thinking person or system of governance, not even to the ruling class if the latter has to pursue its task in a framework of relative stability and minimal participation of affected interests' ('The Yawning Vacuum: A World Without Alternatives,' *Alternatives*, 18, 2, Spring 1993, p. 138).

103.   *Development*, Journal of the Society for International Development, Editorial Note, 3 (1992), p. 4.

104.   The omission of both the terms 'democracy' and 'governance' from the otherwise sharp iconoclastic vision of *The Development Dictionary* points to a void in the crisis and renewal of the discourse. Overwhelmed by the legacy of governing power systems, it is difficult even to conceptualize democracy for all in global terms, which may appear a populist pipedream. Yet it is precisely this old-order straitjacket that needs to be exposed and confronted, at the very least to preserve possibilities for democratic alternatives.

3 Structural Adjustment and the Prospects for Democracy in Southern Africa

Manfred A. Bienefeld

Everyone applauds democracy, those who in practice oppose it applaud most loudly.

(Gills and Rocamora[1])

Nigeria's return to democracy could hardly have come at a more difficult time . . . without substantial debt relief . . . Nigeria has little chance of sustaining an IMF programme. The Shonekan government offers only a brief window of opportunity for western creditors to do a conditional deal with a non-elected civilian authority for the new elected administration to inherit. It is a chance that may not recur.

(E. Balls, *Financial Times*)

Borrowers and lenders often fail to take full account of the institutional, social and political rigidities that restrict a country's capacity to adjust.

(World Bank)

INTRODUCTION

The economic liberalization associated with orthodox structural adjustment is unlikely to permit the consolidation or deepening of democracy in southern Africa. Indeed, by introducing additional tensions and uncertainties into a highly charged political situation, it is far more likely to extinguish the flickering flame of freedom and pave the way for chaos or authoritarianism. If, by chance, democracy should survive, it would be a Guatemalan democracy that merely obscured an authoritarian reality.

The only hope for a genuine, popular democracy lies in the adoption of moderate, conciliatory and egalitarian economic and social policies that recognise the critical importance of social and political stability for democracy and efficiency. But such policies will not materialise without sustained and effective pressure from a politically engaged population, monitoring and influencing government through the institutions of a strong and diverse civil society. Politics and economics are thus utterly interdependent. Either a stable, participatory democracy will foster economic success and further strengthen democracy, or political instability will ensure economic failure.

The disastrous impact of neoliberal adjustment policies in Eastern Europe is a graphic reminder of the centrifugal forces unleashed by their reckless adoption (or imposition?) under inappropriate conditions. And Africa bears the scars of the same errors of judgment because the IFIs (international financial institutions)[2] used the leverage conferred on them by the debt crisis to spread these high risk policies in that impoverished continent. Acknowledging that most African countries were unable to respond constructively to the resulting competitive pressures, the Bank's chief economist for Africa declared, almost ten years after the start of adjustment lending, that 'we did not think that the human costs of these programs could be so great, and economic gains so slow in coming.'[3] This might serve as a fitting epitaph for many a fledgling democracy. Certainly southern Africa's precarious political situation will not afford policy makers ten more years of grace for experimentation.

Structural adjustment is IFI code for the deregulation of national economies. It seeks to promote long run efficiency, welfare and growth by eliminating distortions that impede the 'rational' allocation of resources. But, because its high 'transitional' costs often stimulate political opposition that can lead to policy reversals, the effective political management of adjustment emerged as a major IFI concern. Their work on 'good governance' soon led them to the conclusion that these policies must not appear as external impositions, but must be 'owned' by implementing governments and legitimated by national democratic processes. Democracy thus became an important part of their crusade to spread sound economic policies around the world, further confirming the neoliberal belief that democracy and free markets were but two sides of the same coin. Had not President Reagan, in 1982, launched a world-wide 'crusade for democracy' to accompany his neo-conservative revolution?[4]

This new enthusiasm for democracy is conditional, however. Democracy will lead to good governance, as defined by the IFIs, only if electorates 'choose' to support their neo-liberal policies. Just as Henry Ford once declared his Model-T to be available 'in any colour, so long as it is black,' bemused electorates now find they can choose 'any policy regime, so long as it was the neoliberal one.' In fact they can only choose how to deal with the consequences of that regime and those who demand a wider choice are dismissed as naïve, foolish or subversive, on the grounds that 'reasonable' people understand that this regime is good for them and that 'there is no alternative' in any event.

As social and economic circumstances deteriorate, the coercive part of this argument becomes more prominent. Promises of imminent prosperity give way to ever more forceful reminders that deregulation and globalisation must be accepted, whatever their 'transitional' costs. In a world of diminished expectations, the hegemonic ideology thus seeks to retain its credibility by diluting the promises and emphasising the threats. However, at some point this will destroy its hegemonic status which depends on its ability to achieve voluntary regime compliance.

However, threats cannot achieve compliance unless they are credible. That is why the IFIs and the hegemonic powers go to such lengths to ensure that the alleged inevitability of global economic liberalization turns into a self-fulfilling prophecy. Those adopting sound policies are so openly rewarded that President Reagan chose to publicly 'welcome an increase in the (IMF) practice of lending contingent on countries' turning to more market-oriented policies.'[5] Those who do not, are punished by the world's capital markets, the IFIs and/or the hegemonic powers. And as elections approach, no expense is spared to remind electorates of these rewards and punishments. Where results are still in doubt, large additional sums may be funnelled from abroad to 'acceptable' parties. And if people still elect unacceptable governments, then they may suffer sanctions ranging from a withdrawal of credit, to economic blockade, to subversion by externally funded terrorists, dubbed 'freedom fighters' for the purpose. In this way a Nicaraguan government, elected in an internationally supervised 'free and democratic' election in 1984,[6] became the victim of a campaign that was described by a former director of the CIA 'as terrorism, as State-sponsored terrorism,' in testimony to a US Congressional Committee.[7]

As more and more governments give in to this subtle blackmail, their acceptance of the orthodox policies is hailed as proof of their intrinsic merits, just as if those choices had been freely made. Indeed, according to the IMF's Managing Director, the world is undergoing 'a kind of silent revolution' as 'more and more countries recogni[ze] that removing all structural impediments to growth is the only way to progress.'[8]

Southern Africa has enough experience of this cynical manipulation. Who could miss the message implicit in the contrast between Mozambique's treatment before it saw the light, when political and military support was given to RENAMO terrorists committing indescribable brutalities throughout the land, and its treatment today, when it receives concessional loans from the IFIs? Or that conveyed by the Angolan tragedy, where an externally funded terrorist movement is receiving tacit international support even as it wages a genocidal war to overturn the results of yet another internationally supervised democratic election that produced an unacceptable result?[9] The message is inescapable. Democratic elections are fine when they legitimate 'sound economic policies.' When they do not, almost any alternative is preferred, including the authoritarianism of Guatemala's fascist democracy, or the chaos of liberated Afghanistan.

Unfortunately, genuine democracy is hard to reconcile with neoliberalism's mystical belief in the magic of disembodied markets, its fierce hostility to the notion of state and society as organic entities capable of defining and pursuing a common interest, and its insistence on pervasive deregulation. Under such conditions, states lose the capacity to manage economies in accordance with democratically determined social, ethical or political priorities. Only the shallowest and most meaningless democracy will survive in a 'cowboy capitalism'[10] where property rights become virtually absolute because states and electorates are disempowered by the mobility of capital; because the sanction of competition is diluted by the unregulated growth of monopoly together with an increasing segmentation, manipulation and interdependence of markets; and because money and credit are increasingly subject to speculative manipulation.

Although Eastern Europe's current descent into hell may be the most graphic reminder of the potential conflict between unregulated markets and democracy, the same message is implicit in the unravelling of social fabrics and the destabilisation of political structures around the world. Globalization is diluting and undermining the substance of democracy, even in some stable OECD countries as 'the means of regulating the market system, and thus ensuring social stability and offering genuine political debate, are ... steadily withdrawn.'[11] This is not good news for southern Africa's fledgling democracies.

Under these conditions southern Africa's present may merely be prelude to tragedy, since that which is economically feasible may not be politically feasible, while that which is politically feasible may not be economically feasible. The successful consolidation of democracy may thus depend on an easing of the internationally defined constraints within which this region has to meet that challenge. But such a change does not seem imminent judging by the pig headed intransigence of the IFIs in Eastern Europe; their apparently unlimited tolerance for speculative instability in the world's financial markets;[12] and their current demand for the radical deregulation of the world's labour markets as the next step in their crusade for free markets.[13] Apparently change will have to be imposed on the IFIs by new political realities.

In the meantime the southern African countries will have great difficulty in espousing less risky strategies that emphasise the need for national cohesion; that accept the need to use protection and managed trade to achieve higher levels of employment and domestic resource utilisation and to increase learning effects; and that will be able and willing to deal with income redistribution and land reform. Such a strategy must be developed, but in doing so the region must avoid the errors of the past. It must exercise extreme caution in accumulating foreign debt; it must maintain high domestic savings and investment rates; and it must ensure that domestic growth is not eventually strangled by a foreign exchange constraint because exports were neglected. Although these risks are real, they are not inevitable or necessary, as the East Asian Newly Industrializing Countries (NICs) have shown.[14]

Ironically the hegemonic powers would benefit in the long run if they supported such alternative policies with debt relief, appropriate technical assistance and less conditional flows of concessional funds. Investment could then focus on production for domestic markets, rather than on debt servicing. In the medium term this would lead to the emergence of more stable, reliable and ultimately more profitable trading partners, as it did in 1948, when the Marshall Plan provided highly concessional and largely unconditional finance to European countries whose national reconstruction programs were threatened by an acute foreign exchange crisis.[15] By supporting those reconstruction programs and allowing them to sustain full employment growth, these transfers ultimately also served donor interests much better than if these countries had been forced to expose their fragile economies to US competition while servicing large and growing debts by deflating domestic demand. The point is made in a refreshingly unorthodox IMF technical paper analysing OECD Export Credit schemes:

> There is . . . a growing realization that the earlier tendency to give very large weight to export promotion was not in the debtor countries' interest, and certainly not in the interests of the (export credit) agencies. Moreover, it is becoming apparent that such an approach was also not even in the long-run interests of industrial country exporters, who would be best served by stable, growing markets in the developing world.[16]

Such insights are all too rare in a world where sweeping generalisations about the benefits of trade and export promotion have been so often repeated that they are often mistaken for 'fact.' While trade is important, it is neither an end in itself, nor does it necessarily increase growth or efficiency. Its true importance lies in providing the foreign exchange needed to finance national development. It does not lead to development, industrialisation or prosperity. But it is a vital component of any national development strategy that does.

This highlights the fundamental difference between the truly successful East Asian NICs, and many other NICs (like Brazil, Mexico, Yugoslavia, Philippines), whose export promoting 'miracles' have long since turned to social and economic disasters. South Korea and Taiwan mounted their export drives in support of national industrialisation strategies that emphasised the need to build strong national firms and to develop indigenous technological capabilities. Together with radical land reform, strong support of small-holder agriculture, strategically managed trade and extensive state control of capital and finance, this allowed them to sustain full employment over thirty years and to remain competitive in spite of dramatic and sustained real wage increases.[17] No other strategy could have produced this combination of results.[18]

In southern Africa, the East Asian NIC option would face enormous economic challenges, even if it was politically feasible because of the yawning gap between available investible resources and the sums required to improve education and infrastructure, to finance immediately productive investment and to satisfy the expectations of a large, impoverished and politicized population. And foreign capital will be difficult to attract on terms that would allow the region to reap significant net benefits, since uncertainty raises the cost of capital. Indeed, unless these economies can be protected from the threat of capital flight and from significant speculative instability, both investment and consumption may fall short of expectations; or, even of the levels required to reverse the region's economic decline. That would quickly trigger a vicious circle in which low investment increased political uncertainty which reduced investment.

The political challenge facing the region is equally daunting. Democracy is giving a voice to its people under circumstances that could hardly be less auspicious. Electoral verdicts are always more difficult to accept peacefully when economic instability and decline magnify social tensions and threaten people's economic and physical security. That is why, despite the early euphoria, Latin American

democracy has not been consolidated. The weakness of civil society, the economic crisis, and problems endemic to political elites have all made it difficult for the new political system to stabilize. At the same time, this new-born democracy is shallow. It is characterised by a plurality of political parties and periodic elections, but other elements necessary for an effective political process – such as an independent judiciary, strong parliaments, and military and security forces that respect the law and human rights – are notably absent.[19]

Even in Britain, the so-called cradle of modern democracy, the thirties had led to the creation of a National Government that effectively suspended open political competition because this had become too divisive. While in Africa today, 'three years after the winds of democracy began to blow ... many novice voters feel they have tasted only a dust storm of hypocrisy.'[20]

In southern Africa the achievement of democracy could prove a hollow victory under such adverse conditions. Because large income disparities overlap dangerously with ethnic and regional divisions, political competition might raise ethnic tension and increase political instability. Such concerns are not without foundation, as suggested by places as diverse as Eastern Europe, Algeria and Afghanistan. Within the region, one can see the shadows of such latent conflicts in the cynical manipulation of democracy in Angola; in the uneasy truce between democracy and the one party state in Zimbabwe; and in the ambiguity and tension of a Mozambiquan democracy that has been purchased at the price of allowing RENAMO terrorists to campaign as a 'political party' with substantial external funding.

The only hope lies in political engagement that succeeds in building political coalitions and organisations that can give many people the knowledge and the experience to appreciate the constraints within which policy choices must be made; to relate their specific demands to the needs of the entire community; and to accept compromises because they are seen as contributing to a process of social and political transformation.[21] This is why a strong civil society is rightly deemed important.[22] But it will not be an easy task. And the emergence of active civic organisations and strong social movements could also become a source of conflict and instability, if those movements were not linked by some broad concept of 'the common good,' as it pertains to the larger, national societies of which they are a part.[23]

Internationally, an appreciation of the narrow constraints within which this region embarks on the task of building democracy, should lead to demands for more debt relief, for better market access and for aid that is free of neoliberal conditionality. Such concessions would not secure the region's precarious democracies, but they would improve their chances of surviving as genuine popular democracies. After all, 'in the absence of progressive social reform the term "democracy" is largely devoid of meaningful content. Indeed, it is in danger of becoming a term of political mystification.'[24]

STRUCTURAL ADJUSTMENT AND THE ECONOMIC CHALLENGE

Orthodox structural adjustment tries to eliminate obstacles to the free functioning of competitive markets. It came to prominence with the debt crisis in the early eighties when many countries needed quick disbursing loans to deal with chronic balance of payments crises. In response, 'policy loans' were made available on condition that recipients give global market forces an overriding power to restructuring their economies in accordance with the new global realities which included their accumulated debts, high real interest rates, low commodity prices and sluggish growth. The resulting adjustments were painful and sometimes destabilising since they relied heavily on domestic deflation and import compression. Combined with strong export promotion, these policies effectively maximized debt repayment – in the short term. The promise that they would also restore growth and development in the longer run, was based more on hope than on science. A decade later, those benefits could be demonstrated in a few relatively strong economies. But in many others, the fear that debts were being serviced at a high cost in human welfare and in future development prospects appears to have been borne out by events.

The orthodox adjustment policies are highly inappropriate for the southern African region, whose precarious political situation demands a strategy that minimizes 'downside risks.' Rapid economic liberalisation can trigger potentially disastrous, even irreversible bouts of instability. When introduced under difficult circumstances it can unleash speculative forces that increase uncertainty and income inequality, misallocate resources and foster social and economic polarization.[25] By encouraging the unrestrained pursuit of short term profit it can lead to an excessive accumulation of debt for which society will eventually be held accountable. By encouraging rapid devaluation it can fuel inflation, increase fiscal deficits and create a need for further devaluation. And by reducing the government's ability to respond to domestic social and political pressures, it can lead to conflicts that will undermine even economic efficiency in the end.

These risks are widely acknowledged. A 1987 IMF review of the theoretical foundations of its adjustment policies suggests they should not be applied in 'the presence of a large external debt' since they can lead to instability, 'capital flight . . . higher inflation . . . [and] a further deterioration in the fiscal situation.' It concludes that, for such circumstances, 'the proper mix of policies' still needs to be established through 'further study.'[26] Paul Krugman concludes a detailed analysis of the foreign exchange market with the blunt statement that 'there is not a shred of positive evidence that this market is efficient' and adds that the same is true 'for other asset markets . . . that is, both the bond market and the stock market.' Thus, 'we are freed from Friedman's . . . argument . . . that an efficient market could not exhibit destabilizing speculation.'[27] An IMF study of financial deregulation in the industrial world warns that such policies 'may . . . result in destabilizing and inefficient capital market speculation'[28]; while a World Bank report explains that financial liberalization often ends in disarray because volatile financial flows intensify domestic imbalances and takes this as a reminder that 'market-based financial systems can be unstable and susceptible to fraud.'[29] Based on these facts, one must agree with Dani Rodrik when he argues that adjustment policies must put much more emphasis on economic and political stability if they are to succeed – and to survive.[30] And nowhere is this more true than in a tense and deeply divided southern Africa.

Given the severity and certainty of the risks, the adoption of these policies could only be justified if there was very strong evidence to support the claim that they would eventually yield large and sustained economic gains. But this is simply not the case. Despite frequent claims to the contrary, that evidence remains extremely weak even today. And when adjustment lending first began, it was all but non-existent.

The fact that there was little or no empirical support for these policies when they were first imposed on distressed developing countries sheds light on the motivation behind their introduction. It more or less rules out the possibility that they were primarily intended to restore the development prospects of recipient nations and strengthens the claim that their main purpose was to bail out the banks by maximizing debt service payments. Jeffrey Sachs, now a leading advocate of Eastern Europe's disastrous 'big bang' approach to adjustment, suggested as much when he wrote that:

> from a global perspective . . . liberalisation might be defended not as in the interests of the initiating country, but rather in the interests of the rest of the world . . . However, to the extent that this is the real motivation for the pressures for liberalization then it makes little sense to press poor countries in dire economic difficulties to make rapid structural changes on behalf of the rest of the world.[31]

By giving global economic forces an overriding role in the restructuring of highly indebted economies, adjustment lending made debt repayment

100 Structural Adjustment and Democracy

a first priority. And full debt repayment, or 'no debt forgiveness,' was a central premise of 'policy lending,' even though these debts had been created in speculative markets driven as much by the irresponsibility of greedy lenders as by the profligacy of venal borrowers. This was acknowledged by the World Bank, but only after it had subjected the developing world to a decade of debt bondage. In 1989, it added insult to injury by remarking that the lending spree of the seventies should be seen as 'evidence that even competitive financial markets can still make mistakes'![32]

The rationale for imposing the costs of these mistakes so disproportionately on the developing world, was the need to save the international financial system from collapse and to avoid the moral hazard of giving debt relief to profligate borrowers, to the detriment of prudent borrowers. The moral hazard of rewarding irresponsible, speculative lenders by demanding full repayment for unwise and ill conceived loans does not appear to have been of similar concern.[33] Fears that such intransigence would create untold hardship and compromise future development prospects, and might even trigger political or economic collapse, were dismissed on the grounds that deregulation would unleash such powerful supply side effects that countries could fully service their debts, rebuild their infrastructure and restore growth and development without imposing significant hardship on their people. These outlandish claims were backed by wildly optimistic 'scenarios' that showed how easily gallons could fit into pint pots, if one resorted to 'the magic of the market.' Ten years of massive net resource transfers from the developing to the developed world, have shown that these claims were, at best, exercises in wishful thinking, and, at worst, systematic deceptions. But by then it no longer mattered. The banks had averted their crisis.[34] By 1986, the *Wall Street Journal* could report that:

> Bank profits have grown steadily during the debt crisis, according to a report by the Joint Economic Committee of Congress . . . The Administration's whole approach to the debt crisis has kept the banks solvent but it has sunk the debtor nations further in debt.[35]

The fact that this global usury might be undermining the developing world's long term capacity to service debt or to generate markets and profits went largely unnoticed in a world where policy making had been hijacked by financial arbitrageurs, too highly leveraged to think of any consequences beyond tomorrow. Of course, there were voices in the wilderness, that declared the emperor naked. Early in Mrs Thatcher's reign, a prominent neoclassical theorist lamented that the claims being made in the name of neoclassical theory went far beyond anything that this theory would allow – even in pure theory, let alone with respect to policies in the real world.[36] In his opinion, people had abandoned reason in favour of 'gurus' dispensing 'specious nonsense.' But not any specious nonsense could become the new received wisdom. Only that which served sufficiently powerful interests. Structural adjustment and the outlandish promises of the supply siders qualified because they legitimised the draconian – and very profitable – demand for full debt repayment. Their impact on debt repayment was real. Their developmental promises remain largely hypothetical.

To be fair, the IFI studies commissioned to marshall the evidence for Structural Adjustment Lending (SAL) did candidly acknowledge that its impact on human welfare and on development was largely unknown.[37] They described SAL policies as being too vague and general and suggested that they would have to be much more effectively tailored to specific circumstances, if they were to be plausible. However, this seems to have been more easily said than done. Indeed, ten years into adjustment lending, a World Bank study referred to SAL policies as 'textbook solutions' and expressed the hope that the Bank might finally be in a position to 'move beyond' the dispensation of such ideological nostrums.[38] But pragmatism and realism are hard to achieve by 'six week experts.' Even if 'development' had been the primary purpose of adjustment lending, they are pretty much restricted to textbook advice since they rarely know enough about a society's true adjustment capacity to devise sensible policy. Demands for the universal deregulation of markets can only come to be derived from textbooks; and from rather bad textbooks at that.

It is therefore no surprise that even after fifteen years of adjustment lending, the Bank's central policy prescriptions still appear to take precedence over the evidence. Thus, when a recent Bank study concluded that the success of South Korea's highly interventionist state contradicted many of the Bank's standard policy prescriptions, a 'senior official' explained that the Bank had initially refused publication 'out of fear that it would be misinterpreted as a change in World Bank policy'![39] The concern was understandable since the study attacked the very heart of the orthodox position by suggesting that 'the ability of governments to be economically selective should be assessed on a case-by-case basis rather than assumed absent,' and that 'the need for various types of intervention cannot be governed entirely by normal cost-benefit analysis, because of the problems of quantifying uncertain learning sequences and because of differences in economic strategies pursued by different governments.'[40]

When SALs were first introduced, ignorance of their impact on development was so pervasive that even the effects of most individual policy instruments were largely unknown. In 1987, John Nellis, a senior World

Bank official with responsibility for privatisation policy, stated that 'the empirical evidence for privatisation is virtually nonexistent.'[41] Once again one can only conclude that this policy was not being promoted primarily because of its alleged impact on efficiency, but that other reasons, like the desire to roll back the public sector and to expand the space for private profit, must have been dominant. Finally, Nellis's assurance that studies had been commissioned to fill this gap, was not at all reassuring since an institution cannot be objective in assessing a policy to which it has already firmly committed itself. The recent 'East Asian Miracle' study only confirms the validity of this concern.

In fact, Nellis was quite wrong to say that there was 'virtually no empirical evidence' about privatisation. There was a wealth of such evidence, but it did not support the Bank's broad generalisations about the benefits of privatisation. That may have been why it was ignored. According to that evidence:

> In small-scale enterprise . . . where one deals with firms whose mode of operation is, so to speak, business as usual, private enterprise is likely to have a marked efficiency advantage. . . . The case of large enterprises is quite different. Here the efficiency advantage of private enterprise, apparently, often disappears. One can easily find cases in which a public firm seems much more efficient than its private counterpart, as well as cases where the reverse is true. **Thus, where large industry is concerned one must be pragmatic and be prepared to act differently from case to case in choosing between public and private ownership.**
> (emphasis added)[42]

The empirical foundations for the other policy instruments that make up the orthodox SAL were no stronger, according to a 1985 IMF study. It concluded that:

> the effects of fiscal deficits . . . turn out to be difficult to establish empirically . . . [and] there is . . . uncertainty whether public sector investment raises or lowers private sector investment;
> attempts to eliminate distortions . . . can cause unemployment and in some cases can even reduce welfare;
> it is still uncertain whether an increase in interest rates will, on balance, raise the savings rate;
> the direction and magnitude of the growth effects of exchange rate changes depend crucially on such issues as the extent and duration of the real exchange rate changes, the structure of production, and the responses of trade flows to relative price changes.[43]

If little was known about the effectiveness of individual policy instruments, much less was known about the impact of implementing complex policy packages containing many uncertain policy instruments. Very little was known about possible interactions between these instruments; even less was known about their optimal phasing; and almost nothing was known about how these policies would behave when introduced under difficult and unstable circumstances and, almost always, in the presence of substantial debts. Thus, the World Bank's 1985 'Evaluation of Program Design' lamented the fact that:

> potential conflicts among . . . SAL objectives and policy instruments . . . are not sufficiently elaborated and the trade-offs are not carefully explored . . . The treatment of these issues in SAL documents requires more attention and rigour. In some cases they are not directly addressed. In others they are only casually and superficially treated.[44]

But such earnest injunctions to 'do better' understate the nature of the problem. The impact of such complex policy packages is poorly understood even in the industrial countries, let alone in debt distressed developing countries. The very high degree of uncertainty necessarily associated with their implementation is therefore quite impossible to reconcile with the supreme confidence of the claims made on behalf of these policies by the IFIs. This phoney fervour, once again, suggests a hidden agenda, like the desire to maximize debt servicing at any cost. This suspicion is strengthened when one finds an IFI study actually declaring the evidence irrelevant to its policy conclusions. This astonishing message is delivered by an IMF study commissioned to review the evidence concerning the welfare impact of adjustment. This study informs the startled reader that, because of inherent methodological problems, its estimates of its short term impact are 'primarily based on deductive reasoning and not on the evidence itself,' while those of its long term effect have to be based on 'the axiomatic assumption that the impact of structural adjustment on welfare is subject to a J-curve effect.'[45] So much for pragmatism and science!

Some may be encouraged by the candour of the IFIs in acknowledging the weakness of their position, but these 'honest doubts' rarely seem to moderate the single minded militancy with which they pursue their neoliberal objectives. Thus, it was not long after these disarmingly frank studies had shown adjustment to be no more than living (and uncontrolled) experiments, that the Managing Director of the IMF announced to the world that 'there are good policies and there are bad policies' and that 'removing all structural impediments to growth is the only way to progress.'[46] The yawning gap between such bizarre claims and the freely acknowledged state of ignorance in the IFI technical papers serves as a reminder that, in an Orwellian world, the truth is established more by repetition and power, than by inquiry or research. Once again, the rationale for such grotesque over-statements can only be found by examining the interests that they serve. And, in the short run at least, adjustment policies serve the interests of international and hegemonic capital.

Even after ten years of adjustment lending the evidence to support those policies remains remarkably weak. Despite the best efforts of the IFIs to demonstrate their value, they remain little more than ideological assertions.

In 1988 the Bank published the first comprehensive analysis of its SALs, *Adjustment Lending: An Evaluation of Ten Years of Experience.*[47] The study claims to have 'reaffirmed the basic rationale for adjustment lending';[48] shown that adjustment lending was associated with a 'modest improvement' in economic performance; and established that 'the overall appraisal of adjustment lending is ... generally favourable.'[49] But even a cursory examination of the evidence contained in that study destroys these self serving conclusions and shows the policies to have been remarkably ineffective, even in the short term, when one would have expected a sudden infusion of foreign exchange to have given a measurable boost to the debt distressed recipients. It is as if the authors hoped that readers would just accept their conclusions, without bothering to examine the evidence.

The study compares the performance of each of thirty Adjustment Lending (AL) countries in the three years before and after their first SAL, with the average performance of 48 Non-Adjustment Lending (NAL) countries, in those same years.[50] When performance is compared on nine indicators, for a total of 270 comparisons,[51] 'the 30 AL countries improved relative to the NAL countries in 54 percent of cases.'[52] This result is the main basis for the study's 'generally favourable' conclusions, although it seeks to buttress these by showing that three subsets of AL countries outperformed the NAL countries more decisively. 'The envisaged effects of adjustment lending are more evident for middle-income countries'[53]; 'the performance of the 12 AL-intensive countries is considerably better than that for the larger AL group'[54]; and 'manufacturing exporters ... had the greatest improvement ... with sharp absolute and relative improvements in external and internal balances.'[55] Overall, the report concludes that 'the modestly better performance of the 30 (AL) countries and the substantially better performance of the 12 (AL-intensive) countries is associated with the initiation of adjustment lending.'[56]

But even these weak and tentative conclusions are untenable. It is not possible to say that AL countries did 'modestly better' than NAL countries because 54 per cent of these 270 comparisons came out in their favour.

This result must be interpreted as showing that there is no significant difference between the two groups, especially if one understands that: (i) less than a third of the differences in performance were statistically significant at the five per cent level;[57] (ii) the nine criteria for comparison were arbitrarily selected and included highly interdependent variables like GDP and export growth, or debt/GDP and debt/export ratios; (iii) the choice of time periods was arbitrary; and (iv) no sensitivity analysis was done to test the impact of these arbitrary specifications.

The study's attempt to buttress its main conclusions by showing that middle income, AL-intensive and manufactured exporting countries had all benefitted far more clearly from adjustment, also fails since the same countries turn out to dominate all three groups. In fact, only the nine manufacturing exporters appear to have derived clear benefits from adjustment although one must add that, even this result is heavily influenced by the extraordinarily positive performance of South Korea which has never actually applied the Bank's neoliberal policies even though it has been in receipt of SAL money.[58] The truth is that the 'middle income' and the 'AL intensive' groups are dominated by some of the manufacturing exporters. If these are removed from the sample, all of the remaining groups (all AL, AL intensive and middle income) compare unfavourably with the NAL countries on over 50 per cent of the comparisons; and often by a wide margin.

Ironically, structuralists would have predicted such a result since they would assume that relatively strong and diversified economies, like the manufactured exporters, would be more likely to respond constructively to the challenge of market liberalization. They would also have expected these gains to be short lived in those cases where liberalization was taken so far that it undermined their ability to manage their exposure to external competition to suit changing domestic circumstances. They would, therefore, not have been surprised to find that two thirds of these 'success stories' (the Philippines, Brazil, Hungary, Pakistan, Yugoslavia and Turkey) had run into serious economic difficulties by 1992, largely because they had found it increasingly difficult to maintain political stability in the face of such radical economic liberalization.

The short term success of structural adjustment thus turns out to be limited to one particular type of economy. *According to the Bank's own findings*, the great majority of AL countries derived no net economic benefits from these policies. In the study's own words, 'the hoped for switching and growth-augmenting effects of adjustment lending is [*sic*] not apparent in the low-income countries';[59] while 'in the highly indebted group . . . fewer than half (45 per cent of AL countries) matched the average (performance) of the NAL group.'[60] Since these two groups make up 75 per cent of the AL countries, it is impossible to claim that this study provides general support for adjustment lending. In fact, the opposite is true since only strong positive evidence would be sufficient to justify these risky and experimental policies. The study does not come close to providing such strong evidence.

In speculating on the reasons why almost three quarters of the AL countries performed so poorly, the Bank surmises that it may be 'unrealistic to expect large increases in private savings ... [when] per capita consumption is stagnant or declining,' or that maybe 'the supply response ... has been slow because of ... deep-seated structural problems'![61] This belated and unacknowledged rediscovery of structuralism may qualify the authors for a world record in 'slow learning,' although they appear to believe they have made a new discovery. One can only hope that more such discoveries will eventually produce a more pragmatic approach to adjustment policy – but that would assume that the evidence was actually the basis of the policy prescriptions.

Finally, the relatively dismal performance of most AL countries might represent short term pain for long term gain, but the evidence does not suggest this. Indeed, even this poor performance appears to have been achieved at the expense of future development prospects since, in most cases, investment (I/GDP ratios) fell while external debt ratios rose, despite import compression, restrained private consumption, rapid export growth and reduced public spending. According to the Bank:

Debt service-to-export ratios have risen, except for manufacturing exporters. Moreover, these rises understate the deterioration because they exclude services falling due but not paid ... In most instances, the debt problem is greater now than it was at the start of the 1980s.[62]

Investment–GDP ratios fell for all groups ... This pattern of falling investment shares in GDP suggests that the required reduction in expenditures fell disproportionately more heavily on investment than on consumption, jeopardizing future growth.[63]

Indeed, despite its claim that the 'overall' impact of adjustment had been positive, the study had to admit that the long term implications were worrisome.

Several factors ... bring the sustainability of adjustment programs into question. Investment ratios have declined, and budget deficits are higher in the highly indebted and the Sub-Saharan countries. Although current accounts have been reduced, debt service ratios and especially debt–export ratios have increased. It is not possible to conclude, therefore, that the AL countries are growing out of debt.[64]

No objective observer would support the continuation of adjustment lending based on this evidence. At best, they may be justified in relatively strong economies, already exporting manufactured goods on a significant scale. But even here their long term effects would need to be carefully monitored.

The first decade of neoliberal adjustment has thus failed to vindicate the ideological assertions that swept them to power. Instead, it has vindicated those who feared that these simplistic policy prescriptions would over-whelm societies because they failed to 'recognise the ultimate unity of social, political and economic dimensions of reality.'[65] By 1985 the World Bank had to agree, noting wistfully that 'borrowers and lenders often fail to take full account of the institutional, social, and political rigidities that restrict a country's capacity to adjust.'[66]

Taken as a whole, the story of adjustment lending suggests strongly that it was not primarily driven by concerns about development, and that concerns about globalization and debt repayment were probably of some importance. That helps to explain why their diffusion has had to rely so extensively on coercion rather than persuasion. And that, in turn, explains why the IMF could recently write that 'the structural reforms now being considered in the industrial countries are relatively minor compared to [the] comprehensive stabilization-cum-liberalization programs' already implemented in many developing countries.[67] If these policies had spread primarily because people had understood and accepted their desirability, one would have expected them to have been most rapidly adopted in the more advanced, educated and technically proficient countries. Paraphrasing the South Pacific's brilliant anti-nuclear slogan: 'If it's safe, why not do the testing in Europe?,' one could ask: 'If these policies are so good, why were they not applied first in the industrial countries?' The answer is, because the IFIs did not have sufficient leverage there. Unfortunately, as the unemployment and the debt crises deepen, and as financial deregulation, the GATT and various bilateral agreements like the CUFTA (Canada–US Free Trade Agreement) and the NAFTA (North American Free Trade Agreement) gradually disenfranchise electorates in the industrial countries, their leverage is steadily growing.

The citizens of the developing world were significantly disenfranchised by the advent of 'policy lending' whose main purpose was brilliantly, if brutally, described by Elliot Berg, in an internal World Bank paper as, 'buying a place at the policy high table.'[68] It represented a direct assault on sovereignty. Before 'structural adjustment,' project lending required national governments to make strategic choices through a national political process – choices that reflected the interests and preferences of its citizens. Projects were then selected on the basis of their ability to contribute to the realisation of the objectives thus defined. Although this was not always what happened in practice, it provided a rationale that acknowledged the importance of such sovereign choices. Now, policy lending dispenses both with the substance of sovereignty and the rhetorical niceties. The best development strategy is now determined by the IFIs who claim that this is a technical question to which they have worked out an objective, 'correct' answer: namely, that neoliberal policies serve every country's 'national interest'! They will occasionally even advise and assist client states to defuse or disperse potential opposition to those policies, on the spurious grounds that all such opposition represents illegitimate attempts to seek or to protect the rents of a minority at the expense of the welfare of society as a whole.[69]

Governments and political processes have thus been emptied of political content. Governments have become executive agencies that implement predetermined, sound policies devised by technical experts. This has made it much easier for the IFIs (and the hegemonic powers) to support democracy in the developing world, since it is no great threat to give people the democratic right to elect governments that have no effective power over social or economic policy. Indeed, under such conditions the attainment of democratic rights may turn out to be a mixed blessing that makes it easier to divide and rule. That is why both the struggle and the debate in southern Africa must focus on the substance, not the appearance, of democracy.

If the hegemonic powers insist on imposing the straitjacket of orthodox adjustment on southern Africa, they will increase the risk of political and economic disaster because the resulting 'low intensity democracies' will be unable to maintain a balance between social, political and economic conditions inside and outside the country. They should recall Bhagwati's warning that his fellow advocates of adjustment should 'exercise ... caution lest their prescriptions are counterproductive because of ignored political prerequisites.'[70]

DEMOCRATIZATION AND THE POLITICAL CHALLENGE

The relationship between capitalism and democracy has long been hotly contested.[71] The two seem natural allies since both represent highly decentralised coordinating mechanisms that allow individuals a lot of discretion and freedom in making economic and political choices. This impression is reinforced by the fact that historically capitalism and liberal democracy have often coexisted, but it would be wrong to think that they always reinforce each other. Things are not so simple. Both in the developing world, and in periods of economic crisis, their apparent complementarity often breaks down. In fact, under these conditions neoliberalism is often linked with authoritarianism because the scope for social and political conflict escalates as poor people are directly exposed to volatile, powerful and unbalanced global markets. So when can democracy and capitalism be expected to reinforce each other? And do these conditions exist, or could they be created, in southern Africa?

Classical Marxism suggests that the answer to the first question is: Never! From its perspective the democratic freedoms enjoyed by citizens in capitalist states are mere 'bourgeois freedoms' that do not afford much genuine choice regarding the kind of society in which to live. In a fiercely competitive world always tending towards economic instability and crisis, and characterised by highly unequal and authoritarian property rights, people's finest sentiments and dearest wishes would soon be 'drowned in the icy waters of commercial calculation.'[72] The people might wish for a society in which technology freed them from economic insecurity and from the need to work long hours in stressful jobs, and allowed them to devote more time and energy to social and cultural pursuits. And periodically such gains would be made, but they would always be threatened and undermined when major economic imbalances intensified competition and returned working people to a dog eat dog reality in which technology displaces workers, creates unemployment, reduces wages, increases economic insecurity and intensifies labour – no matter how high the average level of productivity. Reality would then mock their dreams of a leisure society. And should they seek to challenge the constraints that imposed these conditions on them, they would discover the iron fist hidden in the velvet glove of that democracy.

Such a world creates the illusion of freedom without its substance.[73] It pits people against one another in a relentless struggle for economic survival; a struggle that breeds conflict and leaves only limited choices. Such a world regards the notion of economic democracy as foolish and treats global competitive pressures as 'facts of life,' to be accepted at any cost. In this world the drive for efficiency, cost minimisation and competitiveness will dominate all other objectives.

At the other end of the spectrum are pluralists and public choice theorists, who do believe there to be a close, inseparable link between capitalism and democracy, because both maximise the individual's freedom to choose. They see no systemic limits to that freedom but emphasise only the need to establish clear and unambiguous property rights. Outcomes are jointly determined by complex and open-ended processes of political and economic competition in the market place. So long as this competition is free (or 'perfect') the outcomes will be economically optimal and politically legitimate. These conclusions cannot be challenged since they are really tautologies: an optimum economic outcome is defined as that outcome which is (or would be) produced by perfectly competitive markets; and political legitimacy is measured by the extent of political competition.

From this perspective democracy and capitalism require and reinforce each other. Problems arise only when political competition leads to outcomes that constrain the freedom of economic competition, as may happen when economic competition increases economic insecurity, poverty and social conflict. Faced with a choice between the two freedoms, the political right will generally give priority to economic freedom, because it is regarded as the basis for 'democracy' and because property rights are the *sanctus sanctorum* of this religion.[74] Economic crisis and instability can therefore sever the bond between capitalism and democracy even in pluralism's idyllic society, which is why the smell of fascism becomes so quickly pervasive during periods of economic crisis in the industrial world and why stable democracies are such a rarity in the developing world. It is also why the seventies witnessed the emergence of an authoritarian strand of modernization theory which sought to explain and justify the persistence of authoritarian governments in the developing world.[75] And why such ideas are gaining ground so rapidly in Russia where, on the day Yeltsin's troops had gutted Parliament, a senior aide informed CNN's viewers that a 'reforming' Russia would now have to go through a period of 'democratical [*sic*] dictatorship.' If Joe Hill were still with us, he would be singing about:

> Pie in the sky;
> And democracy bye and bye![76]

The early post-war period tilted the debate between Marxists and pluralists strongly towards the latter because Marx's arguments appeared dogmatic and implausible at a time when the capitalist democracies provided citizens with an historically unprecedented capacity to make real choices. In the industrial countries, labour could bargain with capital and enforce the resulting compromises; and it could demand that governments maintain full employment, thereby sustaining the upward pressure on wages that eventually transformed income distributions and laid the basis for the modern welfare state. Though it fell far short of paradise, this form of capitalism gave considerable substance to democracy. But it also led to the fatal illusion that those gains could be taken for granted as the natural and automatic consequence of capitalism's ability to raise productivity through technical progress. This naive illusion allowed the political foundations of that 'golden age' to be destroyed, and this process accelerated when the generation that had experienced the thirties and the war moved into retirement. Meanwhile, Eastern Europe's dramatic implosion was fuelled both by its internal failures and by the spread of an even more simplistic illusion, which led its people to believe that capitalism, the 'forbidden fruit,' would allow them to 'have it all' – freedom, leisure, prosperity – and cigarette lighters that play 'The Star Spangled Banner'.

What was forgotten was that the historically unprecedented conditions of this golden age were made possible by a post-war settlement that had tolerated, even encouraged, the existence of relatively sovereign nation states, linked together by a loose and pragmatic set of rules designed to limit economic conflict between them. These states were able to respond to the demand for full employment. And their capitalist classes were rooted sufficiently within each nation to be obliged to function within politically defined limits. This gave democracy substance and allowed stable regimes of regulation to be established and sustained.[77] Significantly, it was the US and the UK, the two countries in which capital was least nationally rooted, that ultimately took the lead in destroying this system by their headlong pursuit of global deregulation.

The relatively strong states of this period were initially tolerated by the dominant hegemonic power (the US) and by capital: because everyone feared a repetition of the economic turmoil that had followed World War I; because the chaos of the twenties, the spectre of the depression and the horror of the war had created a genuine fear of social breakdown and revolution; and because the existence of the Soviet bloc fanned those fears into the flaming paranoia of the 'Cold War.' But memories are short and with prosperity and stability came complacency and greed, the latter relying on neoliberalism's poisonous promises to give its tawdry claims an air of respectability. And meanwhile, competitive pressures were bearing down on the US and the UK, whose low productivity growth rates threatened their relative standards of living and their power. To counter these trends, they supported a process of financial and economic liberalisation that allowed them to compensate for their internal weaknesses but that also undermined the foundations of the 'golden age,' sending the world's working people back to the world of the twenties, or beyond. Under these conditions, the pluralist vision is losing its resonance as fascism threatens to disrupt the link between capitalism and democracy; and Marx's analysis of that link becomes comprehensible once again.

For the moment, the tide of ignorance and amnesia is in full flood, as the war on national sovereignty escalates. A recent *Business Week* editorial encourages the US to consolidate its foreign policy initiatives by targeting those who still have the temerity to oppose the creation of an unregulated global market.

> With the end of [communist] 'containment,' the main element in any US foreign policy must now be 'enlargement' – unyielding promotion of an open global-market economy.
>
> But to guarantee the spread of market economies overseas, the US must also contain the forces of reaction. This won't be easy . . . Expanding global markets, containing extremists, and building new middle classes overseas is the way to further worldwide prosperity, spread democracy, and ensure the peace.[78]

The 'forces of reaction' that are to be 'contained' are 'those dispossessed on the road to capitalism'! And the ultimate object is 'to preserve . . . nascent market economies **and to contain the nationalists who threaten them**' (emphasis added). Thus we go from communist 'containment' to the 'containment' of those who do not accept the logic or the consequences of globalization. Their views are declared out of bounds, even if democratically derived. As Kissinger put it, in justifying the US's participation in the 1973 overthrow of Allende's democratic government in Chile: 'I don't see why we need to stand by and watch a country go communist due to the irresponsibility of its own people.'[79] But these new cold warriors do not realise that their ambition is only a recipe for more disasters, because markets can only function effectively when embedded in sovereign societies.

Of course, even during the golden age (1948 to 1973) when many in the industrial world were dreaming of the end of ideology and of the leisure society, those living in, or dealing with, the developing world were daily reminded of the limited compatibility between capitalism and democracy. In this part of the world capitalism and democracy have rarely coexisted for long and, where they have done so, democracy has frequently been reduced to the political charades that pass for democracy in Guatemala.

Modernization theorists and Chicago Marxists like Bill Warren,[80] argued it was just a matter of time until development brought both prosperity and democracy, so long as the forces of modernity emanating from the 'modern' world, were allowed a free rein. Dependency theorists were less sanguine, fearing that excessive dependence would distort domestic political processes and prevent them from resolving domestic distributional and political conflicts. They associated economic liberalization and unlimited international integration with authoritarianism, not democracy. Thus, when democracy arrived in many parts of the developing world together with rapid economic liberalization, it seemed that modernization theory had been vindicated.[81] But this is no longer so clear as the initial euphoria gives way to more realistic and balanced assessments.

The flowering of democracy in the eighties must be understood in its global and historic context. It occurred in the wake of Reagan's cynical crusade for democracy; at a time when sovereignty had been sharply contained by the debt crisis and by policy lending; and in a context where the hegemonic powers felt increasingly free and unconstrained to intervene anywhere in the world, as Soviet power and independence waned. This does not suggest that the new democracies were mere foreign implants. They were invariably driven by strong popular democratic forces, but these were suddenly able to succeed in many cases because the dictators who had long suppressed them with the tacit, or active, approval of the hegemonic powers, were being pressured to run the risk of releasing their strangle hold on those democratic forces. They were also forgiven and urged to form political parties and to stand for election. And they were often supported in their born again career by their former friends abroad. No wonder these new democracies are often so limited, shallow and fragile. As Eduardo Galeano has put it:

> There is nothing strange in the fact that the very same people who cheer the trials of human rights violators in Eastern Europe applaud impunity in Latin America. In the South, state terrorism is a necessary evil.[82]

As a result, many people feel they have achieved the shell of democracy, without its substance. Disillusion and voter apathy are rampant. And those who do vote often show little enthusiasm for the choices before them. In Russia's most recent election, 85 per cent of those who voted, 'voted against (Yeltsin's) policies,'[83] which may have something to do with the collapse of the economy (a 40 per cent decline in the GDP!), the dramatic immiseration of workers and pensioners, and the explosive growth of crime, corruption and unemployment. In Latin America, 'all the democracies have a certain fragility' because 'the potential for the kind of social unrest that prompts military intervention is growing as the region undergoes a wrenching shift to free-market economic policies.'[84]

In this harsh world, compromises are made. Democracy is diluted. Sovereignty is constrained. Externally-funded terrorists with little social base and no political program (like Mozambique's RENAMO) reappear as 'democratic' parties, while Haiti's democratically elected president is asked to compromise by giving cabinet posts to the thugs who have been assassinating his supporters and his Cabinet Ministers in broad daylight. And if he does not compromise, then the thugs may be invited to form the government and, so long as they can stage manage a Guatemala-style election, all would be considered well. Haiti would drop out of the news, because it would be regarded as a 'democratic' country that could be relied upon to defend the rights of global capital.

That is how Orwellian democracies are created. Soon such diluted democracies may be all one can realistically expect. The demand for a popular democracy in which well informed people can make real choices may be dismissed as a utopian dream. We may all be asked to 'make do' with purely formal democracies, in which global elites manipulate electoral processes to lend an aura of legitimacy to predetermined policies that protect their power. Electoral victories would be treated as the unquestioned mark of political legitimacy, even if only those with great personal wealth could hope to succeed in elections; even if the media were controlled by a few millionaire ideologues; even if most of the population had been eliminated from politics by ignorance, disillusion or apathy; and even if those with contrary views were terrorised by vigilantes, hired assassins or government sponsored death squads, trained and financed by aid money from powers professing an undying love for democracy, while developing their capacity to wage 'low intensity war.'

In such a world the IFIs can treat Colombia as an economic 'success story' and as a democracy worthy of extensive assistance and aid, while Cuba is pilloried, blacklisted and embargoed for its human rights violations. No matter that before the collapse of Eastern Europe and the intensified US embargo, Cuba's people had achieved welfare levels and social conditions that were the envy of the developing world. And no matter that Colombia's government is engaged in a process of 'political cleansing' which

> rests on the notion that people who hold what are defined as communist or socialist ideas, or who work with grass-roots organizations, are dirty and must be eliminated or forced out to preserve the nation's health
> ... there were more than 4,300 political murders in Colombia last year, an average of twelve a day ... 74 per cent of these [have been attributed to] the police, armed forces and their paramilitary clients ...

The targets are not only guerillas but anyone perceived as helping or sympathizing with them, including human rights monitors, journalists, union leaders and peasant organizers.

The Patriotic Unity Party . . . says it has lost more than 2,200 members to political assassination since 1985, when the party was founded . . . the UP won an astonishing victory in 1986 municipal elections . . . Then the backlash began.[85]

Of course, such violence always has a history that allows each side to blame the other, but that does not make oppressors and oppressed equally guilty. The sequence of events that brought Colombia so low is a chilling reminder of the future that awaits southern Africa, and the world, unless ways are found to narrow the chasms opening up within and between societies. Colombia's descent into hell began after a 1940s populist leader (Gaitan) had

galvanised the popular classes into a new force. The terrified oligarchy reacted fiercely by destroying the unions and reversing the workers' achievements. The assassination of Gaitan on 9th April 1948 caused the angry and frustrated pueblo to erupt into an insurrection.

The ultraconservative . . . Gomez (1950–1953) unleashed the answer to the mob: a mixture of terror, partisan sectarianism, and scorched earth policy. Its extreme modality was pitiless murder, indescribable atrocities, and the mutilation of popular conscience. Raging violence marked for life an entire generation whose attitude to its condition vacillated between fatalism, vengeance, and repressed rebellion. The country lay devastated, on the verge of an irreversible social and political crisis.[86]

To avoid such a fate, let alone undo such a legacy, requires policies that strengthen the sense of community and the belief that inequities will be gradually reduced through policies that are responsive to people's democratically defined wishes. Several of the Fathers of the American Constitution wrote on more than one occasion that the democracy they hoped to fashion could not succeed unless two conditions were met: income and wealth should not be too unequally distributed; and those seeking public office, as well as those electing them, should value 'public virtue'![87] Both of these conditions are undermined by the poisonous consequences of neoliberal adjustment, which allows enormous fortunes to be amassed amidst grinding poverty and which denigrates the very idea of public virtue as a 'rent-seeking' pretension. The IFIs even like to speak of the need to decriminalise parallel markets, implying that the transactions in those markets express people's real preferences more legitimately than the political process. This implies that it would not be legitimate for a society to enforce a rationing system that protected people from those hoarding food to drive up prices in a famine. Such 'specious nonsense' gets a hearing because it serves to undermine the ability of states to restrain market actors in the public interest!

By supporting democracy only so long as it does not pose a challenge to their overriding commitment to the creation of a deregulated global economy, the hegemonic powers are denuding democracy of political content and sowing the seeds of its future destruction. A unified global economy is a contradiction in terms and a recipe for disaster. In such a world income, power and resources would be allocated strictly in accordance with people's ownership and control of property and skills, which is why it is so attractive to those who currently lay claim to the bulk of those property rights. But its achievement would not even serve their interests, because by rupturing the vital link between economy and society it would destroy the very possibility of efficiency. Competitive markets are a powerful positive force for change, but they must be managed and directed if they are to serve humanity. Wealth, like capital, is a social relation that obtains its meaning, its power and its ability to gratify from the social context in which it exists. In an anarchic, deregulated world everyone will be desperately impoverished.

The link between democracy and capitalism therefore depends on the existence of a sovereign political process capable of reconciling social and economic objectives in a competitive environment. The severe difficulties encountered by democracy in the developing world must be traced back to the limited sovereignty enjoyed by states in that part of the world.[88] Exceptions like Costa Rica merely prove the rule that democracy is sustainable only when a sovereign nation is able to create a responsible and responsive capitalism.[89] And in the industrial world, the exception of the post-war 'golden age' teaches the same lesson. The most stable and substantive democracies emerged when sovereign governments were able to maintain full employment and enforce politically determined compromises between capital, labour and other social forces. Far from conflicting with efficiency, this also produced the most rapid and sustained growth of output and productivity and the most widespread diffusion of welfare in history.

That conclusion is further reinforced by an analysis of cross-sectional data on the relationship between economics and democracy in the developing world. This concluded that 'levels of economic inequality are more important to the quality and stability of democracy than levels of

economic output or the rate at which this changes.'[90] Equity is not likely
to be prominent in impoverished societies in which individuals are given
unlimited freedom to exploit the advantages conferred upon them by their
ownership of capital, resources, information or skills. Sustained equity requires the sovereign ability to redistribute income, assets or opportunities
in accordance with politically defined priorities and pressures, even though
the demand for equity must be reconciled with other objectives, like growth.
But, it is precisely because there is no one optimum trade-off between
these competing objectives, that a stable, high equity outcome requires the
presence of a sovereign government that is guided by an effective political
process. In the light of this evidence, our conclusion must be modified.
Instead of suggesting that democracy can be reconciled with capitalism
only in the presence of a relatively sovereign state, we must add that this
sovereign state has to *place a significant emphasis on equity.*

The lessons of development thus reinforce the central lesson of the
industrial world's 'golden age.' Both echo Karl Polanyi's argument that
the agonies of the 1920s and 1930s should have taught us that markets will
serve the social interest and will be compatible with genuine democracy
only when they are embedded in social and political frameworks able to
contain the forces that give unregulated markets 'a tendency to instability
and fraud,' in the World Bank's memorable phrase.

The question of socialism enters when we ask what political and social
controls are needed to manage market economies and to curb their tendency
to 'overaccumulation and crisis.' There is no single answer to this question
and history will record as many answers in the future as it has done in the
past. And yet there are things we can learn from that past. Eastern Europe
clearly relied too heavily on administrative controls and left too little
space for markets and democracy. In the twenties and thirties, the world
relied excessively on deregulated markets and paid a heavy price in wasted
resources, blighted lives and poisoned democracies. And the industrial
world may have come close to 'getting it right' in the golden age between
1948 to 1973, although we clearly need to find ways of protecting such a
model from inter-generational amnesia, greed and excessive international
competition.

In the developing world Cuba, South Korea/Taiwan and Costa Rica
deserve our attention as possible models, despite the vast differences between them. The fact that Costa Rica was the only one of these to sustain
a formal democracy bears witness to the difficulties of protecting democracy in such an environment, but then Cuba serves as a reminder that,
even in the absence of competitive political parties, it is possible for a
government to serve the interests of its people and retain their support over

long periods of time, in spite (or maybe partly because) of extreme external hostility and provocation. There are many roads to development but
they are all rocky and narrow. And it seems that only cohesive, sovereign
nations, capable of defining and pursuing a long term 'national interest'
have any hope of completing the journey. Those who would help them,
must support them in that task.

And so we return to the original question: Can southern Africa build a
meaningful democracy on the basis of neoliberal adjustment policies that
would integrate the countries of the region fully into the international
economy? The answer has to be: 'Almost certainly not!' This leaves policymakers, politicians and the region's citizens with the difficult task of seeking a middle ground that is both feasible and desirable. What remains of
this brief essay can do no more than touch upon some of the main issues
they will have to address.

Neoliberal adjustment will not solve the region's chronic economic
problems. Its tendency to foster economic instability, to heighten social
conflict and to increase political tension would prove politically dangerous
and economically destructive. It is therefore necessary to create the political
space that is needed to pursue alternative policies that can encourage growth
and investment across a broad front, while protecting the economy from
destructive competition and from destabilising speculation by financial
regulations that channel investible resources towards long term national
development. For South Africa, these needs are explicitly addressed in the
Macroeconomic Research Group's *MERG Report*,[91] which has developed
a serious and plausible 'alternative strategy' that should serve as a point
of departure for the economic policy debate in that country. Although one
cannot take the administrative capacity or the sovereignty that such a
strategy requires for granted, the challenge must be confronted if disaster
is to be averted.

Some argue that because such an alternative strategy is impossible,
South Africa must seek its salvation under the full glare of international
competition. This is, of course, the view of hegemonic capital, but it is
shared by some who are clearly committed to the creation of a democratic
South Africa that serves the interests of the majority of its people. The ISP
(Industrial Strategy Project), which arose out of COSATU's Economic
Trends Group, is a case in point. Their pessimism regarding the scope for
a coherent national (or regional) policy is understandable and may even
prove justified. And their strong and innovative focus on the need to
strengthen South Africa's high value added manufactured exports should
remain an important component of any future strategy. But their optimism
regarding the consequences of radical economic liberalisation appears ill

considered and underestimates the difficulties and the risks associated with such a policy.

The ISP believes South Africa's industrial sector must be exposed to unrestricted international competition because this would force it to become efficient, enabling South Africans to enjoy the benefit of competitive international prices. Within that context, the ISP proposes measures to assist South Africa's manufacturers to attain the flexibility and efficiency needed to survive in the global market.[92] Although these efforts are likely to make an important positive contribution to the economy, they are most unlikely to succeed on the scale needed to solve its chronic unemployment problem. Indeed, it is inconceivable that South Africa could maximise internal learning effects or capture important dynamic externalities, without making extensive use of infant industry and other industrial policies that would allow it to nurture strategic firms or industries. That is the lesson of history. It is also the lesson of the successful East Asian NICs. South Africa will not succeed without making use of such policies to a degree.

Radical liberalization would destroy a large part of the existing industrial structure, especially since most industries presently suffer from substantial excess capacity globally, so that the marginal cost of supplying a new market is often very low. To achieve full employment or to sustain rising real wages South Africa must develop nationally based technological capabilities that will eventually allow it to generate and to appropriate technological rents in the form of higher real wages. This will not happen spontaneously.

It may be that the East Asian models can no longer be copied because South Korea and Taiwan were exceptionally 'allowed' to build strong national economies to serve as bulwarks against communism in Asia. In the New World Order there is no need for such exceptions. Moreover, the East Asian NICs were hardly democracies during their formative years, and technology has moved a long way since they began their industrialisation drive in earnest. The train the late developers have to catch is moving much faster and one may no longer be able to jump aboard using the methods of yesterday. But that does not increase the plausibility of the ISP's even riskier strategy, which dilutes national sovereignty and puts a large part of the existing economy at risk, in the faint hope that success at the micro level could offset the inevitable macro level losses.

It is ill advised of the ISP to exclude the possibility of complementing its export promotion activities with measures that could stimulate resource mobilisation in areas of the economy not yet able to withstand international competition. The radical rejection of such possibilities is extremely unwise. There is much to be said for moderation in such matters. The 'big bang' approach to policy change is rapidly losing credibility, and for good reason. Gradual policy changes allow learning to occur and minimise the risks of disruption. Even if South Africa chose to liberalize its economy, it should do so gradually and carefully, following the lead of Asia's successful and gradual transitions from central planning (China, Vietnam),[93] and from nationalism (Japan, South Korea, Taiwan). By the same token, any future moves to strengthen national sovereignty should also proceed gradually.

These are difficult choices. A more nationally focused strategy would face enormous difficulties, including the hostility of the hegemonic powers. Pragmatism must be the order of the day. South Africa cannot confront those powers head on, but it must exploit the available room for manoeuvre by devising feasible policies that minimise the risk of failure. The MERG report is an excellent first step in such a process. Although its discussion of financial intervention might unsettle some investors, one should remember that those same people would be the first to pull the plug on South Africa if economic policies led to social and political unrest. Ultimately, only a stable and expanding domestic economy can hope to attract the long term investment that South Africa needs. If some capital is to behave as national capital, it must see long term advantages in building a strong national economy in which it has a strong position. Ironically, such advantages may come to appear more important as international markets become more unpredictable and predatory. To abandon any attempt to create a pool of (relatively) 'national capital' would be a grave mistake. In its absence, labour will only be able to bargain with international capital, where its bargaining leverage is, and will remain, desperately weak.

A stable democracy will not be easy to achieve in southern Africa. The only hope resides in the possibility of building stable institutions and political parties that can negotiate for significant sections of the population while maintaining a clear sense of the interests of society as a whole. Much will depend on the kinds of economic policies adopted by – or imposed upon – the states of the region. If these destroy the ability of domestic parties and institutions to determine patterns of growth and development in accordance with the region's social and political realities then political failure will be inevitable. And political failure will ensure economic failure.

CONCLUSIONS

The possibility of consolidating democracy in southern Africa depends on whether economic growth can be achieved through policies that focus

simultaneously on efficiency, welfare and political stability. This requires
a degree of sovereignty that is not easy to reconcile with orthodox adjustment policies, which tend to fuel social conflict and political tension and
reduce the state's ability to mediate between different regions or social
groups. Such policies would therefore lead to political, and then to economic, failure.

Economically they would fail: because they would not elicit a large
enough supply response to offset the loss of large parts of the economy to
international competition; because speculation would increase uncertainty,
misallocate resources, undermine social and political cohesion and inhibit
long term investment; and because the resulting ideological climate would
destroy any chance of persuading people to accept painful and difficult
decisions because they were seen to be part of a process that was ultimately
fair and responsive to their needs and interests. As a result, the costs of
contract enforcement would escalate and efficiency would ultimately take
a back seat to survival.

The chances of success would be greatly enhanced if the IFIs and the
international community eased the economic constraints by making more
resources available on a relatively unconditional basis. To those who say
that this is an unrealistic demand under today's economic circumstances,
one can only say that South Africa's future is also our future. The world
can only survive so many open wounds like Liberia, Angola, Colombia,
Yugoslavia, Afghanistan, the Sudan, Russia, Georgia, the Ukraine,
Nicaragua, Haiti, Zaire, Palestine, Panama, Rwanda, Mozambique . . . !

The challenge of consolidating democracy in southern Africa has been
accepted by its people under the most difficult conditions. The world must
help them to meet that challenge. Its future, as well as theirs, may depend
on the outcome.

Notes

1. B. Gills and J. Rocamora, 'Low Intensity Democracy,' *Third World Quarterly*, 13, 3 (1992).
2. IFI refers primarily to the World Bank and the International Monetary Fund
although, with increasing 'policy coordination' in the eighties, the policies
of these institutions were increasingly reflected in the activities of the regional development banks, the OECD and even most of the bilateral donors.
3. O'Brien, the World Bank's chief economist for Africa as cited in John
Raymond, 'Worth repeating,' *Toronto Globe and Mail*, 22 June 1988.

4.   The 'crusade for democracy' was launched just as the US government was escalating its 'low intensity conflict' against the democratically elected government of Nicaragua by arming CONTRA terrorists. In 1987 the Central American governments, despite their enormous differences, issued the Contadora peace accords calling for 'simultaneous steps to halt outside assistance to insurgent forces, prohibit the use of one's territory for aggression against other states and implement ceasefires,' H. Sklar, *Washington's War on Nicaragua* (Toronto: Between the Lines Press, 1988), p. 376. The accord called for 'an authentic democratic, pluralist and participatory process that includes the promotion of social justice, respect for human rights, (state) sovereignty, the territorial integrity of states and the right of all nations to freely determine, without outside interference of any kind, its economic, political, and social model' (*Central American Peace Accord*, as reprinted in ibid., p. 402). The US response was delivered by President Reagan when he told the Organisation of American States: 'I make a solemn vow; as long as there is breath in this body, I will speak and work, strive and struggle for the cause of the Nicaraguan freedom fighters'! (ibid., p. 379).

5.   Ronald Reagan, cited in 'President Urges Creation of Global Economy Open to "Uninhibited" Trade and Investment,' *IMF Survey*, 20 October 1986.

6.   This included the Latin American Studies Association of the United States, the International Human Rights Group, and the British Parliamentary Human Rights Group (see Sklar, op. cit., pp. 200–2).

7.   Testimony given to the House Subcommittee on Western Hemispheric Affairs on 16 April 1985, as cited by P. Kornbluh in T. Walker (ed.), *Reagan vs. the Sandinistas* (Boulder: Westview Press, 1987).

8.   Michel Camdessus as cited in *IMF Survey*, 18 October 1989, p. 290.

9.   Victoria Brittain, 'Angolan Democracy: The International Betrayal,' *Southern Africa Report*, 9, 3 (January 1994).

10. This evocative phrase was used by Nell to describe the neoliberal revolution under Reagan. See E. J. Nell 'Conclusions-Cowboy Capitalism: The Last Round-up,' in Nell (ed.), *Free Market Conservatism: A Critique of Theory and Practice* (London: Allen & Unwin, 1984).

11. W. Hutton, 'Markets threaten democracy's fabric,' *Guardian Weekly*, 16 January 1994, p. 21.

12. The chronic problems generated by these volatile and irrational markets were acknowledged in *The Economist*, 19 September 1992, p. 46, when it warned that 'just as the new international dimension of finance has added to some risks that may help to start a crisis – greater instability in currencies, faster transmission of economic disturbances across borders, new opportunities for leverage, increased susceptibility to the illusion of liquidity and so on – so it has also weakened (or anyway complicated) the traditional remedies of economic policy. In the new world of finance, the seas are rougher and the life-rafts flimsier.' For further discussion of these issues, see M. A. Bienefeld, 'Financial Deregulation: disarming the nation state,' *Studies in Political Economy*, 37 (Spring 1992).

13. See *IMF World Economic Outlook* (Washington: IMF, October 1993, Chapter IV), pp. 48–67.

14. The case for the view that the experience of these countries shows 'intervention' to have been both beneficial and important is made in R. Wade,

Governing the Market (Princeton: Princeton UP, 1990); in World Bank, 'World Bank Support for Industrialization in Korea, India and Indonesia,' *A World Bank Operations Evaluation Study* (Washington: World Bank, 1992); in M. A. Bienefeld, 'The Significance of the Newly Industrialising Countries for the Development Debate', *Studies in Political Economy*, 25 (Spring 1988); and in Paul Romer, 'Two Strategies for Economic Development: Using Ideas vs. Producing Ideas', *Proceedings of the World Bank Annual Conference on Development Economics 1992* (Washington: World Bank, 1993).

15. A. S. Milward, *The Reconstruction of Western Europe: 1945–1951* (London: Methuen, 1984).

16. K. B. Dillon and L. Duran-Downing, *Officially Supported Export Credits: Developments and Prospects, IMF World Economic and Financial Surveys* (Washington: IMF, February 1988).

17. This debate continues as the neoliberals struggle to reconcile their 'beliefs' with the contradictory evidence of East Asia. The most recent effort was contained in the so-called 'miracle study' (World Bank, *The East Asian Miracle: Economic Growth and Public Policy*, Policy Research Department, World Bank: Washington, 1993). This study attempts to achieve this reconciliation by isolating education and export promotion as *the* key explanations of the success of these economies. Several reviews have challenged and effectively destroyed the tortured logic of this last ditch defence. S. Lall, ' "The East Asian Miracle" ' Study: Does the Bell toll for Industrial Strategy? *World Development*, 22, 4 (April 1994), and D. Rodrik, 'King Kong meets Godzilla: The World Bank and the East Asian Miracle,' paper presented to the Overseas Development Council, (mimeo), January 1994.

18. Paul Romer makes this point in juxtaposing 'Two Strategies for Economic Development,' op. cit. He contrasts Taiwan, which has used a highly interventionist 'industrial policy' to create a national technological base that allows it to create ideas, with Mauritius, which has merely persuaded foreign producers to 'use ideas' within its borders by offering cheap labour and other inducements. Romer concludes that most countries have no choice but to pursue the Mauritius strategy even though this leaves them in a low wage trap, unable to sustain rising real wages. Indeed, with increasing competition from countries like China and India they must expect wages to fall. 'What is particularly worrisome about a strategy merely of pursuing factor price equalisation for labour is that the equilibrium wage for unskilled labour may be very low, lower even than the average wages now earned on Mauritius' (pp. 26–7). 'Development' as it is generally conceived, is thus simply ruled out. Ironically, Romer sees the Mauritius strategy as the only one that is compatible with 'democracy,' arguing that a Taiwan strategy could only be implemented by an authoritarian regime. But history would suggest that the Mauritius strategy is only rarely compatible with democracy for any length of time; while the Taiwan strategy will, at least, create some space for democracy in due course and need not be incompatible with it even in the earlier stages.

19. R. B. Manaut 'Identity Crisis: The Military in Changing Times,' *NACLA Report on the Americas*, 27, 2 (September/October 1993), p. 15.

20. R. Stackhouse, 'Freedom remains only a promise,' *Toronto Globe and Mail*, 18 March 1993, p. A9.

21. See J. Saul, 'South Africa: Between "Barbarism" and "Structural Reform",' *New Left Review*, 188 (July/August 1991), for a fuller discussion of this point.

22. This point is frequently made in the literature, although sometimes in ways that are rather vague and ill-defined. Peter Gibbon 'Social Dimensions of Adjustment and the Problem of Poverty in Africa,' Paper presented to SIDA, Stockholm, Autumn 1991; '"Civil Society" and Political Change, with Special Reference to "Developmentalist" States,' paper presented to Nordic Conference on 'Social Movements in the Third World,' University of Lund, Sweden, 18–21 August 1993; Gibbon, Yusuf Bangura and Arve Ofstad (eds), *Authoritarianism, Democracy, and Adjustment: The Politics of Economic Reform in Africa* (Uppsala: The Scandinavian Institute of African Studies, 1992); S. P. Riley 'Political Adjustment or Domestic Pressure: democratic politics and political choice in Africa,' *Third World Quarterly*, 13, 3 (1992). The point must be carefully qualified to be really persuasive (see R. Saunders, 'A Decade of Power in the Dock,' *Africa South*, August 1992). Otherwise it is indistinguishable from modernization theory's earlier claims that stable pluralist societies will emerge so long as most people were simultaneously involved in many cross-cutting activities and interest groups; or from public choice theory's conviction that if enough groups compete in the 'political market place' optimal outcomes are assured.

23. The neoliberals once celebrated Mancur Olson's claim that in prosperous societies the growth of 'distributive coalitions' would inevitably lead to stagnation and conflict, because it allowed them to argue for 'deregulation.' In doing so, they chose to ignore the fact that the historical record had forced Olson to acknowledge the possibility that this outcome could be averted by the formation of 'encompassing coalitions' driven by a commitment to 'the common good.' See M. Olson, *The Rise and Decline of Nations* (New Haven: Yale UP, 1982).

24. B. Gills and J. Rocamora, 'Low Intensity Democracy,' op. cit., p. 502.

25. The IFIs frequently acknowledge the reality of such dangers. See M. A. Bienefeld 'Structural Adjustment: Debt Collection Device or Development Policy?', ADMP Series No. 5 (Tokyo: Institute of Comparative Culture, Sophia University, 1993).

26. IMF 'Theoretical Aspects of the Design of Fund-Supported Adjustment Programs,' IMF: Occasional Paper No. 55 (Washington: IMF, 1987), p. 45.

27. P. Krugman, 'The Case for Stabilizing Exchange Rates,' *Oxford Review of Economic Policy*, (Autumn 1989), pp. 65–6.

28. IMF, *Staff Studies for the World Economic Outlook* (Washington: IMF, August 1989), p. 4.

29. World Bank, *World Development Report 1989* (Washington: World Bank, 1989), pp. 4–5 and p. 131.

30. Dani Rodrik, 'How Adjustment Policies should be Designed,' *World Development*, 18, 7 (July 1990).

31. J. Sachs, 'Trade and Exchange Rate Policies in Growth Oriented Adjustment Policies,' in V. Corbo (ed.), *Growth Oriented Adjustment Programs* (Washington: 1987).

32. World Bank, *World Development Report 1989* (Washington: World Bank, 1989), p. 4.

33. This is no trivial point. The World Bank accepts that these loans were pushed onto the Third World when investment opportunities in the OECD were highly constrained. Moreover, once the resulting loans had been socialized through government guarantees, lenders were no longer very concerned about the viability of the projects they were financing. Since these lenders had a lot of leverage and were assumed to be best placed to assess the commercial viability of these projects, it is not surprising that they had little difficulty 'selling' their schemes to poor and beleaguered governments. See World Bank, *World Development Report 1985* (Washington: World Bank, 1985), pp. 114–15.

34. For a fuller discussion see M. A. Bienefeld, 'A Time of Growing Disparities,' in Tomlin and Molot (eds), *Canada Among Nations: The Tory Record 1988* (Toronto: Lorimer, 1988).

35. *The Wall Street Journal*, 31 December 1986.

36. F. Hahn, 'Reflections on the Invisible Hand,' *Lloyds Bank Review* (April 1982).

37. M. S. Khan and M. D. Knight, 'Fund Supported Adjustment Programs and Economic Growth', IMF Occasional Paper No. 41 (Washington: IMF, 1985); and World Bank, *Structural Adjustment Lending: A First Review of Experience* (Washington: World Bank Operations Evaluation Department, September 1986); and F. Yagci *et al.*, 'Structural Adjustment Lending: An Evaluation of Program Design' World Bank Staff Working Papers No. 735 (Washington: World Bank, 1985).

38. World Bank, *Adjustment Lending: An Evaluation of Ten Years of Experience* (Washington: Policy and Research Series, World Bank, 1988), p. 66.

39. *Far Eastern Economic Review*, 2 March 1992, p. 49.

40. World Bank, 'World Bank Support for Industrialization in Korea, India and Indonesia,' A World Bank Operations Evaluation Study (Washington: World Bank, 1992), pp. 53–7. The points raised in this study were so fundamental that the Bank agreed to publish this paper only in response to Japanese pressure and only on condition that Japan finance a major Bank study to draw the lessons of the East Asian NICs 'once and for all.' The resulting 'miracle study' (see fn 17 for references) was clearly designed to reconcile the NIC experience with the Bank's neoliberal policy prescriptions. It achieved this result by claiming that, of all the interventionist measures used by those governments, only export promotion and the finance of education could be 'clearly' shown to have had a significant positive impact on their economic success. This conclusion is used by a tortuous logic that is clearly committed to a certain answer from the outset. The study has been subjected to devastating critiques from various quarters. Since nothing can be conclusively proven in the social sciences, it merely proves that people can always cling to certain beliefs if they wish to do so. But such exercises in self-justification must not be confused with careful, open ended scientific inquiry.

41. This statement was made in the plenary session of a workshop on 'Privatization: Fact, Fad or Fantasy?' organised by Carleton University's School of Public Administration in conjunction with the Pearson Program at Carleton University, Ottawa, Canada on 22 and 23 June 1987.

42. W. J. Baumol, 'On the Implications of the Conference Discussions' in

W. J. Baumol (ed.), *Public and Private Enterprise in a Mixed Economy* (London: Macmillan, 1980), p. 301.

43. Khan and Knight, op. cit., pp. 12–17.

44. Yagci *et al.*, op. cit., pp. 1, 2 and 22.

45. A J-curve effect is one in which an initial decline is inevitably followed by an increase. When the slopes of the curve are not specified, this improvement occurs after an unspecified period of time. The 'axiomatic' belief in such a pattern makes one immune to empirical evidence since negative outcomes can be dismissed as merely reflecting the initial downward slope of the J. The quotations are from P. S. Heller, A. L. Bovenberg, T. Catsambas, K. Y. Chu and P. Shome, 'The Implications of Fund-Supported Adjustment Programs for Poverty: Experiences in Selected Countries,' IMF Occasional Paper No. 58 (Washington: IMF, May 1988).

46. Michel Camdessus, as cited in *IMF Survey*, 18 October 1989, p. 290.

47. World Bank, *Adjustment Lending: An Evaluation . . .* , op. cit.

48. Ibid., p. 3.

49. Ibid., p. 31.

50. The results of this study are especially difficult to interpret because most of the NAL countries were also in receipt of IMF loans in the relevant periods so that they were also implementing many of the orthodox policies.

51. GDP growth; investment/GDP; export growth; real exchange rates; current account/GDP; budget balance/GDP; inflation; external debt/exports; and debt service/exports. See World Bank, ibid., p. 25.

52. Ibid., p. 24.

53. Loc. cit.

54. Ibid., p. 31.

55. Ibid., p. 24.

56. Ibid., p. 31.

57. Loc. cit.

58. These countries are so classified on the grounds that the 1988 *World Development Report* showed at least 35 per cent of their exports as manufactured goods. The nine countries are: Pakistan, Thailand, South Korea, Philippines, Brazil, Morocco, Turkey, Uruguay and Yugoslavia. Ibid., p. 21.

59. Ibid., p. 24.

60. Ibid., p. 24.

61. Ibid., p. 3.

62. Ibid., p. 30.

63. Ibid., p. 28.

64. Ibid., p. 31.

65. M. A. Bienefeld, 'Dependency in the Eighties,' *IDS Bulletin*, 12, 1 (December 1980).

66. World Bank, *World Development Report 1985* (Washington: World Bank, 1985), p. 2.

67. R. A. Feldman *et al.*, 'The Role of Structural Policies in Industrial Countries,' *Staff Studies for the World Economic Outlook* (Washington: IMF, August 1989), p. 7.

68. E. Berg and A. Batchelder, 'Structural Adjustment Lending: A Critical View,' paper prepared for the World Bank Country Policy Department, Elliot Berg Associates: Alexandria (Va), January 1985.

69. An entire literature based on this premise has been financed by the IFIs. It all began with A. Krueger's 'The Political Economy of Rent-Seeking Society', *American Economic Review*, 64, 3 (1974). A typical example that provides references to many others is K. Anderson and R. Baldwin, 'The Political Market for Protection in Industrial Countries,' *World Bank Staff Working Paper No. 492* (Washington: World Bank, 1981).

70. J. Bhagwati 'Rethinking Trade Strategy' in J. P. Lewis and V. Kallab (eds), *Development Strategies Reconsidered* (New Brunswick: Transaction Books, 1987), p. 101.

71. A brilliant summary of some of this literature is contained in Ian Robinson, *North American Trade As if Democracy Mattered: What's wrong with NAFTA and what are the Alternatives?* (Ottawa and Washington: Centre for Policy Alternatives and International Labour Rights and Education Fund, 1993).

72. This evocative phrase stems from the *Communist Manifesto* of 1848.

73. A classic statement of this argument can be found in C. B. Macpherson, *The Political Theory of Possessive Individualism: Hobbes to Locke* (Oxford: Oxford University Press, 1964).

74. If one defines 'the political right' as those who will choose economic freedom over political freedom whenever there is a conflict between the two, then this argument also turns out to be a tautology.

75. The authoritarian tendencies among modernization theorists were analysed by Donal Cruise O'Brien, 'Modernization, Order, and the Erosion of a Democratic Ideal,' *Journal of Development Studies*, 7 (1971), pp. 141–60; and Colin Leys, 'Samuel Huntington and the End of Classical Modernization Theory,' in Hamza Alavi and Teodor Shanin (eds), *Introduction to the Sociology of 'Developing Societies'* (New York: Monthly Review Press, 1982), pp. 332–49. In the seventies similar concerns about 'excessive democracy' in the industrial countries surfaced in the work of the Trilateral Commission. (See M. Crozier *et al.*, *The Crisis of Democracy: Report on the Governability of Democracies to the Trilateral Commission* (New York: New York UP, 1975).)

76. Joe Hill was the 'bard' of the International Workers of the World (the 'IWW') who 'rode the rails' in the United States around the turn of the century bringing the union message to workers in that country. Persecuted by the feds and by armies of Pinkerton security agents, they were 'defeated' in the 1920s, but many of their ideas resurfaced in the successful union initiatives of the thirties.

77. Unfortunately, the regulation school has done some disservice to our understanding of these issues by treating the achievement of stable regulatory regimes as a matter of chance, or 'serendipity,' and putting the main blame for the break-down of the post-war 'order' on technologically induced changes in productivity or on excessive wage increases. See A. Lipietz, *Miracles and Mirages: The Crisis of Global Fordism* (London: Verso, 1987).

78. 'Editorial,' *Business Week*, 17 January 1994, p. 102.

79. D. Munro, *The Four Horsemen: The Flames of War in the Third World* (Don Mills, Ont.: Mission Book Co., 1987), p. 23.

80. B. Warren, *Imperialism: Pioneer of Capitalism* (London: Verso, 1982).

81. R. Gastil, *Freedom in the World: Political Rights and Civil Liberties 1985–1986* (New York: Greenwood, 1986).

82.   Eduardo Galeano, 'The Corruption of Memory,' *NACLA Report on the Americas*, 27, 3 (Nov–Dec 1993).

83.   K. van den Heuvel and S. F. Cohen, 'Last Chance,' *The Nation*, 24 January 1994, p. 76.

84.   L. Whittington, 'Doubts about Democracy: Some leaders feel they must first destroy it in order to save it,' *The Ottawa Citizen*, 19 April 1992, p. B5.

85.   Robin Kirk, 'A War Against Ideas, not Drugs,' *The Nation*, 256, 19 (17 May 1993), pp. 664–5: the data is attributed to the Andean Commission of Jurists (Colombian Section).

86.   H. Krombach, 'Can tolerance be taught?', *London School of Economics Monitor* (London: LSE, 1993).

87.   See the last chapter of R. N. Bellah *et al.*, *Habits of the Heart: Individualism and Commitment in American Life* (Berkeley: University of California Press, 1985).

88.   To avoid misunderstanding it is important to emphasise that sovereignty is seen as a necessary, **not** a sufficient, condition for achieving stable 'regimes of accumulation' or successful democracies in the developing world.

89.   Jose Figueres had led a successful nationalist and anti-Communist peasant revolution in 1948. The two most significant actions of his new government were the nationalization of the banks and the consolidation and strengthening of the country's small-holder agricultural base in coffee, the primary export crop.

90.   Ian Robinson, op. cit., p. 11.

91.   MERG (Macroeconomic Research Group) *Making Democracy Work: A framework for macroeconomic policy in South Africa* (Cape Town: Centre for Development Studies, distributed through Oxford University Press, 1993).

92.   David Lewis, 'Markets, Ownership and Industrial Competitiveness,' ISP Background Paper for June and July Presentations, Cape Town, 1993 (mimeo).

93.   P. B. Rana and J. Dowling, 'Big Bang's Bust,' *The International Economy*, September/October 1993.

4 From African Socialism to Scientific Capitalism: Reflections on the Legitimation Crisis in IMF-ruled Africa

James Ferguson

> Give us rain. Give us bananas. Give us sugar cane. Give us plantains. Give us meat. Give us food. You are our king, but if you do not feed us properly we will get rid of you. The country is yours; the people must have their stomachs filled. Give us rain. Give us food. . . .
>
> (Ritual greeting of late 19th C. Shambaai
> commoners to their newly installed king.[1])

> I think the economic logic behind dumping a load of toxic waste in the lowest-wage country is impeccable and we should face up to that.
>
> (Lawrence Summers, Chief Economist, World Bank[2])

> The exploiters of Zimbabwe
> were cannibals drinking the masses' blood,
> Sucking and sapping their energy.
> The gun stopped all this.
> Grandmother Nehanda,
> You prophesied.
>
> (From a song by the ZANU-PF Ideological
> Choir, broadcast on ZBC radio on the occasion
> of Zimbabwe's independence (17 April 1980).[3])

INTRODUCTION

In the summer of 1989, I travelled across a Zambia reeling from the effects of a newly imposed IMF structural adjustment regime.[4] Prices of essential goods were skyrocketing, employment declining, and real incomes rapidly shrinking. Many wondered how they would manage to make ends meet. Many, indeed, were failing to make ends meet: with high food prices, many went hungry; with free medical care abolished, many sick could not receive treatment. For my part, I was trying to buy some blankets for a trip to the countryside; but everywhere I went, blankets were either unavailable or selling for preposterously high prices. Finally, after days of looking in the major centers of Lusaka and Kitwe, we found abundant, cheap blankets at a shop in the provincial town of Mansa. I wondered how it was that this merchant had in such abundance what was in short supply throughout the country. My research assistant, a young, educated Zambian man, had the answer: this merchant was widely known as a powerful sorcerer. He obtained his supplies by making potent medicines from the organs of human beings whom he murdered. It was the hearts, in particular, that he was after; this was what gave him his special supply lines, and had enabled him to grow very rich.

On December 12 of 1991, Lawrence Summers, the chief economist of the World Bank, sent an internal Bank memorandum (later leaked to the press) in which he argued that the export of pollution and toxic waste to the Third World constituted an economically sound, 'world-welfare enhancing trade' that should be actively encouraged by the Bank. Since 'the measurement of the costs of health-impairing pollution depends on the forgone earnings from increased morbidity and mortality,' 'a given amount of health-impairing pollution should be done in the country with the lowest cost, which will be the country with the lowest wages.' Furthermore, he suggested, carcinogens associated with, say, prostate cancer are of less concern in countries where people are not likely to live long enough to develop such diseases. In economic terms, he suggested, 'the underpopulated countries in Africa are vastly *under-polluted*.' Summers rejected criticisms of this position on the grounds that they were based on such things as 'moral reasons' and 'social concerns' that 'could be turned around and used more or less effectively against every Bank proposal for liberalization.'[5]

Summers was correct in this last assertion. The World Bank/IMF structural adjustment programmes that have been forced down the throats of African governments in recent years are based on precisely the sort of spurious economistic 'proofs' and implausible suspension of moral and social values that are displayed so conspicuously in the memorandum. It is possible to show that these structural adjustment programmes have already had enormously destructive social consequences and human costs.[6] It is also possible to argue, as Henry Bernstein has in an incisive critique, that the World Bank's structural adjustment project is 'a fantasy' likely 'to generate results that are as brutal as they are ineffectual in terms of its stated goals.'[7] But my concern here is with neither the effects nor the efficacy of structural adjustment, but rather with the style in which it is legitimated. For the cold, technocratic, economistic reasoning deployed to justify dumping toxic waste in Africa is in reality just the raw form of a literally 'demoralizing' logic of legitimation that, I will show, is pervasive in 'development' accounts of 'structural adjustment.'

And yet, as the story of the merchant with which I began hints, the social world into which this de-moralizing mode of legitimation is inserted is one in which economic realities are routinely apprehended in fundamentally moral terms. The question I want to ask, then, is what happens when such an economistic, technicizing style of legitimation meets the insistent moralizing that is so much a part of discourses on the economy across wide areas of Africa.

PROSPERITY, POWER, AND AFRICAN MORAL DISCOURSE

The relation between matters of wealth, production, and prosperity, on the one hand, and moral and cosmological order on the other, has been a pervasive theme in the ethnography of Africa, or at least of southern and central Africa, which are the ethnographic regions I know best. Though the ethnographies mostly deal with local particularities, I will here try to draw out some broad themes that seem to be very widely shared over a broad culture region. In the process, many subtleties will be lost; but my point is not to describe accurately a local system, but to sketch with a broad brush a set of moral themes that are quite widely distributed across a vast region. I emphasize that these themes constitute not a rigid and specific system of belief, but a flexible repertoire of key metaphors, contrasts, and discursive themes that provide a rich moral vocabulary for talking and thinking about issues of wealth, prosperity, profit, and exploitation in a variety of specific contexts.

Most generally, the production of wealth throughout wide areas of southern and central Africa is understood to be inseparable from the production of social relations. Production of wealth can be understood as pro-social, morally valuable 'work,' 'producing oneself by producing people, relations, and things';[8] or, alternatively, as an anti-social, morally illegitimate appropriation, exploitative and destructive of community. A common axis of contrast is an opposition between honest 'sweat,' which builds something shared and socially valued, and trickery or artifice through which one exploits or 'eats the sweat' of another. The ubiquitous notion of sorcery or witchcraft can play a number of roles here; it can be the sanction that checks anti-social accumulation (the familiar 'levelling' role); but it can just as well be understood as the fearsome power that makes it possible for exploiters to exploit with impunity.[9] There is no need to romanticize sorcery here. Even sanctions that enforce norms of generosity are not necessarily egalitarian in their effects – as Moore has pointed out, since only the rich can afford generosity, 'prescriptive altruism' may hit the poor hardest, by 'translat[ing] the many manifestations of the stinginess and craftiness of poverty into moral faults.'[10] What is important for my purposes, however, is simply the fact that the social meaning of production and accumulation is widely interpreted in fundamentally moral terms.[11]

The same is often true of exchange and consumption. Key domains of wealth such as cattle, lineage land, and bridewealth are often at least partially blocked off from or sheltered from commodity exchange.[12] Along with such restrictions on exchange commonly come moral valuations; against a realm of cash and commodities conceived as intrinsically 'selfish' and associated with individual acquisitiveness and exploitation, there stand specially valued domains of sociality and solidarity. Thus, for instance, wealth in cattle in Lesotho is understood as a uniquely social domain, associated with sharing and helping the poor, whereas money, as one informant put it, 'is just closed up there [in the bank]; it will work for you alone, and not for the mutual help of all us Basotho.'

In all of this, it is often possible to discern an underlying contrast between powers that create social prosperity versus powers that destroy it. A number of recent studies of chiefship[13] show a key contrast between two aspects or moments of chiefly power. On the one hand, it can provide for the people and bring peace and prosperity; on the other, it can destroy the land and feed off the blood of the people. Key metaphors appear again and again: the chief as both man and lion, rain-maker and witch, feeder of the people and eater of the people. These two modalities of power usually correspond to two kinds of wealth; broadly, the kind that feeds the people and the kind that eats them. The first type is a kind of collective wealth, bound up with a prosperity that is general and shared. Key metaphors for this kind of pro-social prosperity are rain, and feeding the people (the key connection is well expressed in the Sotho trinity of chiefship: khotso [peace, product of a healthy chiefship], pula [rain], nala [prosperity]). The second kind of wealth is selfish, anti-social, exploitative. Key metaphors are cannibalism, blood-sucking, and witchcraft. Pro-social, collective wealth provides the basis for community and mutuality; anti-social, exploitative wealth is the dangerous and destructive temptation for which people's hearts may be cut out.[14]

Marx had Africa in mind when he made his famous analogy between the savage's 'fetishism,' entailing belief in the magical powers of an object, and a capitalist 'fetishism' that disguised the social origins of the value of the commodity, imputing value to the object itself as a natural property. The insight into capitalism was undoubtedly profound, but with respect to Africa, Marx could not have been more wrong. For the idea that keeps cropping up in the ethnography of Africa is not that the human world is ruled by powerful objects, but that all of the world, even the natural, bears the traces of human agency.

The best-known example of such thinking, of course, remains Evans-Pritchard's account of Azande causal reasoning.[15] When a large granary fell on a man who happened to be walking beneath it, killing him, Evans-Pritchard's informants insisted that witchcraft had to have been involved. When Evans-Pritchard argued that it was simply termites that had caused the mishap, the Azande agreed that the termites were involved, but insisted that the termites were only the means – they were how the granary had fallen. The important question, however, was why it fell. Why did it fall at that moment rather than another? Why did that man happen to be under it at just that second? Surely termites were present, but the real question was: Who sent the termites?

This famous anecdote is usually told in the context of arguments about rationality and so-called closed systems of thought. But my point here is rather different. For what is crucial to our purposes here is neither the rationality nor the mysticism of the Azande line of thinking, but rather the determination to arrive at specifically human causes. Capitalist fetishism is here neatly inverted – where capitalism naturalizes the human world by imputing powers to objects, the Azande were busy humanizing the natural. And what is true of mortal fate is also true of economic and political destinies. Not only among the Azande, but throughout the region, disparities of power and wealth, like fluke accidents, never 'just happen'; they demand to be explained in terms of meaningful human agency.

Such apprehensions of issues of power and wealth in broadly social and moral (i.e. human) terms are not only found in popular understandings of pre-colonial or 'traditional' systems; recent scholarship shows that capitalist forms of accumulation and modern state economic activities are very widely understood in similar terms. Feierman's study of chiefship in Tanzania[16] reveals that key discursive themes concerning the healing and harming of the land, the bringing of rain, the productive or destructive nature of central power, continue to be brought to bear on the activities of the modern state. Lan[17] shows dramatically how an indigenous moral discourse on chiefship and power was central to the legitimacy of the Zimbabwean revolution. And Geschiere[18] has shown that fundamental moral ideas about sorcery and wealth are pervasive in the relations of state officials with villagers in Cameroon. Jean-François Bayart has made a compelling general argument that the power of the state and urban elites in Africa must be understood in terms of indigenous moral cosmology. His wonderfully evocative phrase, 'la politique du ventre' ('the politics of the belly'), refers both to the material processes of élite appropriation, and to the widespread symbolic association of 'eating' with both political domination and sorcery. In this perspective, Bayart argues, the stereotypical figure of the big-bellied African bureaucrat takes on a special significance.[19]

In this context, I would add only that African socialism, as a language of legitimation, spoke in terms that drew upon many of these key popular moral themes. Where European socialism often insisted on a language of 'objective necessities' and 'empirically observable contradictions' (so-called 'scientific socialism'), socialism in Africa was distinguished by its insistently moralizing tone.

For Julius Nyerere of Tanzania, to take only the best-known example, socialism was first of all an attitude of mind. The key oppositions, for Nyerere, were not primarily between rival economic systems or modes of production, but between conflicting moral orientations: selfishness versus sharing, exploitation versus solidarity, individual acquisitiveness versus communal mutuality. Socialism, for Nyerere, was the rejection of selfishness; a capitalist, in contrast, was defined as 'the man who uses wealth for the purpose of dominating any of his fellows.'[20] Exploitation was thus understood as a moral fault rather than as an aspect of a mode of production or an economic structure; socialism, in response, constituted an ethical commitment to foreswear the temptation to exploit one's fellow man. As the Arusha Declaration put it: 'a genuine TANU leader will not live off the sweat of another man, nor commit any feudalistic or capitalistic actions.'[21] The TANU creed drew not only on the rhetoric of international socialism, but also on central moral oppositions that would be familiar to any ethnographer of the region: selfishness versus sociality, sharing versus exploitation, benevolence versus malevolence. And in his avowed refusal to 'eat' his fellow man, Nyerere's conspicuous lack of a belly was perhaps as symbolically potent as his rejection of material luxury.

Socialist discourses of legitimation in Zambia were, if anything, even more explicitly oriented to morality than they were in Tanzania. President Kenneth Kaunda's elaboration of African Socialism, which he called Humanism, explicitly declared itself an ethics. The heart of socialism, for

Kaunda, was the fight against 'the exploitation of man by man.' Such exploitation could take place in class terms, as powerful people abused their power; or it could occur in a geographical sense, as urbanites exploited rural villagers. In any case, however, the policies of the socialist state were largely justified as a way of preventing the selfish from engaging in such exploitation, preventing exploiters from getting fat off of their fellows.[22]

Let there be no mistake here: I am in no way arguing that such exploitation was in practice prevented, or that such legitimating discourses can be taken at face value as accurate statements of policy. African socialism was from the start an ideology of rule, and state moralizing, in Tanzania, Zambia, and elsewhere, was intensely interested, self-serving, and very often fraudulent. The point is not that the African socialist state stamped out selfishness or did away with exploitation, but that it spoke in a comprehensible local moral vocabulary; its economic arguments were always moral arguments, in a familiar popular idiom. And it is in terms of these popular idioms that African socialism was both attacked and defended.

Mineworkers in Zambia during my fieldwork in 1985–86, for instance, attacked the government most vigorously not for specific policies or acts, but for its general 'selfishness'; officials were faulted, often in highly personal terms, for immorality, exploitation, and enriching themselves at the expense of the people. What mineworkers said of their government officials largely echoed what Hutu refugees in Tanzania were saying, more economically, of government officials there: 'they eat our sweat.'[23] When government or party officials came to exhort Zambian mineworkers to accept wage increases far below inflation rates, the miners scoffed at the big-bellied parasites who lectured them on the national need for belt-tightening. And along with the focus on the 'appetite' of the elites went a parallel emphasis on the 'hunger' of the people. Hunger is an all-too-real phenomenon in contemporary Zambia; but it should be recognized that it is also a powerful metaphor for a failure of government – the ultimate political bankruptcy being the failure to 'feed the people.' It is in this context that we should understand the repeated claims of employed mineworkers (who are, even today, among the better paid workers in Zambia) to be going hungry. Consider the following lament from a letter I received from a young mineworker in Kitwe, describing the aftermath of the Copperbelt food riots of 1986. Note that an explicit rejection of state ideology is here directly tied to questions of hunger, family mutuality, and morality:

On the day of reverting to the old price of mealie meal all milling companies were nationalized under those two books he (Kaunda) has written under the heading Humanism parts I & II; but for god's sake this was not the root cause and all these books have not brought anything [for] a Zambian to enjoy. So personally, how dare we toil over a book which has brought hunger on my body – imagine I got two boys, not knowing what was to come. I am unable to meet their needs, then to hell with humanism or socialism and according from wherever they have been imposed on the people these ideologies just downgrade the moral freedom of its citizens and believe me they are bound not to succeed.

SCIENTIFIC CAPITALISM

The coerced adoption of 'structural adjustment' programmes by African states over the last decade has been accompanied by a fundamental shift in the way these states seek to legitimate their policies. Leaving behind the moral language of legitimation that was shared by African socialism and its critics alike, African politicians and bureaucrats increasingly seek to explain and justify their new policies (for audiences both foreign and domestic) in the economistic language of international technocracy (a shift inevitably recorded in the West as a move toward 'pragmatism' and 'moderation' in matters economic). 'Structural adjustment' policies, often adopted only under extreme duress, are thus rationalized retrospectively as 'necessary' for 'economic growth' and 'efficiency.' They are, in fact, rarely justified at all (in the sense of a developed argument that the policies are in fact just); they are claimed to be 'right' only in the sense that they are claimed to be 'economically correct.' This regime of 'economic correctness' is far more oppressive in its effects than any amount of the over-discussed 'political correctness' on college campuses; indeed, it is as rigid and dogmatic in its reasoning as any 'scientific socialism' ever was. It is in acknowledgement of this fact that I speak of the new regime of IMF/ World Bank governance in Africa as 'scientific capitalism.'

I will illustrate the language of legitimation of 'scientific capitalism' with the World Bank report of 1981, entitled *Accelerated Development in Sub-Saharan Africa* (the so-called 'Berg Report').[24] I focus on this document, not because it is an accurate guide to the Bank's actual economic policies (it is not), but because it has been arguably the single most central text in a coordinated strategy of ideological legitimation.[25]

What is most noteworthy in this report is the way that extremely controversial and widely disputed claims are blandly asserted as simple, incontestable, scientific facts. For example, many thoughtful analysts in and out of Africa are concerned about a loss of food production and food security associated with the expanded cultivation of export crops. Yet Berg flatly declares, with all the authority of a high-school textbook: 'Empirical evidence does not support the hypothesis that expanding export production leads to declines in food production' (p. 62). Moreover, even if export crops are produced at the expense of food, we are told, careful measurement of the 'domestic resource costs (DRC)' of different commodities proves that African countries' 'comparative advantage' is in export crops, and that the cultivation of food crops is 'inefficient' (pp. 64–5). There is no room for discussion, let alone political debate or moral contemplation – the statistics are clear: growing food is just economically incorrect.

'Efficiency' likewise demands that efforts at industrialization be dismantled; it is not economically correct for African countries to seek to escape the niche the world market has provided for them. What is 'necessary' is for African economies to concentrate on their areas of 'comparative advantage,' which are to be found mostly in shrinking and unstable agricultural export commodity markets (pp. 91–7). (The report did not yet anticipate, of course, that hosting toxic waste dumps might become another such area of 'comparative advantage.') Similar technical justification is offered for other drastic policy dictates, such as doubling and tripling urban food prices, scrapping free health care, abolishing higher education scholarships, and so on (pp. 64, 43–4).

The effectiveness of the whole package of prescribed policy changes is definitively demonstrated through a 'simulation' which projects, with the Bank's usual fraudulent pseudo-precision ('Source: World Bank projections'), the exact percentage increases that the specified reforms will bring in GDP, Agriculture, Exports, and Imports (p. 122). What is there to argue about, after all? It's all right there in the numbers.

It is true that in recent years there has been some dissatisfaction even within the Bank with purely economistic approaches. Indeed, the fashionable view now among enlightened insiders is that just as important as 'getting the prices right' is 'getting the politics right.' But although this shift is an interesting one, and worth analyzing in its own right (see section on 'Politics and Responsibility', below), it is clear that it does not introduce any real break with the logic of 'economic correctness.' For it is all too obvious that in the quest to 'get the politics right,' 'politics' is understood as just another technical 'factor' – not an arena for public participation and moral discussion, but only another 'input' to be fixed at a 'correct' level.

REMORALIZING ECONOMIC DISCOURSE

The focus of the analysis is on the efficiency with which resources are used. Economic growth implies using a country's scarce resources – labor, capital, natural resources, administrative and managerial capacity – more efficiently. Improving efficiency requires, first, that a country produce those things which it can best produce as compared with other countries and, second, producing them with the least use of limited resources. . . . [T]he record of poor growth in most Sub-Saharan African countries suggests that inadequate attention has been given to policies to increase the efficiency of resource use and that action to correct this situation is urgently called for.

(The World Bank, 'The Berg Report'[26])

The masses knows just as them guys know, enough is enough. . . . Whoever is there to represent, is there to tow their system's policies, but the masses know the purposeful of this system – secure their status politically, economically and socially and leave the masses to poverty. . . . there is a gloom in the nation because of the lack of medicines in hospitals and children are dying like nobody's business and [there is a] scarcity of essentials since the IMF programmes . . .

(From a Zambian mineworker's letter, 1987)

I have shown that scientific capitalism seeks to present itself as a non-moral order, in which neutral, technical principles of efficiency and pragmatism give 'correct' answers to questions of public policy. Yet a whole set of moral premises are, of course, implicit in these technicizing arguments. Notions of the inviolate rights of individuals, the sanctity of private property, the nobility of capitalist accumulation and the intrinsic value of 'freedom' (understood as the freedom to engage in economic transactions) lie just below the surface of much of the discourse of scientific capitalism. Often, too, there seems to be a puritan undertone of austerity as punishment for past irresponsibility: having lived high on the hog for so long, say the stern bankers and economists (safely ensconced in their five-star hotels and six-figure incomes), it is time for Africans to bite the bullet and pay for their sins.

But the larger point is that these moral premises on which the technicizing justifications of structural adjustment depend almost always remain implicit. The moral and cosmological assumptions on which ideological justifications of structural adjustment often rest are unacknowledged and even actively denied by those who hold them. Like Lawrence Summers, the legitimizers of scientific capitalism in Africa scrupulously distance themselves from any explicitly moral or 'value-laden' claims; it is all a matter, they insist, of objective economic correctness, of how the equations work out. This is not to say that capitalist ideologies are somehow incapable of speaking in a moralizing voice; in many times and places they have done just that, and with great success. But in contemporary justifications of structural adjustment in Africa, the legitimizing discourse of technical economic expertise does not speak, as Ronald Reagan once did, of the glory of individual freedom and the shining city on the hill; it speaks, instead, in the grey language of economic 'pragmatism.' The morality of the market thus denies its own status as a morality, presenting itself as mere technique.

Recent experience shows, however, that the economic policies of scientific capitalism continue to be understood by Africans in moral terms, and that they are received and sometimes resisted accordingly.

In Zambia, the establishment of 'correct prices' and 'efficient' markets resulted, quite predictably, in a series of food riots, and eventually in the fall of the government. Informants told me that the 1986 Copperbelt riots had been, effectively, popular uprisings, in which a wide range of respectable people – including, in one account, policemen – had joined in. Many of those who participated in the looting were unashamed, even proud. T-shirts were even printed in the townships, reading 'Looters' Association of Zambia.' For many Zambians, what was truly illegitimate was not the theft by the looters, but the rise in prices itself.

Similar events have occurred all over the continent, where IMF-sponsored policies have provoked legitimation crises for African states. Scientific capitalism's claim that prices are 'economically correct' apparently has little meaning when, as one informant put it, 'children are dying like nobody's business.'

Such observations may serve to remind us that, as Henry Bernstein has noted, however little democratic accountability African states may have, 'they do have to confront the consequences of their actions – if only by the exercise of repression – in ways that the World Bank or IMF do not.'[27] Technocratic reason may be good enough to sell World Bank/IMF dogma in the international arena. But someone, somewhere down the line, has to implement these policies, at which point questions of legitimacy and popular reception must be addressed. In Africa, capitalism will have to learn, as socialism learned, to drop its 'scientific' pretensions and speak a local language of moral legitimation. How (and whether) what is going on in places like Zambia can in fact be legitimated in locally meaningful, moral terms must remain an open question.

Wealth in Africa has long been understood as first of all a question of relations among people. This, I would suggest, is a politically and theoretically rich understanding, vastly more so than the IMF/World Bank's impoverished conception of the economy as an amoral, technical system. Against the truly fetishized view that would see 'the market' as a natural force to which human life simply must submit, the African insight that markets, prices, and wages are always human products is a powerful one. In the worst case, of course, the attribution of economic ills to human agency may degenerate into crude scapegoating and demonization – blaming the 'greed' of Indian traders for a rise in prices, for instance. But the fundamental perception that economic facts are moral and human facts may also provide a resource for a much deeper critique. After all, when one's society is being systematically destroyed by 'the market,' that old Azande question is an acute one: 'Who sent the market?'

African traditions of moral discourse on questions of economic process may thus be understood not as backward relics to be overcome, but as intellectual and political resources for the future. Geschiere has rightly noted that a whole range of 'forms of politics held in contempt by most Western observers can only be comprehended in relation to a rich world of images and conceptions.'[28] What needs to be added is that this rich world of images and conceptions may itself enable and energize a potent popular politics.

The claims of technical capitalistic reason, which seem to be so readily accepted (for the time being) in Eastern Europe and the former Soviet Union, may not win the day so easily in Africa. Instead, there is reason to believe that the issue of 'structural adjustment' will eventually have to be taken up in a moral key, in a way that recognizes the inevitable connection of social, economic, and cosmological orders. This may offer a ray of hope, in what is indeed a de-moralizing era, that Africans may yet find ways to do what neither socialist nor capitalist states have managed: to create an economic order genuinely responsive to popular moral sensibilities. As the IMF and World Bank fail (as they must) in their project of 'de-moralizing' African economies, it is just possible that the seeds may be being sown for a different kind of economic reform, another 'structural adjustment' – one that would unabashedly speak a moral language, open an honest debate on economic priorities and moral values, and, who knows, maybe even end up 'feeding the people,' instead of 'eating' them.

POLITICS AND RESPONSIBILITY

I have thus far argued that the rhetoric of 'scientific capitalism' does not provide effective legitimation for the imposition of 'structural adjustment' in Africa, and that the attempt to reduce questions of public policy to questions of economistic technique runs afoul of a well-developed African talent for understanding questions of poverty and wealth in a social and moral frame that foregrounds questions of human agency and responsibility. In this final section of the paper, I will attempt to sketch some of the implications of this analysis for thinking about practical political alternatives and effective strategies of resistance to IMF/World Bank rule.

First, it should be clear that such alternatives should not be expected to come from within the IMF/World Bank apparatus itself. Extraordinary amounts of ink have been spilled in recent years in advertising the emergence from within this apparatus of a 'new paradigm,' focusing not only on economic growth and expansion of markets, but on such things as 'governance,' 'participation' and 'sustainability.'[29] This is supposed to be the 'liberal' ('with a human face') version of 'structural adjustment' – the velvet glove, as it were, over the iron fist of 1980s-style market discipline. Yet it not clear that there is really much that is 'new' in this 'new paradigm.' It is easily enough demonstrated that the ideological program of 'governance' (at least in its dominant versions) is little concerned with substantive democracy, still less in the 'empowerment' of the poor (Schmitz, this volume). But this can hardly be surprising, since what the 'new paradigm' seems to be principally about is getting African governments to accept, implement, and legitimate policies made in Europe and North America largely in the interests of Western banks.

The very existence of this literature, however, shows that the IMF/World Bank planners have taken notice of the legitimation crisis I have described. In the first wave of criticisms of African governments (beginning with the Berg Report), Western governments and lenders sought to place the blame for the failure of 'modernization' on the shoulders of 'inefficient,' 'mismanaged,' 'corrupt' African states. As Bernstein has pointed out, of course, the failed policies for which African governments were being blamed were themselves largely pressed upon them by those same Western governments and lenders now denouncing them, in a process that created much of the corruption and mismanagement now decried.[30] Yet this denunciation of the African state provided a ideological charter for the first round of draconian 'structural adjustment' reforms enforced by the IMF and its associated capital cartel.

The second, now-current wave of criticism of African governments (associated with the idea of a crisis of 'governance') takes note of the fact that the governments responsible for imposing the IMF/World Bank 'reforms' suffer from a crisis of legitimacy. This is then blamed on the fundamentally non-democratic and unaccountable nature of African governments (no mention being made of the non-democratic and unaccountable nature of the IMF and the World Bank). The crisis of 'structural adjustment' thus becomes a crisis of 'governance,' for which the appropriate remedy is a reform of African governments, with a new attention not only to 'good management' and 'good government,' but also to 'democracy' and 'human rights.'

What friends of democracy need to bear in mind in all of this is that however democratic an African government may be in formal terms, its scope for making policy is very radically constrained by the non-democratic international financial institutions themselves. No matter what party is elected to power in a country like Zambia, they will have to come to terms with the IMF, and the voice of the Zambian electorate will have precious little say over those terms. Effective IMF rule over huge areas of economic and social policy is thus papered over with an appearance of popular sovereignty. The current ideological frothing over 'democracy in Africa' in this way ends up serving a profoundly anti-democratic end – that is, the simulation of popular legitimation for policies that are in fact made in the most undemocratic way imaginable.

Whether this cynical strategy for legitimating 'structural adjustment' can succeed, however, is another matter. 'Good government,' as defined by the lending agencies, may help to legitimate IMF/World Bank policies within the West, but it is not at all clear that it will get to the heart of the crisis in Africa. For as I have argued, popular legitimacy in Africa requires a perception not simply of 'good government' (efficient and technically functional institutions) but of a government that is 'good' (morally benevolent and protective of its people). An efficient and effective government is not necessarily a 'good' one in this second sense, and a regime that presides over the efficient and effective pauperization of its people is not likely to acquire much legitimacy, no matter how many elections may be held.

What Lemarchand has referred to as 'the moral discredit incurred by the state, both as concept and institution'[31] thus remains a potent political fact across most of Africa, one which current shifts in legitimation strategies do little to address. Africans continue to regard the state largely as a malevolent and ever-hungry predator, and to perceive it not as an expression of their collective will but as an instrument of the exploiters, the tool of those who get fat 'eating' the sweat of honest working people. It would be difficult to argue that they are wholly mistaken.

Moreover, Africans are increasingly aware of the inability of national governments to control either macro-economic processes or the day-to-day living conditions of the people. No longer do they expect that a new government will solve their problems, or that a shift in regime can make much of a difference to the grim slippage in their standards of living. Increasingly, they seek to find expressions of collective solidarity, social order, and moral beneficence outside of the state altogether – e.g. in local, kin-based social systems, in ethnic separatism, in religiously inspired social movements, in millenarian cults, and in various other movements aimed at cleansing the world of its only-too-evident corruption and evil. Thus Zambia has seen a revival of witch-cleansing movements[32] and localist social identities,[33] Mozambique a renewal of kin-based traditions of political leadership, Uganda an extraordinary succession of millenarian cults (also evident in Mozambique), North and West Africa powerful Islamic funda-mentalist movements, and so on.[34] All of these movements (for all their differences, and whatever their political merits and demerits) address the fundamental moral questions that I have suggested are at the heart of the crisis of African societies today. And it is just this fundamental moral question that the reformers and ideologists of 'governance' have so con-spicuously not addressed, and perhaps cannot address.

What this suggests for progressive political strategy is quite complex. On the one hand, there is a clear need to insist on the 're-moralization' of political discourse at the national level. It will not be sufficient to settle for 'good government' without an explicit and public discussion of what 'good-ness' consists in, and what state policies would best serve the public 'good.' It will not be sufficient to combat 'corruption' in government with-out asking the larger question of whether the very aims and purposes of state rule are not corrupt. Such an opening up of political discourse will probably not lead to very dramatic changes in public policy, since, as I have argued, the range of possible action of African states is very severely constrained by the vice-grip of international finance. But it would at least allow the real moral and ethical issues at stake in policy decisions (who will eat, and who will go hungry?; whose sickness will be treated, and whose allowed to fester?) to be openly aired and honestly considered. And it might, ultimately, result in a more radical questioning of the whole bank/state complex, and even of the legitimacy of international debt itself. Such questioning has apparently begun in a place like Zaire, where the very radical question has already been posed: If a corrupt CIA-installed general gets billions from Western banks and squanders it, according to what moral or ethical principle are the working people of Zaire liable to repay these billions? Just whose debt is it, anyway?

On another level, however, the assessment of the political situation in Africa must move beyond the state-centered framework entirely. The question of alternatives must move past the stultifying form: 'Well, then, what should Zambia do?'[35] For the cast of relevant political actors extends far beyond the roster of national governments and political parties. Indeed, many of the most important political processes on the continent are occurring, as I have suggested, at sub-national and trans-national levels. The local institutions and grass-roots social movements referred to above must be taken seriously, understood not as regressions or throwbacks, but as potentially formidable political responses to contemporary realities. Where political legitimacy has been achieved by such non-state movements and institutions, it is crucial to understand how this has occurred, and to see how the moralizing frames of reference I have analyzed here may be engaged with viable and effective political structures. It is possible, too, that a better understanding of these movements may make a contribution to the crucial tactical goal of forging links and alliances among them, suggesting a beginning to a real alternative form of 'governance.'

At the same time, attention must be paid to the formidable institutions 'governing' Africa from afar, the transnational financial institutions (World Bank, IMF, foreign banks) and development agencies (USAID, UNDP, UNHCR, etc.), as well as the churches, missions, and so-called 'non-governmental organizations' (NGOs). These transnational institutions continue to be very little studied, in spite of the fact that they clearly play a very central role in the de facto governance and administration of the continent today.[36] We will not have a balanced understanding of the actual processes through which Africa is governed until we move beyond the myth of the sovereign African nation-state[37] to explore the powerful but almost wholly unaccountable transnational institutions that effectively rule large domains of African economy and society.

Finally, a consideration of the moral politics of structural adjustment must make its way from the moral dilemmas facing African people and governments back to the moral questions the crisis in Africa raises for 'the West' itself. For it is not only Africans who have traditions of moral discourse capable of generating critique, cleansing, and renewal. As David Cohen has recently pointed out, the West has its own traditions of accounting moral responsibility that might well be dusted off and put to work as we survey the landscape of the post-Cold War world. Rather than accepting the marginal status ascribed to Africa by much current, end-of-the-Cold War punditry, Cohen suggests the historical moment calls instead for a sober assessment of responsibility:

> Rather than lamenting the loss of an era of donors and investors interested in winning allies in a global struggle, one could begin to account the losses to those prospective allies of participation in four decades of

this most costly global game, whose rules and results were largely conceived and tabulated elsewhere.[38]

Just as contemporary Germans have had to assess their collective moral responsibility for the Holocaust, Cohen suggests, both sides of the cold war will have to assess their responsibility for 'the militarization and impoverization of three-quarters of the globe' as well as for the creation of 'conditions, interests, orientations, institutions, routines, and cultures that define the possibilities of much of the globe.'[39] If African traditions of moral discourse are, as I have suggested, capable of posing profoundly moral questions of human agency and causation, Western traditions may lead us to the equally profound question of historical responsibility. Where Africans may ask, drawing on an indigenous intellectual tradition, 'who sent the market?', it remains for us in the West – as we survey the carnage left in the wake of colonization, cold-war, and the forced march of 'development' – to ask an equally profound moral question, itself also embedded in a local cultural tradition: 'My God, what have we done?'

One may well be wary, as Cohen notes, of the historic tendency to reduce the causes of African social problems to the doings of outside powers. But the generally salutary emphasis in recent Africanist scholarship on the centrality of African actors must not be an excuse, either, for evading the complex ethical and historical question of transnational responsibility.

History, Cohen insists, is not 'at its end,' but at a beginning, 'a new and critical moment of responsibility.' What this responsibility means in the case of the crisis in Africa, and how it is to be translated into concrete political action and public policy, must be at the heart of the continuing battles over the moral politics of 'structural adjustment,' as they are fought both in Africa, and outside of it.

Notes

1. Cited in Steven Feierman, *Peasant Intellectuals: Anthropology and History in Tanzania* (Madison: University of Wisconsin Press, 1990), p. 46.
2. 'Let Them Eat Pollution,' *The Economist,* February 8, 1992, p. 66.
3. David Lan, *Guns and Rain: Guerrillas and Spirit Mediums in Zimbabwe* (Berkeley: University of California Press, 1985), p. 217.
4. Relations between Zambia and the IMF/World Bank were officially resumed only in September of 1989. But many of the austerity measures the IMF was demanding (including a 37 per cent devaluation of the *kwacha*, a

sharp rise in food prices, and the removal of most price controls) were already being implemented in the months following the visit of an IMF delegation to Zambia in April and May of 1989.

5. 'Let Them Eat Pollution,' op. cit., p. 66.

6. John Clark and Caroline Allison, *Zambia: Debt and Poverty* (Oxford: Oxfam Publications, 1989).

7. Henry Bernstein, 'Agricultural "Modernisation" and the Era of Structural Adjustment: Observations on Sub-Saharan Africa,' *Journal of Peasant Studies*, 18, 1 (October 1990), p. 3.

8. Jean and John L. Comaroff, *Of Revelation and Revolution: Christianity, Colonialism, and Consciousness in South Africa*, Volume One (Chicago: University of Chicago Press, 1991), p. 143.

9. See Peter Geschiere, *Village Communities and the State: Changing Relations among the Maka of Southeastern Cameroon since the Colonial Conquest* (London: Kegan Paul International, 1982), and 'Sorcery and the State: Popular Modes of Action among the Maka of Southeast Cameroon,' *Critique of Anthropology*, 8, 1 (1982).

10. Sally Falk Moore, *Social Facts and Fabrications: 'Customary' Law on Kilimanjaro, 1880–1980* (New York: Cambridge University Press, 1986), p. 301.

11. Compare with, from among a huge literature, Jean and John L. Comaroff, op. cit.; Peter Geschiere, op. cit.; E. Ardener, 'Witchcraft, Economics and the Continuity of Belief,' in Mary Douglas (ed.), *Witchcraft Confessions and Accusations* (London: Tavistock, 1970), and the whole of this book; Max Marwick (ed.), *Witchcraft and Sorcery: Selected Readings,* second edition (Harmondsworth: Penguin Books, 1982); John Middleton and E. H. Winter (eds), *Witchcraft and Sorcery in East Africa* (London: Routledge and Kegan Paul, 1963); J. R. Crawford, *Witchcraft and Sorcery in Rhodesia* (London: Oxford University Press for the International African Institute, 1967); Victor Turner, *Schism and Continuity in an African Society: A Study of Ndembu Village Life* (Manchester: Manchester University Press, 1957); Wim van Binsbergen, *Religious Change in Zambia: Exploratory Studies* (London: Kegan Paul International, 1985).

12. James Ferguson, 'The Bovine Mystique: Power, Property, and Livestock in Rural Lesotho,' *Man*, 20 (1985); James Ferguson, 'Cultural Exchange: New Developments in the Anthropology of Commodities,' *Cultural Anthropology*, 3, 4 (1988); James Ferguson, *The Anti-politics Machine: 'Development,' Depoliticization, and Bureaucratic Power in Lesotho* (Cambridge: Cambridge University Press, 1990); James Ferguson, 'The Cultural Topography of Wealth,' *American Anthropologist*, 94, 1 (1992); Parker Shipton, *Bitter Money* (Washington, DC: American Ethnological Society Monograph Series, 1990); Sharon Hutchinson, 'The Cattle of Money and the Cattle of Girls among the Nuer, 1930–83,' *American Ethnologist*, 19, 2 (1992); Jean and John L. Comaroff, 'Goodly beasts and beastly goods: cattle in Tswana economy and society,' *American Ethnologist*, 17, 2 (1990); Sally Falk Moore, op. cit.

13. See Steven Feierman, op. cit.; David Lan, op. cit.; and Randall M. Packard, *Chiefship and Cosmology: An Historical Study of Political Competition* (Bloomington: Indiana University Press, 1981).

14. Cf. David Lan, op. cit.; Steven Feierman, op. cit.; Randall M. Packard, op.
cit.; Audrey Richards (ed.), *East African Chiefs* (London: Faber, 1960); Max
Marwick, op. cit.; Peter Geschiere, *Village Communities* . . . and 'Sorcery
. . . ,' op. cit.; Cyprian F. Fisiy and Peter Geschiere, 'Sorcery, Witchcraft
and Accumulation: Regional Variations in South and West Cameroon,'
Critique of Anthropology, 11, 3 (1991); Wim van Binsbergen, op. cit.; Jan
Vansina, *Paths in the Rainforests: Toward a History of Political Tradition
in Equatorial Africa* (Madison: University of Wisconsin Press, 1990).
15. E. E. Evans-Pritchard, *Witchcraft, Oracles, and Magic among the Azande*
(Oxford: Clarendon, 1976).
16. Steven Feierman, op. cit.
17. David Lan, op. cit.
18. Peter Geschiere, *Village Communities* . . . and 'Sorcery and the State: Popu-
lar Modes . . . ,' op. cit.; Cyprian F. Fisiy and Peter Geschiere, 'Sorcery,
Witchcraft . . . ,' op. cit.
19. Jean-François Bayart, *L'Etat en Afrique: La Politique du ventre* (Paris:
Fayard, 1989). Cf. also Bayart's 'Civil Society in Africa', in P. Chabal (ed.),
Political Domination in Africa: Reflections on the Limits of Power (New
York: Cambridge University Press, 1986); Peter Geschiere, '*L'Etat en Afrique*:
Book Review', *Critique of Anthropology*, 9, 3 (1989); Cyprian F. Fisiy and
Peter Geschiere, op. cit.; David Lan, op. cit.; Steven Feierman, op. cit.; Wim
van Binsbergen, op. cit.
20. Julius K. Nyerere, *Ujamaa: Essays on Socialism* (New York: Oxford University Press, 1968), p. 1.
21. Ibid., p. 17.
22. Kenneth D. Kaunda, *Humanism in Zambia and a Guide to its Implementation, Parts I and II* (Lusaka: Zambian Information Services, 1968. 1974); cf.
James Ferguson, 'The Country and The City on the Copperbelt,' *Cultural
Anthropology*, 7, 1 (1992).
23. Liisa H. Malkki, *Purity and Exile: Historical Memory and National Consciousness among Hutu Refugees in Tanzania* (Chicago: University of Chicago Press, in press).
24. The World Bank, *Accelerated Development in Sub-Saharan Africa: An
Agenda for Action* (Washington, DC: The World Bank, 1981).
25. Henry Bernstein, op. cit., p. 16.
26. The World Bank, op. cit., p. 24.
27. Henry Bernstein, op. cit., p. 28.
28. Peter Geschiere, 'L'Etat . . . ,' op. cit.
29. See The World Bank, *Governance and Development* (Washington, DC:
The World Bank, 1992); The World Bank, *Sub-Saharan Africa: From Crisis
to Sustainable Growth* (Washington, DC: The World Bank, 1989). Also
compare with Goran Hyden and Michael Bratton (eds), *Governance and
Politics in Africa* (Boulder: Lynne Rienner Publishers, 1992); The Carter
Center, *African Governance in the 1990s* (Atlanta: The Carter Center, 1990).
30. Henry Bernstein, op. cit.
31. René Lemarchand, 'Uncivil States and Civil Societies: How Illusion Became
Reality,' *Journal of Modern African Studies*, 30, 2 (1992).
32. Mark Auslander, ' "Open the Wombs": The Symbolic Politics of Modern
Ngoni Witchfinding,' in Jean and John Comaroff (eds), *Modernity and Its*

148   *From African Socialism to Scientific Capitalism*

    Malcontents: Ritual and Power in Postcolonial Africa (Chicago: University of Chicago Press, 1993).

33. James Ferguson, 'Cultural Dualism and the Micro-political Economy of Style on the Zambian Copperbelt' (manuscript, forthcoming).
34. Cf. René Lemarchand, op. cit.
35. Cf. James Ferguson, *The Anti-politics Machine: 'Development', Depoliticisation and Bureaucratic Power in Lesotho* (Cambridge: Cambridge University Press, 1990), pp. 280–8.
36. Cf., for example, Joseph Hanlon, *Mozambique: Who Calls the Shots?* (Bloomington, Indiana: Indiana University Press, 1991).
37. Cf. James Ferguson, 'Paradoxes of Sovereignty and Independence: "Real" and "Pseudo-" Nation-States and the Depoliticization of Poverty'. Paper presented at a conference on 'Space, Culture, and Community' at the Institute of Anthropology, University of Cophenhagen, December 1993.
38. David Cohen, 'Forgotten Actors', *PAS News and Events* (Evanston: Northwestern University Program of African Studies, 1993), p. 4.
39. Loc. cit.

5 Urban Social Movements, the Housing Question and Development Discourse in South Africa

Patrick Bond

INTRODUCTION

Urban South Africa offers fertile case study material in the application of political-economic theory to contemporary policy and practice, mediated by the twists and turns in the discourse which surrounds development.[1] Political debate, policy analysis and contestation of development processes are as advanced in South Africa's cities as in any present-day setting. The 1994 election of the African National Congress (ANC) to lead the first democratic 'government of national unity' was, in important respects, the culmination of the first round of debate over post-apartheid development discourse. In brief, this transition period witnessed a contest between proponents of three distinct policy ideologies – neo-liberal, social democratic and radical – all of whom can claim to have won certain significant concessions.

A developmentalist, populist ANC-led regime is the apparent outcome: intent on putting down left-wing challenges (public sector strikes, land invasions and the like); relatively protective of national sovereignty against Washington financial bureaucrats; logistically and ideologically uneven at the level of the nine new federal provinces (seven of which it controls); and throughout the country, never quite firm enough to hold together its multi-class coalition and achieve clear consensus, under increasingly difficult conditions of international economic integration. In these respects, all three camps may claim satisfaction from the please-all discourse of the ANC, yet each is likely to be dissatisfied with the new ruling party's practice. That practice will be particularly difficult in the context of a long-term structural downturn in the South African economy which has created a development impasse of grave proportions (see section on 'The Development Impasse').

149

The conflicting discourses are more than evident in answers to the 'housing question' provided by the market-oriented World Bank, the consensus-based National Housing Forum, and the more radical-popular urban social movements (all discussed later in this chapter). But to judge the discourses and to draw out their implications for political-economic practice in the recent and coming periods, requires prior background deliberation – not of policy, but of theory. Of particular interest is the Left's evolving perspective on race and class, which bequeaths future radical development strategists a strong but nonetheless contradictory intellectual legacy (section on the Race–Class Debate). Characteristic of high theory over the past couple of decades across the world, much of the South African analysis was rather disconnected from practice, and was also questionable on its own terms.

Thus it is in the same critical spirit of Moore's review of the disputed concepts 'sustainability,' 'equity' and 'participation' that South Africans must 'link discourses emanating from the academic realm of development studies and the "practical" development practice as articulated in the development agencies in the western world' – as well as those discourses articulated in the soot-filled matchbox houses in black townships where leaders of urban social movements strategise. Moore concludes that in part because of the failure of intellectuals to make these links, the analysis advanced by such 'counter-hegemonic movements' has been 'too easily co-opted into the dominant discourse,' and that as a result, 'new delineations of terms and new strategies are required.'[2]

THE DEVELOPMENT IMPASSE

Moore's pessimistic assessment rings broadly true, but probably deserves reappraisal in South Africa based on the strength of 2,000 vibrant, counter-hegemonic, 'civic associations' (community groups) organised under the rubric of the South African National Civic Organization (SANCO). SANCO has generally taken a firm stance against conceptual and policy slippage on matters of basic need, particularly the struggle for access to housing as a fundamental human right. Consistent with Moore, I would argue that ultimately there is in fact no real crisis in the underlying concepts of sustainability, equity and participation, merely a distraction in terms of the success of establishment development agencies – the World Bank, US AID, various UN bodies, international foundations and the like – in coopting progressive discourse while applying ineffectual policies inspired by neo-liberal economic theory.

The far deeper crisis is to be found in the world capitalist economic system. Failing to achieve growth on even limited quantitative terms, the main agents of international economic integration – financial institutions and development agencies – have through structural adjustment and project conditionality set impossible constraints on Third World developmental practice. At the same time, largely through trade liberalisation and financial deregulation, they push and pull speculative flows of capital into outlets which appear most profitable in the short-term but which have a debilitating impact upon development.

These conditions fully pertain to South Africa. In the wake of several decades of apartheid planning, import-substitution industrialisation and state control of large sections of the economy, the ascendance of neo-liberal thinking was unmistakable in the white government during the 1980s. Yet simultaneously the limits to the market as a force for development, and the danger of speculative, footloose finance (taking forms such as a volatile and vastly overvalued stock market, inordinate corporate and consumer debt, hugely overbuilt commercial property markets, and massive capital flight), emerged to bedevil the transition from apartheid. The objective of South Africa's ruling *verligte* ('enlightened') Afrikaaners, backed by key corporate and military forces, was to move from race-based socio-economic segregation to class-based segregation. In local parlance, the 'securocrats' gave way to the 'econocrats.' But what seemed to be a clear-cut strategy when the ANC and other political parties were unbanned in early 1990 quickly disintegrated.

Aside from two major trade union strike waves (1990 and 1994) and 'Third Force'-related violence involving state surrogates such as the Inkatha Freedom Party, perhaps the most obvious terrain of conflict during the early 1990s was housing. Rent boycotts were the norm for township public housing, reflecting the challenge to apartheid-puppet local authorities. In the private market, only 10 per cent of the black population could afford to acquire homes (which for middle-income workers able to raise credit bear a minimum price of roughly $12,000 per house), while at the same time housing finance brimmed over in the white suburbs and massive inflows of funds to banks and institutional investors generated speculative investment pools that in turn could find few productive outlets.

To illustrate the scale of the contradictions, it should be noted that South Africa is second in the world (to the United States) in the percentage of bank assets held in the form of mortgage credit (39 per cent). Yet of $15 billion in total 'housing bonds' (mortgage loans) on the banks' books in the early 1990s, just $2.3 billion (15 per cent) was invested in the township market, while blacks make up three quarters of the population.

As black people were allowed to own homes beginning in the late 1970s, the state phased out new public housing construction and brutally repressed civic associations from 1985–1986.

Most of the bank loans were granted over just four years, until mid-1990, when a variety of factors – market saturation, an increase in nominal interest rates from 12.5 per cent (–7 per cent in real terms) to 21% (+7 per cent), poor construction and lack of community facilities, a massive retrenchment wave, an upsurge of political violence in key areas, and a decline in township housing values leading to widespread 'negative equity' (in which bond value exceeds house price) – converged to end the flow of new loans and to reduce repayment rates on outstanding loans to as low as 67 per cent. In sum, housing finance flowed in and then ebbed out of the black townships in a manner devoid of sustainability, equity or community participation.

Meanwhile, capital market funds continued to swell by $10 billion per year, thanks in large part to billions of dollars in black worker pension contributions and insurance premiums. During the 1980s, the Johannesburg Stock Exchange share value rose by a factor of ten to in excess of $150 billion, and indeed was for several years the fastest-growing major stock market in the world. Speculative construction of commercial property also exploded, leaving 20 per cent vacancy rates and artificially-high land prices in central business districts by the early 1990s. Then, during the late 1980s and early 1990s, real economic activity dwindled, as South Africa suffered through the longest depression in its history. The official unemployment rate climbed above 50 per cent, and net fixed capital investment dropped to just 1 per cent of GDP in 1992 (in comparison to 16 per cent per year during the 1970s). The apartheid state's response was to deregulate and privatise, run real interest rates of approximately 7 per cent, and introduce a regressive Value Added Tax while lowering corporate taxes. The banks' response was to open more branches in the Cayman Islands, Panama, the Isle of Man, Guernsey, Jersey, Zurich and other hot money centres than in all of South Africa's black townships combined.

In short, the country's economy has faced an accumulation crisis of serious proportions, characterised by productive sector stagnation and untenable financial speculation, under conditions of state-led monetarist austerity, rapidly-growing official corruption and substantial capital flight – conditions not terribly dissimilar to so many other semi-peripheral national economies in recent years. The one widely-acclaimed social democratic route out of the impasse, a housing and basic needs economic kick-start, was barricaded by the failure of the state to apply its inordinately large budget ($40 billion in 1993, amounting to 35 per cent of

GDP) to housing, which received just $0.5 billion in 1993, far short of the $1.5 billion required for an 'Affordable Housing for All' subsidy system.

The development cottage industry emerged from deep remission and adapted to such contradictions in various ways. Progressive forces were initially led into the *culs-de-sac* of negotiating fora and sectoral social con-tracts (such as the National Economic Forum), most of which were soon unveiled as business-dominated experiments in low-grade corporatism ex-onerating top-down neo-liberal policies (such as the endorsement by even trade unionists, through the Economic Forum, of GATT – which will cost South Africa an extra $400 million per year by 1992, according to the OECD – and of an onerous IMF loan). The National Housing Forum falls into this category, as noted below. A national-scale social democratic deal, which might have been expected from such an unstable capitalist class, was dashed by the parameters of 'macroeconomic stability' advanced by the orthodox development agencies. If not rejected, such parameters will exacerbate already acute processes of uneven development.

Yet the shallowness of the recent social democratic thrust may just provide the ground for such a refusal. The conspicuous failure of the neo-liberal approach in the late 1980s and the inability of business elites to convincingly win ANC hearts and minds in the early 1990s has created the conditions by 1994 for a renewed round of more radical developmental discourse which submerges respect for the market by stressing the urgent provision of basic need goods (not commodities) for all. This is witnessed by a largely-successful backlash against neo-liberal ideas in the formula-tion of the ANC Reconstruction and Development Programme in the early months of 1994, prior to the first democratic election.

Just this sort of broad development impasse is evident across the world. Continually intensifying uneven development in the economic sphere, 'low intensity democracy'[3] in the political sphere and 'global apartheid' (as some have termed it) in the socio-spatial sphere must be addressed with far more gravity and strategic coherence by social movements. Here South Africa can perhaps convey lessons in ideologies, strategies and tactics. The first phase of the civic movement's national-level activity – a relent-less critique of the apartheid-capitalist social reality during the 1980s through an 'ungovernability' strategy, and tactics such as rent boycotts and mass stayaways – has moved to a second phase: bottom-up construction of a development discourse capable of winning over wary ANC policymakers. A third phase, namely the implementation of the radical policy during the 1994–1999 period of the first ANC government, will be less a problem of establishing the new hegemonic discourse of development, and more a function of two overriding constraints: external pressures and limited local-level delivery capacity. The latter cannot be addressed here; the former is taken up below. But in exploring the potentials and possible pitfalls of the radical project, this chapter moves next to a theoretical commentary setting the stage for a discussion of selected developmental discourse in South Africa.

THE RACE–CLASS DEBATE

The 'crisis in developmental discourse' at the international scale stems from disjunctures between theory and recent development experience which have called into question modernisation and dependency theories, as well as their descendants.[4] Some influential critiques of structuralist theory have drawn sustenance from the excesses of Marxism[5] (and from some straw Marxist arguments).[6] This is not the place to review the theoretical impasse in international development theory. The purpose of revisiting the South African race–class debate is, instead, to draw parallels which may shed some light on the problems of historical materialism and developmental discourse.

To begin, there is much to be said for a dependency analysis of South Africa in the world economy, based upon the high-growth era of the relatively autarchic 1930s and 1940s[7] and upon structural changes which occurred in the post-war years. Indeed it was the post-war reintegration of South Africa into international capitalist circuits which fostered the crisis conditions that are so overwhelming today: a near-exhausted raw materials export sector; an overproductive luxury goods sector hosting overprotected local monopoly capital and multinational corporations; an inadequate capital goods sector; and a hopelessly under-resourced basic needs sector. As in many semi-peripheral countries, import-substitution industrialisation was geared to the desires of the local bourgeoisie and ended up generating serious balance of payments tensions. Under such structural conditions, as rising levels of class struggle combined with local processes of uneven development, an accumulation crisis surfaced during the 1970s and became acute during the late 1980s.

But South Africa's own development debate was consumed nearly entirely by the internal question of race/class conflict, as opposed to either issues of international economic relations posed by dependency theory, or classical Marxist concerns with accumulation crisis. The well-known South African equivalent of modernization theory was the traditional 1960s liberal thesis that racially-inscribed underdevelopment would succumb to the market's incessant drive to growth and progress. Radical social scientists contested this vigorously during the 1970s, arguing that the evolutionary paths of apartheid and capitalism were interwoven, and to break from one required breaking from the other. In retrospect it appears neither liberals nor radicals were correct.

From the late 1970s leading elements of the ruling bloc made clear their desire to jettison apartheid. But, as this was occurring in a slow and extremely painful way, it also became evident that the condition for reform was not capitalist growth, but rather stagnation (and hence the need for capitalists to explore a new export-oriented route to accumulation unhindered by political unrest and their global pariah status). Hence it is ironic that while the ANC's strategy of weakening the economy through international sanctions (especially financial) as one pillar of the national democratic struggle appears to have been correct, for many radical intellectuals the combination of state reforms and repression in the 1980s represented a debilitating paradox.

The strengths and weaknesses of the legacy of historical materialism in South Africa may explain the present ambivalence many feel towards an older, more explicitly Marxist discourse. South African Communist Party (SACP) cadres had, since the early 1960s, based their call for a 'two-stage revolution' (bourgeois democracy followed by socialism) on the idea that the South African social formation represented 'colonialism of a special type' (CST).[8] But the CST framework, which was essentially an internal form of dependency theory, came under repeated questioning from Left intellectuals over a period of two decades, through several intellectual stages.[9] A version of CST was rescued by Wolpe's application of 'articulations of mode of production' theory in the early 1970s, with the conclusion that South African capitalism required the superexploitation available by harnessing colonial-style dominance of pre-capitalist modes of production.[10] Subsequent research and theoretical argumentation suggested there was ample room for contesting Wolpe's chronology and understanding of the dynamics of capitalism.[11]

Meanwhile, international trends in historical materialism – especially the success of Althusserian and Poulantzian structuralism – were by the mid-1970s making a decisive impact on South African development debates. From articulations of modes of production emerged a fascination with which 'fractions of capital' controlled the state at particular moments of political change. Although the various fractions had become increasingly blurred as South Africa's big mining finance houses diversified into manufacturing, several leading neo-Marxist researchers identified earlier distinctions between capitals in terms of their sector of production (mining, manufacturing or agricultural), their location within the circulation of capital (industrial, financial, commercial, landed), or their 'nationality' (Afrikaaner, English-speaking, British, other European, or US).[12]

The Poulantzian analysis itself came under sharp attack. Whereas focusing on fractions of capital highlighted questions of power, the costs of this single-minded focus were excessive: the capital accumulation process was downplayed, capital-labour conflicts dismissed, and thus any sense of necessity and contingency in the development of the social and economic formation lost.[13] In any event, very little further work was done in this tradition during the 1980s. Part of the reason was a frontal attack on the fractions perspective from a new school of South African social history which prided itself for looking at society and economy not from the top (state and capital), but from the very lowest levels of the voiceless majority. As rich and interesting as the particularities of the social history case studies proved, however, they added up to very little that was generalisable as development theory.[14] The broader theoretical discourse about race and class in South Africa seemed to peak in the 1970s, and with rigorous detailed probing underway in the 1980s in the context of the search for specificity, tailed off markedly.[15]

In the late 1980s the larger questions were again placed on the agenda. It was a time when South Africa's capitalist class demanded, more sincerely and energetically than ever before, an end to formal apartheid. The reasons for this are relatively clear (again, related directly to capitalist stagnation and financial crisis) but what was disconcerting was how dramatically this shook many Marxist theorists who, earlier, so profoundly rejected the liberal thesis that apartheid and capitalism were incompatible. As Gelb put it, reality demanded that radicals would have to 'develop a substantial and consistent analysis of capital accumulation which preserves their view of the earlier relationship between apartheid and capitalism, explains the transformation from long run apartheid boom to economic crisis and then analyses the crisis itself.'[16] To support such an intellectual project, Gelb introduced French 'regulation theory' to dissect the relative stability of South African capitalism from 1948 through the early 1970s. The concept of South African 'racial Fordism,' as Gelb termed it, captures the post-war combination of formal apartheid with import-substitution industrialisation:

> As with Fordism in the advanced countries, accumulation in South Africa during this period involved the linking of the extension of mass production with the extension of mass consumption, but in a manner that was restricted on both sides of the equation, as is very familiar.[17]

With the crisis in racial Fordism understood as a breakdown in the institutional apparatus that regulated capitalism and limited structural instability – a breakdown heralded by 1970s strikes and social unrest, the import of international inflation, and the oscillating gold price – the key practical task for regulationists has now become how to stitch together a new set of 'post-Fordist' norms, practices and institutions within a social democratic political framework. Wage restraint, productivity *quid pro quos*, and even Taiwan-style export-orientation have, since the late 1980s, been advocated by a group in the Congress of South African Trade Unions (COSATU) who gain inspiration from this particular discourse. Enormous controversies over trade union policy – particularly social contracts and shopfloor flexibility – have begun to emerge.[18] But, reminiscent of some earlier neo-Marxist analyses which were ultimately discredited, regulation theory has subsequently come under attack by historical materialists aiming to debunk heuristic concepts which lead to false hopes of capitalist competitiveness, and to recover an analysis of more durable aspects of capitalist development which elude the easy French typologies.[19] Meanwhile the earlier critical mass of Marxist scholars all but gave up on class analysis by the early 1990s, favouring instead policy analysis, a dash of post-Marxist (especially Laclauian) theory, and the politics of (generally mythical) social contracts.[20]

What, then, is a more appropriate framework for capturing the development processes which have deradicalised so many erstwhile South African Leftists? If we seek to understand why the condition for political reform was not capitalist growth, but rather stagnation (and hence the need for capitalists to explore a new export-oriented route to accumulation), a classical Marxist approach to cycles of capital accumulation may be helpful. Cycles of accumulation are the waves of investment and growth which are invariably followed by periods of excess capacity and stagnation, often referred to as 'overaccumulation crisis.' South Africa experienced such cycles throughout its modern history, and has suffered persistent, worsening symptoms of overaccumulation since the late 1960s.

Under such conditions, crisis displacement occurs to a large degree through intensified uneven development. This is because overaccumulated capital in its most liquid form, finance, flows easily across space in search of more profitable outlets. The advent of overaccumulation crisis across the world in the early 1970s was, not uncoincidentally, the same point at which the Bretton Woods institutions (the World Bank and IMF) assumed added global economic management power. Conditions of uneven development already underway between different regions of the world economy rapidly sharpened under the dominance of neo-liberal policy, in a process not restricted to any particular national balance of forces. Instead, there is a deeper underlying meaning. In his authoritative study of the topic, Neil

Smith concludes that while uneven development dates to the time of
'primitive accumulation and the opposition of capital against pre-capitalist
societies,' modern-day global capitalism retains a 'dichotomous form. But
today it is less an issue of the "articulation of different modes of production,"
more an issue of development at one pole and development of underdevelopment at the other.'[21] If this analysis is correct, uneven development
is not likely to be overcome through application of market mechanisms,
which are at the root of the overaccumulation problem. Nor will social
democratic promises of a new, supposedly more harmonious regime of
post-Fordist accumulation solve the problem.

Of course, neither neo-liberalism nor social democracy have patience
for such analysis. For analysts in both these camps, capitalism *will* perform
the developmental project. And, according to Moore, 'if capitalism [is] not
"spontaneous," it . . . could be implemented through bureaucratic reform,
acculturation and even co-optation' – pushed along by the development
agencies and their officials.[22] The next two sections provide pointers as to
how this was meant to be accomplished in post-apartheid South Africa
through township housing, based on strategies geared to the market and to
a social compact.

HOMAGE TO THE SOUTH AFRICAN TOWNSHIP HOUSING MARKET: THE WORLD BANK

From the late 1970s, the South African state set in motion a series of
programmes aimed at inserting market rationality into apartheid residential
location. As noted above, the lamentable results of a market-led development strategy were already clear a decade later. To a significant degree the
state's new-found commitment to the market was based on prodding by
the parastatal Development Bank of Southern Africa (DBSA) and by the
Urban Foundation (UF), a large, privately-funded think-tank and housing
developer set up by the Anglo American Corporation in the immediate
wake of the 1976 Soweto riots. In turn UF strategists were inspired by the
World Bank, especially during the late 1980s/early 1990s drafting of the
UF *Urban Futures* policy series. One direct result of their lobbying was
a $200 million site-and-service programme implemented by the Independ-
ent Development Trust (IDT), a parastatal-cum-QUANGO itself founded
in early 1990 (by the then-UF chairperson) to channel funds into townships
and rural areas to foster social contracts, concomitant with the rapid
political liberalisation then underway.

The practical results of these and numerous other township housing initiatives conformed, however, far less to a social contract aimed at achieving political stability and kick-starting the economy, and far more to a market-mediated transition from apartheid race segregation to neo-liberal class segregation. This was obvious not merely in the housing field (where 'toilet policy' – the widely-derided site-and-service developments – replaced traditional state housing policy), but in related areas: the phasing out of economic decentralisation subsidies for outlying small towns (at the behest of the DBSA and UF); DBSA market-aided land reform proposals aimed at fostering a black small commercial farming class; the IDT's university loan (not bursary) scheme; and a variety of other substantial attempts to channel grassroots demands into individualised commodities that would soon split the market achievers from those losers who ultimately would drop into the huge lumpenproletariat, living far from the cities in, at best, serviced shack-slums.

Definitive statements concerning the role of the market in township housing allocation can be found in the World Bank's first two 'Urban Sector Aides Mémoire' (May and December 1991).[23] The documents encompass social-democratic sentiments and are reminiscent of classic discourse co-option on various fronts. Illustrating how far the Bank can bend over to please, rhetorically, the second 'Aide Mémoire' carries the following philosophical commentary:

[Housing sector intervention] will involve more than just changing the overt mechanisms of apartheid and then 'letting the market work.' It requires an active role for government to help markets to work in the interests of all citizens and when, as is likely to be the case for some time, markets are unable to provide for the needs and best interests of the most disadvantaged, it requires active intervention in the form of well-designed systems of transfers.[24]

Such pleasing rhetoric was initially treated with misgivings by both oppressed civic associations and the oppressive white local authorities, and the World Bank was well aware of that fact.[25] As Bank urban development division chief Michael Cohen noted at an international conference in 1991:

We are trying to enter the debate in South Africa with a full awareness that virtually anything that we do will have an unhappy outcome for one side or the other ... there are some important ways of demonstrating that reform and changes are to be to everyone's advantage, but politically this is going to be difficult. I do not have any difficulty in being regarded with suspicion – that's the way it goes.[26]

However, the Bank's commitment to enter the urban restructuring debate through widespread 'consultation' and 'participation' with community groups would not be sufficient on its own. In considering the Bank's efforts in Johannesburg in 1992, Swilling and Mashinini explain why this is so:

> To gain wider legitimacy for its own programme, the Bank correctly made strenuous efforts to consult with the civics. What happened?
>
> The discussion began with the Bank asking the civics the same set of technical questions that were posed to white local government officials, but obviously in a simpler form: population, level and standard of services, what is expected and what are the priorities. The answers, however, were not forthcoming. Instead, every civic representative emphasised the need for capacity building.
>
> The problem lay in the way Bank staff asked the questions. As technical experts who deal in hard quantitative data every day, they related to the leaders of social movements as if they were local government officials whose every-day activity is the manipulation of organized data captured through established research methods. This is not what civic leaders do every day.
>
> No one with community organizing experience would sit down at a first meeting with local leaders and ask: What are your needs? Instead, the questions would be: Comrades, what organizational structures do you have here? What struggles have you embarked upon? What were your demands when you went on the rent boycott? What were the demands in the petition you handed to the administration when you marched? What were your short-, medium- and long-term demands at the negotiations? What compromises did you accept, and why? What research are you doing to back up you demands?
>
> Questions are asked in this way in order to tap organic knowledge about socio-economic conditions. Knowledge is inseparable from the rhythms of the daily struggle to transform local and regional conditions.[27]

Many civic leaders sensed that 'participation,' in the Bank's practice, was really a vulgar co-option process innocent of historical social struggles, community-oriented planning, gender-sensitive design, affordability for all community residents, relationship to surrounding economic, social and cultural facilities, and other areas where real consultation would end up increasing delivery costs. One illustration of the one-sided approach to community participation envisaged by the Bank is the proposal that housing finance 'risks must be mitigated through agreements between lending institutions and community members of the townships' which would stress greater 'provision of collateral services to borrowers than is now the case, in exchange for banks being able to enforce provisions of lending agreements.' The collateral envisaged as the basis for community participation is group credit based on joint borrower liability. Unfortunately, this approach was attempted by the IDT in 1991–92 but was rejected quickly when the loans were not being repaid.[28]

If participation on World Bank terms (commercial bank risk-reduction) was not achieved with township activists, the Urban Missions' research programme design during the transition period nevertheless succeeded in attracting progressive intellectuals into a working alliance. This was considered an 'essential condition' of policy formation.[29] Urban technical experts affiliated to the ANC and SACP accompanied Bank Urban Mission staff in their travels between 1991 and the 1994 election, providing legitimacy and contacts. As a result, even radical civic associations were ultimately drawn into the Bank's didactic briefing sessions, though not without occasional disruptions and challenges. (The country's most powerful metropolitan civic federation set out a 'Protocol' to control Bank activity in Johannesburg – including an exhaustive list of conditions with respect to sharing of data, commitment to redistribution of wealth, and a non-racial, non-sexist philosophy – which the Bank promptly rejected.)

But while the Bank was as transparent and open to debate in South Africa as it has been anywhere, a closer look at its framework for analysis and ultimately for sectoral lending reveals many orthodox features. For while on the one hand there is talk of social contracts and participation in research, on the other hand the overall Bank analysis and agenda remains wedded to neo-liberal principles. Bank reports continually stress the point that 'effective demand is low for the black population because of the effects of apartheid,' and never because of the exercise of class power. So central was market dogma to the World Bank's leading housing expert (Steven Mayo) that the consequence was a failure to distinguish between rather different forms of non-market determinations of housing:

The legacy of apartheid policies is felt in terms of both macroeconomic distortions, similar to those experienced in a number of Eastern European countries, and in underperformance of the housing sector . . . One of the most evident features of housing policies for non-whites in South Africa has been their resemblance to the housing policies of the command economies of Eastern Europe and other socialist countries. In such countries, an ironic consequence of the determination that housing was a 'right' rather than a commodity, and, as such, a product confined to the 'non-material' and 'non-productive' sphere of economic activity was that housing markets were not permitted to develop.[30]

To solve this problem – namely that apartheid was functionally equivalent to socialism – the Bank's first 'Aide Mémoire' advocated

> greater efforts to persuade the private financial community to extend mortgage financing to well-located housing for the upper end of the black market, with which the private financial community, and especially the Perm [Bank], has had genuine success in mortgage lending.[31]

Similar faith was expressed in the second 'Aide Mémoire,' to the extent of claiming that 'both the Perm and the South African Housing Trust appear to have been more responsive than most other mortgage granting institutions to interacting on the ground with black township borrowers.'[32]

In reality the SA Housing Trust (a parastatal backed by market-rate investments from several of the country's largest corporations) was at that very time facing fifteen separate township 'bond boycotts' (collective community refusal to repay mortgages), while suffering a 50+ per cent arrears rate due in large part to the institution's well-known lack of credibility. At the same time the Perm was losing tens of millions of rands to township foreclosures which could not be consummated due to refusal of the defaulting borrowers (supported by the community) to vacate their houses. Its holding company (Nedcor) lost 20 per cent of its Johannesburg Stock Exchange share value (in excess of $150 million lost) in a single week in September 1992, following a threat of a national bond boycott from SANCO, which threw into question the Perm's $700 million black housing loan exposure. (A subsequent social contract with SANCO reduced the Perm's troubles, with very little payoff, however, to the civic movement.)

That the market so blatantly failed on its own terms did not deter Mayo from further praise at a 1993 international housing conference:

> The South African housing finance system clearly represents a world-class system, which is capable of providing for the needs of the vast majority of the population, if conditions are put in place which provide for secure tenure, reasonable standards, a housing delivery system that provides well-located and sound quality housing, and a regulatory framework which protects the interests of both housing purchasers and financial institutions.[33]

Note the one crucial variable consistently omitted in Mayo's calculus: borrower affordability. With monetarist-determined interest rates for housing bonds remaining at 16 per cent (7 per cent in real terms) even during the fragile transition, South African development practitioners tried and failed so many times to overcome the limits to the market through financial engineering that even lenders themselves (such as the chief housing officer for the country's largest bank) were finally willing to accept the obvious: 'Banks are able and prepared to provide finance to those who receive a regular income and enjoy stable employment.'[34] Such clients represent at best only 35 per cent of those families in need of housing, a far cry from Mayo's 'vast majority.'

For the Bank to accept the fact that the threshold to engage in purchase of formal housing is too high for most South Africans, would be to confess a profound flaw of capitalism. One solution is simply to define shacks as houses. This Mayo did, arguing that South Africa ranks quite respectably in comparison to other countries in the 'production of houses' (with its increase of 3.6 per cent per annum). In reality, according to Mayo's own data, a third of such 'houses' are made of 'temporary materials' such as straw, cardboard or cloth (most of the balance are of more 'permanent' substances like plywood and zinc sheets). Moreover, 89 per cent of the new homes are 'unauthorised' (illegal shacks subject to demolition at any time). In other words, faced with overwhelming contradictions between what the market promises and what it can deliver, the neo-liberal discourse resorts to semantics to define away the problem.

The problem, in short, is that the Bank is fundamentally opposed to societies determining that a sufficient share of their social surplus should be dedicated to ensuring that all citizens are provided minimal decent shelter. Mayo's conclusion from Bank policy experience across the world is that housing finance 'should complement user charges and other cost-recovery mechanisms in mobilising private savings, thereby contributing to reducing the overall role of government in the sector.'[35]

Will such advice find its way into loan conditionality in South Africa? Such conditionality by the Bank, US AID and similar institutions, is the preferred back-door way to policy, and has been extremely effective in settings (such as neighbouring Zimbabwe) in undermining socialist-sounding government philosophy – without even paying lip-service to transparency.[36] But even setting aside the dangers of conditionality, it is difficult to understand why Pretoria would, in the mid and late 1990s, borrow dollars from the Bank in order to finance low-cost housing at a time of excessive domestic financial system liquidity. The import costs of housing are virtually nil, while the effective interest rate on a foreign loan (once likely inflation-linked devaluation is accounted) is 83 per cent higher than a domestic South African loan.[37] Such arguments meant that the most recent ANC policy statement (the Reconstruction and Development Programme, or

RDP), influenced by trade union and urban social movements, took an extremely strong stance against the Bank:

> The RDP must use foreign debt financing only for those elements of the programme that can potentially increase our capacity for earning foreign exchange. Relationships with international financial institutions such as the World Bank and International Monetary Fund must be conducted in such a way as to protect the integrity of domestic policy formulation and promote the interests of the South African population and the economy. Above all, we must pursue policies that enhance national self-sufficiency and enable us to reduce dependence on international financial institutions.[38]

If neo-liberalism can be kept somewhat at bay through such policy struggles is social democracy ready to fill the void?

IN SEARCH OF SOCIAL DEMOCRACY: THE NATIONAL HOUSING FORUM

Since political parties were unbanned in 1990, South Africa has been overwhelmed with rhetoric promoting the role of social contracts in fostering a political spirit of social democracy (here meaning a market-oriented system tempered by state social welfare support).[39] The formation of the National Housing Forum in mid 1992, encompassing a range of stakeholders including civics, the ANC and other political parties, trade unions, NGOs, developers, materials-suppliers, bankers, and parastatal agencies, was emblematic of these attempts. By far the greatest influence was that of the UF, whose technical experts dominated most of the proceedings. The NHF experienced numerous conflicts with the conservative government housing minister, Louis Shill (who had been seconded to the National Party government from the large insurance company he had founded), but the forum generally backed down when the confrontations appeared debilitating.

Typical of the circumscribed nature of such forums for the Left was the agreement on housing subsidy policy reached between the NHF and a campaigning Shill just weeks prior to the 1994 election. The $26 billion, ten-year housing plan was heralded by the government, but the developer-led site-and-service policy lacked a number of aspects which had been raised by the Left as issues: it included no explicit commitment to eliminating gender bias; no support for squatters' rights; no commitment on ending bank loan discrimination; no assurance of end-user and bridging finance availability; no protection against downward-raiding of subsidies; no possibility of land banking for future development; no means of developing higher-cost inner-city areas; and no attention to pricing of building materials.

The main problem, however, continued to be the size of the NHF-Shill subsidy itself. For those earning below $430 per month (roughly 75 per cent of all South Africans), the state provides a maximum $3,600 capital grant which apply to individually-titled sites, as opposed to what is actually required: low-interest rate loans of a larger amount (say, $7,500) for full-fledged dwelling units. Hence in the name of sustainability, transparency and efficiency (i.e., not interfering in market determinations of interest rates and hence avoiding financial market distortions), the capital subsidy approach to serviced sites fills various market-related functions, not least of which is limiting fiscal outlays on housing subsidies.[40]

The NHF's insistence upon once-off grants makes it difficult to raise recurrent flexible interest rate funding for housing that would match recipient affordability. Once-off capital grants – as opposed to long-term loan commitments – also reduce popular pressure on subsequent government budgets to sustain sufficient subsidies.[41] In sum, the NHF's application of the notion of 'sustainability' mainly means sufficiently market-oriented and insufficiently threatening to the government budget so that the subsidy system is replicable.

'Equity' has also been the subject of inordinate debates surrounding housing subsidy policy, in which the NHF promotes both 'vertical equity' (relatively wealthier households get a lower subsidy than the very poor) and 'horizontal equity' (households of the same income group get the same subsidy). Although the NHF–Shill agreement was far more generous to the upper five percent of the black market than is warranted (a $1,400 housing grant is provided those earning as high as $1,000 per month), in practice the mobilisation of the concepts of vertical and horizontal equity has led to a 'width versus depth' debate in the NHF. This has the effect of emphasising supply of massive numbers of serviced sites, especially to the very poor, rather than embarking upon a Housing for All programme.[42]

Thus the NHF-brokered compromise, and the discourse underlying it, was subject to extensive criticism by former SANCO president Moses Mayekiso:

> It is a major scam. In my view, the whole subsidy scheme must be reworked, because the $3,600 maximum that is offered is just not sufficient to pay for anything more than a plot, a toilet and some few building materials. We say the subsidy must include a core house with

full services and infrastructure. It must be at least 40 square metres in size, with good quality construction. There must be community facilities such as schools, clinics and creches. We have had to compromise, and we are getting far less than that. But we feel this is a temporary arrangement, until we have a humane government policy in place.

   There are other problems with the interim scheme. We don't want those subsidies to encourage speculation and immediate sale of the plot. Our country must not be left bankrupt by people selling their plots to the middle-class, leaving us with a low-income housing crisis. The subsidy should not be meant to enrich individuals, but to solve the homelessness crisis.[43]

Even the World Bank recognised this latter point. In the wake of countless failed low-cost site-and-service projects, it noted that 'in cases where very poor families obtained plots, they frequently sold them to middle-income people to gain a windfall.'[44]

   As the new government was on the way to installation, a debate emerged as to whether to respect the NHF agreement or to instead rapidly develop a more generous, appropriate housing policy. Key provincial leaders in the new federal structure began to recognise the weakness of the compromise, given ANC election promises for a much more substantive housing programme. With the failure of social democratic precepts, a new discourse – based on the principle that housing is a right, delivered through highly-subsidised but community-controlled forms of social housing (community land trusts, housing associations and cooperatives) – proved to be the only viable approach. SANCO was its primary advocate prior to democratic government, and would continue to be in coming years.

A RADICAL HOUSING PROGRAMME: THE CIVIC MOVEMENT

It was not only top-down market failure and the limits to social democratic compromises that forced SANCO to engage in housing policy debates. Grassroots struggle – especially resistance to the broader financial crisis – also played a significant role in the township housing market, and added to already growing dissatisfaction with an individual ownership model, backed by bank credit, as the basis of housing policy. The civic movement began to experiment in selected locales with the bond boycott tactic. The first such boycott was in the Port Elizabeth area in 1988 during a union struggle against Volkswagen, on grounds that ES striking workers could not reasonably be expected to make monthly bond payments. Subsequently the strategy was adopted by civic associations in struggles over the quality of housing in townships near Cape Town, Bloemfontein, Johannesburg and several other cities. In spite of politicians as diverse as (then-housing minister) Hernus Kriel and (ANC leader) Thabo Mbeki stating that such actions were irresponsible, they continued, and in several cases resulted in substantial concessions by banks, developers and parastatal agencies.

The bond boycott must be understood against the backdrop of militant township strategies which continued into the early 1990s. During the previous decade, the civic movement had used the philosophy of 'ungovernability' to politically and financially cripple illegitimate black local governments. Residents' refusal to pay rent on township houses also conformed to local grievances and waning household economics. Such struggles played a large role in forcing the Botha and De Klerk regimes to contemplate power-sharing, and by 1991 had resulted in the resignation of most of the apartheid township councils. But in mid-1992, attempts by SANCO to channel the bond boycott threat into national political gains – by demanding banks cease funding homeland dictators, in much the same spirit as the ANC's financial sanctions campaign – met with firm opposition from ANC moderates. Nevertheless, through bond boycotts and rent boycotts, as well as land invasions on apartheid buffer zones, the civic movement established a capacity to utilise mass protest actions of various sorts to advance residents' interests.[45]

This history of adapting local grievances to highly visible political campaigning gave the civic movement an important stake in the Mass Democratic Movement alliance of ANC, SACP, trade unions, and other anti-apartheid groupings within civil society. This led to an invitation in late 1993 for SANCO to join the RDP policy drafting process, which set the framework for subsequent ANC policy. The RDP housing programme, in particular, was based on SANCO policy nearly word-for-word, which in turn was based on a year-long workshopping process. Thus housing is deemed a 'human right,' and one million low-cost homes are expected to be built over the first five years of ANC rule, with 300,000 houses a year thereafter. These houses, complete with a full set of internal services, would carry sufficient state subsidies (more than three times the amount budgeted by the last National Party government) so as to be affordable to even the poorest residents. A few clauses of the RDP make clear the scope of the new, more radical discourse:

> The housing problems created by apartheid and by the limited range of the capitalist housing markets have been aggravated by the absence of a coherent national housing policy . . . Although housing may be provided by a range of parties, the democratic government is ultimately responsible for ensuring that housing is provided to all. It must create a policy

framework and legislative support so that this is possible, and it must allocate subsidy funds from the budget – to reach a goal of not less than five per cent of the budget by the end of the five-year RDP – so that housing is affordable to even the poorest South Africans. The approach to housing, infrastructure and services must involve and empower communities; be affordable, developmental and sustainable; take account of funding and resource constraints, and support gender equality.[46]

The RDP continues with attacks on land speculation and on the construction and building materials industry, with a pledge to support 'public, worker and community-based ownership where the market fails to provide a reasonably priced product.' But it is in contesting housing finance that the RDP makes its most serious inroads against market determinations of basic needs goods. Thus rather than a nuclear-family subsidy arrangement, as with the Housing Forum model, the RDP insists that 'Mechanisms (such as time limits on resale, or compulsory repayment of subsidies upon transfer of property) must be introduced to prevent speculation and downward raiding.' Moreover, quite contrary to the deregulatory spirit of the World Bank, the RDP determined that 'A national housing bank and national home loan guarantee fund must be initiated to coordinate subsidies and financing most efficiently.' And the existing financial sector requires state intervention:

> 'Redlining' and other forms of discrimination by banks must be prohibited. Community-controlled financing vehicles must be established with both private sector and government support where necessary. Locally controlled Housing Associations or cooperatives must be supported, in part to take over properties in possession of banks due to foreclosure. Unemployment bond insurance packages and guarantee schemes with a demand-side orientation must be devised. Interest rates must be kept as low as possible.[47]

Thus the housing question in South Africa enables us to understand the potential for profound challenges to orthodox development discourse. To further such insight we must consider why the demands advanced in the RDP for community-control of housing and capacity-building financial resources for community-based organizations arose. It is not merely for the obvious reason alluded to above: the failure of private sector developers and financiers, or parastatals working to the World Bank model, to establish a truly sustainable, equitable and participatory model for delivery. There is also, here, a distrust of the new government, and a sense of a future 'watchdog' role for the civic movement, as part of a vibrant, postapartheid civil society.

THE CIVIC MOVEMENT AND 'WORKING-CLASS CIVIL SOCIETY'

According to Petras and Morley, the South African urban movement, along with those of many other countries,

> emerged to break the bonds of authoritarian politics and the constraints of police state regimes, to overcome the passivity and paralysis of the traditional opposition, and to forge a new political reality. What makes these social movements different from those in the past is that they are independent of traditional party-electoral political machines. They are led and directed by grassroots leaders. Policy is constantly debated in democratic popular assemblies. The strong ties to local communities and the intense but profoundly democratic political life has enabled these new social movements to mobilize previously unorganised strata: the unemployed, young women, squatters, indigenous peoples. The new social movements combine with and transcend the action of organised labour movements; street action surges beyond the wage issues toward enlarging the areas of freedom for people to act and realise their human dignity.[48]

This is an optimistic account, but does capture the spirit of the civic movement at its finest. It is a highly political movement, but not tied to party-politics. It is capable of working with the Pan Africanist Congress and the Azanian People's Organization, alongside the ANC. Yet it also recognises intrinsically the class character of Third World nationalism: all too often comprador, petty bourgeois. Thus it continually re-establishes its footing in civil society and takes care to remain representative of working-class and poor peoples' interests, capable of withstanding neo-liberal processes aimed at dividing and conquering a privileged fraction of workers from the masses.

The primary organiser of the Alexandra civic movement, Mzwanele Mayekiso, has long advocated 'organs of working-class civil society which both serve the oft-discussed "watchdog" function and provide the raw material and energy from which to construct socialist building blocks.' In particular, Mayekiso argues,

> The examples of Africa and elsewhere tell us that simply because nationalist organisations like the ANC are apparently progressive today, does not mean they will remain so. The fact that there are, within the ANC, numerous class forces is a reason in itself for strengthening independent organs of working-class civil society. Class struggle will continue into the post-apartheid era. The ANC will lead a so-called

'mixed economy,' and if that means supporting private property rights, then there will necessarily be conflict with the working-class. On the other hand, an ANC government that in principle is strongly supportive of working-class interests will, in turn, need a strong working-class civil society to safeguard a progressive approach.[49]

This sort of analysis, based not on a harmony model of social democratic modernization but on a street-smart historical materialism, is not uncontroversial. Such an approach, which stresses the continuities between urban social movement struggles from past to future, has come under considerable attack from orthodox observers who explain the post-1990 carnage in many townships in South Africa's industrial heartland by reference to the legacy of 1980s 'politics of protest' (in contrast to the 1990s 'politics of development' which ostensibly involves no protest). Mayekiso defends the earlier strategy of ungovernability against such charges:

Within the decay of the old apartheid order, we knew that there were opportunities to plant the seeds of a new approach. We would seek out, through discipline, democracy and accountability, concrete alternatives to apartheid rule. Ungovernability led to the vision of building 'organs of people's power' in townships. This required us to carefully assess how much power we had to challenge the very basis of the regime, and how to develop community-controlled organs of power such as the embryonic structures of the Alexandra Action Committee, People's Courts, and economic, developmental and cultural institutions.[50]

It is in this context that the attempt to establish a radical development discourse has so many implications for grassroots political practice. The awesome ideological vacuum on the Left, in a country like South Africa which has paid so many unnecessary intellectual debts to Third International Stalinism, may well be filled now by a truly internationalist, non party-political civic ideology. When translated into development discourse such as a Housing for All campaign, this could well offer the best means of challenging the hegemony of the orthodox agencies, which can provide no convincing answer to the housing question in either political or practical terms.

CONCLUSION

If SANCO remains a vibrant, community-oriented national coalition, even while many of its leaders are drawn into the new governments, and if the traditional South African civic perspective is maintained even under conditions of corporatism elsewhere in the polity, the movement will remain relatively inaccessible to co-optation. Indeed this chapter has argued that the 'sustainability' required to provide basic needs goods to all South Africans must entail a strengthening of civics and other organs of working class civil society. 'Equity' is an unstated, enduring premise, but one which requires further work to assure that 'width versus depth' debates do not sidetrack progress. The notion of 'participation' has recently been elevated by the civic movement to 'community control.' In each of these areas, it should be clear that the radical project is to continually strive for non-reformist reforms that reward the efforts of organised communities to fight market forces.

None of this is terribly new – what we continually need to be reminded of, however, is the nature of the intellectual challenge: naming capitalism as the principal barrier to development. Indeed, the same underlying analysis of the housing question can, in fact, be traced to Engels:

> In reality the bourgeoisie has only one method of solving the housing question after its fashion – that is to say, of solving it in such a way that the solution continually reproduces the question anew ... No matter how different the reasons may be, the result is everywhere the same; the scandalous alleys disappear to the accompaniment of lavish self-praise from the bourgeoisie on account of this tremendous success, but they appear again immediately somewhere else and often in the immediate neighbourhood! ... The breeding places of disease, the infamous holes and cellars in which the capitalist mode of production confines our workers night after night, are not abolished; they are merely shifted elsewhere! The same economic necessity which produced them in the first place, produces them in the next place also.[51]

In translating this analysis to contemporary policy debates, David Harvey makes clear the direction in which development discourse must go:

> Although all serious analysts concede the seriousness of the ghetto problem, few call into question the forces which rule the very heart of our economic system. Thus we discuss everything except the basic characteristics of a capitalist market economy. We devise all manner of solutions except those which might challenge the continuance of that economy. Such discussions and solutions serve only to make us look foolish, since they eventually lead us to discover what Engels was only too aware of in 1872 – that capitalist solutions provide no foundation for dealing with deteriorated social conditions.[52]

New discussions and new solutions are part, it would seem, of a radical development discourse which urban social movements across the world may be ready to grapple with at last, not merely through 'IMF riots' but through more sustained strategies.[53] And it is in South Africa during the portentous mid and late 1990s – with well-tested social movements demanding 'Affordable Housing for All' (and other such) programmes on the basis of well-considered policy inputs drawn directly from grassroots struggle – that many radical intellectuals may find a means to overcome their own development impasse and re-link theory and practice. If so, their/our challenge remains, as ever, to explore and to publicise the ideological and practical vulnerabilities of state, capital and development agencies; to carefully track the surfacing of crisis tendencies and adapt analysis and strategy accordingly; and to be prepared to internationalise the most effective new principles and programmes of social movements (such as the South African civic movement's ideology and strategies). For nothing less than a unified internationalist effort, based on strong national-scale movements grounded in grassroots organisation in urban and rural centres of resistance, can end the tyranny of both the hegemonic developmental discourse and uneven capitalist development.

POSTSCRIPT

This chapter was written in the turbulent period around the April 1994 election. It should be rewritten. Subsequent policy-making confirms pessimism on the transition. Negotiations rule. Radicalism – even that of the Freedom Chapter – is marginalized. Notwithstanding that the best RDP discourse, stressing that basic needs should be met through 'people driven development,' was hegemonic (even for big business), the politicians and bureaucrats abandoned its feasible and urgent proposals.

Predictably, by August 1994 the World Bank was promoting market-oriented housing finance. It discouraged a national housing bank and loan guarantee plan for pension investments in housing (for which, anyhow, the selected models had strayed far from RDP guidelines). Predictably, too, the UF and many of its capitalist allies advocated the NHF's social contract model – including the insufficient apartheid-inherited subsidy.

Unpredictably, the new Department of National Housing ignored the RDP and took the social democratic approach, sponsoring an all-in 'Housing Accord' conference in October 1994. More unpredictably, the vanguard in the turn right was Housing Minister (and SACP chair) Joe Slovo, who resorted to demagogic discourse against ongoing rent and bond boycotts:

'It's clear who the boycotters are knocking: Nelson Mandela.' Most unpredictably, reflecting the deep descent into social contract politics and the movement leaders' separation from their base, high-profile ANC MP Moses Mayekiso endorsed the 'toilet-and-a-small-pile-of-bricks' policy. Such developments shocked SANCO and trade union members who vowed to campaign for the original RDP housing programme.

It all shows that winning development discourse debates – here the RDP's housing promises – is far from material victory. Attaining a true 'Affordable Housing for All' policy will require a quantum leap in pressure strategy and tactics from SANCO and its allies, perhaps leading to that second stage of revolution Engels considered a prerequisite for the answer to the housing question.

Notes

1. This paper could not have been prepared without the comradeship of my Planact and SANCO colleagues (especially Mzwanele Mayekiso and Barry Pinsky), or the inspiration of David Harvey and Neil Smith. It was initially presented at the 1992 Canadian Association for the Study of International Development meetings in June 1992, at the University of Prince Edward Island in Charlottetown, and I am grateful to David Moore and the IDRC for financial support. The usual disclaimers apply.

   In the terminology adopted for convenience in this paper — which is that most often used in the development industry — the 'black' townships are specifically the 'African' townships, even though many lower-income 'Coloured' and 'Indian' people (who are considered 'black' in common progressive political terminology) face similar conditions, and have organised urban movements along similar lines to those of the African townships. This terminology is not meant to justify apartheid race categories, but rather to most simply and accurately reflect the nature of policy debates.

2. David Moore, 'The Crisis in Development Discourse and the Concepts of Sustainability, Equity and Participation: A Way Out of the Impasse?'. Paper presented to the Canadian Political Science Association Annual Meeting, Queen's University, Kingston, Ontario, June 2–4, 1991.

3. Barry Gills, Joel Rocamora, Richard Wilson (eds), *Low Intensity Democracy: Political Power in the New World Order* (London: Zed Press, 1993), and see Gerald Schmitz, 'Democratization and Demystification: Deconstructing "Governance" as Development Paradigm,' in this volume.

4. The seminal paper was David Booth, 'Marxism and Development Sociology: Interpreting the Impasse,' *World Development*, 13, 7 (1991). This was followed by important works such as Stuart Corbridge, *Capitalist World Development: A Critique of Radical Development Geography* (Totowa, NJ: Rowan & Littlefield, 1986); Leslie Sklair, 'Transcending the Impasse:

Metatheory, Theory and Empirical Research in the Sociology of Development and Underdevelopment,' *World Development*, 16, 6 (1988); Nicos Mouzelis, 'Sociology of Development: Reflections on the Present Crisis,' *Sociology*, 22, 1 (1988); P. Vandergeest and F. Buttel 'Marx, Weber and Development Sociology: Beyond the Impasse,' *World Development*, 16, 6 (1988); Stuart Corbridge, 'Marxism, Post-Marxism and the Geography of Development,' in R. Peet and N. Thrift (eds), *New Models in Geography* (London: Unwin-Hyman, 1989); Michael Edwards, 'The Irrelevance of Development Studies,' *Third World Quarterly*, 11, 1 (1989); B. Stauffer, 'After Socialism: Capitalism, Development, and the Search for Critical Alternatives,' *Alternatives*, 15 (1990); F. Schuurman (ed.), *Beyond the Impasse: New Directions in Development Theory* (London: Zed Press, 1993).

5. Of greatest importance was the switch by Laclau from Marxist critic of dependency theory (Ernesto Laclau, 'Feudalism and Capitalism in Latin America,' *New Left Review*, 166 [1971]), to leading post-Marxist (Ernesto Laclau and Chantal Mouffe, *Hegemony and Socialist Strategy: Towards a Radical Democratic Politics* (London: Verso, 1985)); as well as the oft-cited reversal from Althusserianism performed by Barry Hindess and Paul Hirst, *Mode of Production and Social Formation: An Autocritique of Pre-Capitalist Modes of Production* (London: Macmillan, 1977).

6. Some of the more effective rebuttals include Ellen Meiksons Wood, *The Retreat from Class* (London: Verso, 1986); Norman Geras, *Discourses of Extremity* (London: Verso, 1990); R. Peet, *Global Capitalism: Theories of Societal Development* (London: Routledge, 1991) pp. 171–83. At least one defense of dependency theory can be found in Ronaldo Munck, 'Political Programmes and Development: The Transformative Potential of Social Democracy,' in F. Schuurman (ed.), *Beyond the Impasse* (London: Zed Press, 1993).

7. William Martin, 'From NIC to NUC: South Africa's Semiperipheral Regimes,' in Martin (ed.), *Semiperipheral States in the World-Economy* (New York: Greenwood Press, 1990). Simply stated, as South Africa delinked from the world economy from roughly 1933 to 1945, its secondary manufacturing industry (beyond the traditionally-strong mining equipment sector) burgeoned. Moreover, the rate of growth of the black wage share rose more than 50 per cent during this period (from 11 to 17 per cent – the black share had reached only 21 per cent by 1970). And the overall GDP growth rate (8 per cent) was the fastest recorded in modern times (J. Nattrass in *The South African Economy* (Cape Town: Oxford University Press, 1981)).

8. SACP, *The Path to Power* (London: South African Communist Party, 1989).

9. A Trotskyist rebuttal is provided by Alex Callinicos, *South Africa: Between Reform and Revolution* (London: Bookmarks, 1988).

10. Several statements of this theme are found in Harold Wolpe (ed.), *Articulations of Modes of Production* (London: Routledge, 1980). Wolpe's more recent *Race, Class and the Apartheid State* (New York: UNESCO, 1988) backtracks substantially from the earlier position that apartheid was necessary to capitalist development; he now suggests that aspects of their mutual evolution were contingent.

11. Some of these are reviewed in Patrick Bond, *The Theory of Economy* (Johannesburg: Phambili Books, 1991).

12. See R. Davies, D. O'Meara and S. Dlamini, *The Struggle for South Africa*, Volume 1 (London: Zed Press, 1986).
13. Criticism emerged from a variety of angles. The most important Marxist contribution on South Africa was Simon Clarke, 'Capital, Fractions of Capital and the State,' *Capital and Class*, 5 (1978).
14. Michael Morris, 'Social History and the Transition to Capitalism in the South African Countryside,' *African Perspective*, 1, 5/6 (1987).
15. A notable contribution was an approach to understanding the social formation known as 'racial capitalism,' in John S. Saul and Stephen Gelb, *The Crisis in South Africa* (New York: Monthly Review, [1981] 1986).
16. Stephen Gelb, 'Making Sense of the Crisis,' *Transformation*, 5 (1987).
17. In 'Making Sense of the Crisis' and his edited collection *South Africa's Economic Crisis* (Cape Town: David Philip, 1991), Gelb explained that expensive imported machinery was paid for by a relatively stable flow of foreign currency provided by mineral exports. Although political turmoil disturbed the economic boom in 1960, growth was relatively secure for at least two decades after apartheid was introduced, and this qualifies as the longest uninterrupted period of prosperity that the country's entire white population had ever had. Even short-term business cycle downturns helped correct imbalances in the system, says Gelb, in a 'reproductive' rather than destructive way. But white mass consumption only goes so far – an entire industrialised economy with South Africa's aspirations could not build on so small a base.
18. This is best documented in the *South African Labour Bulletin* and the Toronto-based *Southern Africa Report*.
19. A thorough critique of the theory is to be found in Robert Brenner and Mark Glick, 'The Regulation Approach: Theory and History,' *New Left Review*, 188 (July–August 1991), as well as in Simon Clarke, *Keynesianism, Monetarism and the Crisis of the State* (Aldershot: Edward Elgar, 1988). For a Marxist critique of South African regulation theory, see Charles Meth, 'Productivity and the Economic Crisis in South Africa: A Marxist View,' Occasional Paper, University of Natal Economics Department, Durban, 1991; Patrick Bond, *Commanding Heights and Community Control: New Economics for a New South Africa* (Johannesburg: Ravan Press, 1991); Alex Callinicos, *Between Apartheid and Capitalism* (London: Bookmarks, 1992).
20. V. Pillay, *The Social Contract* (Johannesburg: Phambili Books, 1992).
21. Neil Smith, *Uneven Development* (Oxford: Basil Blackwell, 1990), pp. 141, 156.
22. David Moore, 'The Dynamics of Development Discourse: Sustainability, Equity and Participation in Africa,' report to International Development Research Centre, West and Central Africa Regional Directorate, Dakar, 1991, p. 19.
23. Southern African Department, World Bank 'Urban Sector Aide Memoire,' (Washington, DC: World Bank, May 1991); and idem., 'Urban Sector Aide Memoire,' (Washington, DC: World Bank, December 1991). A full critique of the Bank's urban analysis can be found in Patrick Bond and Mark Swilling, 'World Bank Financing for Urban Development: Issues and Options for South Africa,' *Urban Forum*, 3, 2 (1992).

24. 'Urban Sector Aide Mémoire,' December, Section II, pp. 5, 7.
25. Patrick Bond, 'From the Boardrooms to the Townships,' *BankCheck*, January, 1994.
26. Michael Cohen, 'Comment,' in N. Harris (ed.), *Cities in the 1990s* (London: UCL Press, 1992), p. 59.
27. Mark Swilling and T. Mashinini, 'The Bank's Shopping List,' in *BankCheck*, January 1994, p. 10.
28. Steven Mayo, 'Housing Policy Reform in South Africa: International Perspectives and Domestic Imperatives'. Paper presented to the Euromoney Financing Low Cost Housing Conference, Midrand, 25–26 January, 1994, p. 9. Mayo noted that the IDT group credit approach 'should be encouraged' two years after it was abandoned. This lapse, and others in Mayo's recent work (such as the incomprehensible remark in the same paper that 'at the present time,' banks have had 'a generally favourable lending experience with borrowers in black townships') reflects the enormous distance between H Street in Washington, DC and South Africa.
29. 'Urban Sector Aide Mémoire,' May 1991, p. 2.
30. 'Urban Sector Aide Mémoire,' May 1991, Section CC, p. 11.
31. 'Urban Sector Aide Mémoire,' May 1991, Section CC, pp. 25–6.
32. 'Urban Sector Aide Mémoire,' December 1991, Section II, p. 8.
33. Steven Mayo, 'South African Housing Sector Performance in International Perspective,' paper presented to the 21st World Housing Congress, Cape Town, 10–14 May 1993, p. 16. The reference to the world-class nature of white housing finance reflects the influence of 'dualism,' which allows Mayo to posit that by bringing the existing white suburban market institutions into the institution-less black townships, underdevelopment can be resolved. But the Bank's internal lack of consistency is revealed in Cohen's comment, consistent with the political project noted earlier, that 'One of my colleagues [Mayo] has managed to desegregate housing indicators by race, and one of the conclusions being brought out is that the white sector is not doing very well either, because of the results of apartheid policy as it operates in housing and urban services' (Cohen, op. cit., p. 59).
34. P. Marais, 'The Latest Developments on Experiences in Making Available End-User Finance in the Affordable Housing Market'. Paper presented to the Euromoney conference on 'Financing Low Cost Housing,' Midrand, 25–26 January, 1994, p. 4.
35. World Bank, *Urban Policy and Economic Development* (Washington: World Bank, 1991), p. 65. For a summary of the emerging urban management approach to market-oriented housing and finance, see Urban Institute, Office of Housing and Urban Programmes, *Urban Economies and National Development* (Washington: US Agency for International Development, 1991); and Nigel Harris (ed.), *Cities in the 1990* (London: UCL Press, 1992).
36. Patrick Bond, 'Finance and Uneven Development in Zimbabwe,' Unpublished Doctoral Dissertation, Johns Hopkins University, Department of Geography, Baltimore, Chapter 10.
37. Details of the debate over using high-cost foreign loans as opposed to (highly liquid) domestic funds are provided in Bond and Swilling, op. cit.
38. African National Congress, *Reconstruction and Development Programme* (Johannesburg: 1994).

39. Patrick Bond, 'Scenario Plundering,' *Southern African Review of Books*, July–August, 1993.
40. R. Burgess, 'Petty Commodity Housing or Dweller Control? A Critique of John Turner's Views on Housing Policy,' *World Development*, 6, 9–10 (1978); and Burgess, 'The Limits of State Self-Help Housing Programmes,' *Development and Change*, 16 (1985).
41. Patrick Bond, 'The World Bank Likes Capital Subsidies Too,' *Work in Progress/Reconstruct*, December 1993.
42. In contrast, the two leading practical applications of collective community-controlled subsidies in South Africa – a land invasion in Wattville-Tamboville to the east of Johannesburg which led to the formation of a community land trust serving 700 households; and an inner-city Johannesburg 'Seven Buildings Project' slum tenement purchase, upgrade and co-operative housing conversion of 460 apartment units – violated both types of equity. In each case the subsidy applied to the working-classes as well as the very poor within the community, and in each case the fact that the community was well-organised meant that they received a subsidy beyond that of their income-peers. In each case both types of violations were the result of extensive community mobilisation following a rigorous education process which considered a variety of available housing tenure and financing options.
43. 'Interview with Moses Mayekiso,' *Cross Sections* (Toronto), June 1994.
44. World Bank, *Urban Policy and Economic Development*, p. 65.
45. Patrick Bond, 'Money, Power and Social Movements: The Contested Geography of Finance in Southern Africa,' in Stuart Corbridge, Ron Martin and Nigel Thrift (eds), *Money, Power and Space* (Oxford: Basil Blackwell, 1994).
46. African National Congress, op. cit.
47. Ibid.
48. James Petras and M. Morley 'Declining Empire, Passing Theories: Notes Toward the Definition of a New Development Paradigm,' in Petras and Morley, *US Hegemony Under Siege: Class, Politics and Development in Latin America* (London: Verso, 1990), pp. 52–3.
49. M. Mayekiso, 'Working Class Civil Society: Why we Need It and How we Get It,' *African Communist*, Second Quarter (1992).
50. M. Mayekiso, 'The Legacy of Ungovernability,' *Southern African Review of Books*, 5, 6 (November–December 1993).
51. F. Engels, *The Housing Question* (New York: International Publishers, 1935).
52. David Harvey, *Social Justice and the City* (Baltimore: Johns Hopkins University Press), p. 144.
53. Franz Schuurman and T. van Naerssen (eds), *Urban Social Movements in the Third World* (London: Routledge, 1989); P. Wignaraja (ed.), *New Social Movements in the South* (London: Zed Press, 1993); J. Walton and D. Seddon, *Free Markets and Food Riots* (Oxford: Basil Blackwell, 1994).

6 From 'Equity' and 'Participation' to Structural Adjustment: State and Social Forces in Zimbabwe

Lloyd M. Sachikonye

INTRODUCTION

This chapter reassesses the concepts of equity, participation and structural adjustment with reference to the specific national context and experience of post-independence Zimbabwe. The global context in which these concepts have been defined and appropriated into current developmental discourse has been laid out succinctly elsewhere.[1] Here, I consider the political context in which this discourse on development has been shaped and interpreted in a young developing nation of ten million.

The chapter begins by elaborating on the contradictory ideological context upon which the post-independent state's development strategy drew, resulting in an ambivalent populist variety of 'socialism.' I argue that the fragile commitment to this programme and the social redistribution policies which came out of it soon came under strain as a result of the combined opposition of international and domestic capital. With the shift towards economic liberalization under the auspices of the World Bank-sponsored structural adjustment programme (SAP), the tenuous hegemonic capacity of the ruling elite was undermined further – rather than enhanced.

The chapter then critically assesses the 'growth with equity' policy and argues that the ambiguity of its conceptualization and operationalization contributed to the incapacity of the Zimbabwean state to reconcile and accomplish the two goals. Similarly ambiguous, if not contradictory, was the conceptualization of 'participation.' To some social groups, the concept of participation legitimized their accumulation tendencies; to others, it strengthened the case for democratization of economic and social relations.

In the last section, the main elements and internal contradictions of SAP are then outlined, together with the growing opposition to it by various social forces. It is argued that the unsustainability of the SAP project, like growth with equity before it, is now a real possibility.

THE IDEOLOGICAL CONTEXT OF ZIMBABWEAN DEVELOPMENT DISCOURSE

In his assessment of the limitations of the ideology of nationalism, Frantz Fanon identified two contradictory processes which emerge in nationalist movements on the morrow of independence. After carrying out a prolonged analysis of colonialism and its international context, intellectual elements 'begin to question their party's lack of ideology and the poverty of its tactics and strategy. They begin to question their leaders on crucial points: 'what is nationalism? . . . Independence for what?'[2] The common reaction of nationalist leadership was to isolate these elements which sought to define independence in radical social terms. The resultant ideological deficiency of the nationalist movement was subsequently defined by Cabral as one of its major weaknesses. The lack of ideology on the part of national liberation movements was basically explained by ignorance of the historical reality which these movements aspired to transform; this was one of their greatest weaknesses in the struggle against imperialism.[3]

The ideological cleavages within the Zimbabwe liberation movement have been extensively discussed elsewhere.[4] *Contra* Fanon and Cabral, however, the question in Zimbabwe was not so much the lack of an ideology, but the way in which the conservative and populist factions within the nationalist movement stifled ideological struggle and debate. In Zimbabwe, the March 11 Movement and the short-lived Zimbabwe People's Army (ZIPA) represented attempts to radicalize the ideology of the national liberation movement by subscribing to Marxism-Leninism and envisaging socialist transformation in the post-independence period. This radical ideological tendency was soon isolated and undermined by the 'old guard' conservative nationalists in both ZAPU and ZANU with the collusion of the Front-line States in the 1970s. As has been observed:

> by the beginning of 1977 the 'old guard' with its 'new language' had reasserted its position of nationalist leadership . . . The fate of the March 11 Movement and ZIPA indicates the deepening of the ideological contradictions within Zimbabwe's developing ruling class. However, their movement from the blurred divisions of populism versus elitism formed in the early years of the nationalist movement to the sharper ones inherent in the Marxist challenge did not extend significantly beyond the

intelligentsia on the road to power, and thus did not gain hegemony within the popular classes. As a result, the 'passive' fractions of the new ruling class were able to eliminate the threat and absorb the discourse of their more radical class-mates.[5]

One legacy of the marginalization of the socialist cadres in the ideological struggles was that ZANU-PF's rhetorical socialism was emptied of radical content. Another was the muddled class analysis utilized to justify 'socialist' policy in the post-independence period. A consequence of these legacies has been the weak capacity of the ruling elite to exert its hegemony on the Zimbabwe society. Nationalism has not constituted an adequate hegemonic ideology.

It was in the context of the exigencies of the national liberation struggle that socialism was adopted as a guiding ideology. However, the assumption of the petit-bourgeoisie leaders of the liberation movement was that socialist cadres and party members were largely moulded through ideological education. Tracing his evolution as a Marxist-Leninist, Mugabe explained that:

> in my own study of politics, I had done quite a lot of reading about Marxism-Leninism. When I went 'outside' to try and lead ZANU, that became an environment in which I felt – with the background our cadres then had of being associated with the Chinese and Mao Tse-Tung philosophy and his version of Marxism-Leninism – that I could develop my own thinking in a practical way. I saw Marxism-Leninism as an explanation and as a tool, but also as a most desirable state of things at the end of the day in our socio-economic system.[6]

The elements of choice and voluntarism underlay this rationale for the adoption of socialism from amongst a menu of ideologies. The notion of class contradictions is thus absent in the imperatives of struggle for socialism, as is the concept of class struggle. Lumped in one class category, for example, were intellectuals, students, urban and farm-workers, subsistence farmers and entrepreneurs. It was asserted that:

> the common characteristic of this group is that it depends directly upon the sale of labour to earn a living. Accordingly, it stands to benefit from the implementation of socialism in Zimbabwe. It thus has the potential to spearhead the process of transition to socialism.[7]

On the contrary, the class interests of these social groups are not identical; potential resistance to socialism by entrepreneurs and some intellectuals is not taken into account, for example. Mugabe's analysis goes on to combine the agrarian bourgeoisie, professionals and again entrepreneurs as distinct capitalist groups constituting the petit-bourgeoisie. Finally, a third social category consisting of 'managers of capitalist enterprises, monied public bureaucrats and professionals' is 'neither socialist nor capitalist.'[8] This muddled class analysis reveals the theoretical ambiguity, if not confusion, of what stood as the intellectual rationale for Zimbabwe's 'socialist' project.

We have observed that the ideological contestation between the young Marxist-Leninists and the conservative nationalist 'old guard' marginalized the former while the latter emptied the adopted Marxism-Leninism of its radical social content. Marxism-Leninism was reduced to rhetoric; there was more of a ritual genuflection to the objectives of socialism and egalitarianism than a serious attempt to design a development strategy in which equity and participation were integral elements. A hard-nosed negotiator, for example, summed up the ambiguities of Zimbabwean Marxism with reference to Mugabe's own ambiguous ideological position in these terms: 'his Marxism was compounded of a great deal of common sense as well as ideology.'[9]

The Marxism-Leninism appropriated from the young radicals of the March 11th Movement and ZIPA became a diluted version, if not the caricature, of the original.

If post-independence development thinking was not infused with socialism, and if the concepts of equity and participation had been evacuated of their radical context, what remained was a version of developmentalism fraught with undemocratic, authoritarian connotations. The ideology of developmentalism lays great stress on the primacy of the imperative of national development but subordinates democratization and equity to this primary imperative. Development is conceptualized as an overriding but neutral project in which class conflicts are absent. Developmentalism is an ideology of modernization: 'its logic is quite simple: we are economically backward, we need to develop very fast. In this task of development, we cannot afford the luxury of politics.'[10]

The populist undertones of developmentalism are apparent. Zimbabwe's development planning and especially the expansion of its parastatal sector were infused with a version of this developmentalism. State participation in the economy through the acquisition of shares or the total ownership of specific enterprises was viewed as enhancing that developmentalism. But this developmentalism statism also represents what Gibbon has termed as 'accumulation from above, defined as a form of state-organized and co-ordinated extraction of surplus-value, in which political means (ultimately resting on force) are used.'[11] These political means may involve unpaid participation in certain 'development' activities, state-organized resettlement schemes and regulations stipulating commodities to be produced, minimum hectarages and so on.[12] The resultant accumulation, mainly but not exclusively from peasants,

> may be in the form of state property and revenues or both. This accumulation is typically supplemented by appropriation of revenues from natural resources such as minerals and by overseas development assistance.[13]

However, this form of accumulation may be modified through the extent to which the ruling classes accumulating on this basis are internally differentiated or their accumulation sources diversified, and the degree to which accumulation from above is accompanied by accumulation from below. In Zimbabwe, a prominent role was accorded to increased state participation in the economy in the 'growth with equity' strategy. The founding of new state enterprises such as the Zimbabwe Tourist Development Corporation, Zimbabwe Mining Development Corporation, Zimbabwe State Trading Corporation, Minerals Marketing Corporation and the Zimbabwe Development Corporation (ZIDCO) was reflective of the seriousness with which the goal of increased state participation in the economy was pursued.

The proliferation of state development corporations should not be viewed as an altruistic strategy of the newly-installed state bourgeoisie to limit or pre-empt the expansion of the private sector. It can be interpreted as a conscious attempt by the state-based bourgeoisie to carve a niche for itself for its own accumulation requirements. What originally sounded as a potentially radical manifesto for participation and redistribution was appropriated and blunted by the state-based bourgeoisie for its own class material interests. Furthermore, the expanding parastatal sector provided resources and opportunities to the regime to dispense patronage and to co-opt sections of the petit-bourgeoisie.

However, it soon became clear that the capacity of the newly-installed state sector to provide adequate employment opportunities and patronage was substantially limited. The limits of clientelism (defined as a personalized relationship between two individuals or groups belonging to different classes or class fractions, based upon reciprocal exchange of goods or services, entailing the extraction of labour power, surplus, and political loyalty in return for economic, political, military and religious services[14]) were obvious.

In Zimbabwe, clientelism has resulted in widespread nepotism in recruitment and promotion practises, embezzlement of funds and corruption. We need, however, to relate clientelism to the question of hegemony. In neo-colonial states, the organization of hegemony within the power bloc differs from that in the metropolis, due to their social and spatial location and to their internal class composition.[15] In these states the national bourgeoisie is an underdeveloped one:

> the transnational bourgeoisie is [therefore] the dominant force in the economy. There are entrepreneurs, but no local class with an economic base and ideological project aiming to do what national bourgeoisies elsewhere have done: organize a national-popular bloc and develop auto-centred accumulation and industrialization. Rather, the local dominant classes are divided into many fractions . . .[16]

We would concur with the broad thrust of this argument relating to the very limited capacity of the ruling elite to exert hegemony over society. The implication of this argument is that the concept of hegemony in the Gramscian model has to be modified when applied to the social formations in Africa, because the concept assumes the separation of civil and political societies which occurred in Western European countries with the onset of the bourgeois epoch; in the former colonial societies, there has been a different process of development.[17] The concept of 'hegemony' should more correctly be restricted to the process of legitimating the exercise of state power rather than referring to the moral, intellectual, aesthetic and philosophical leadership of civil society.

However, with respect to Zimbabwe, we need to point out that there does exist a national bourgeoisie, although it should be acknowledged that a substantial proportion of this class consists of erstwhile white settlers.

The very limited capacity of the petty bourgeoisie to be hegemonic organizers would explain why the Zimbabwe ruling elite found it a formidable exercise to have its rhetorical socialism and top-down developmentalism gain currency in the broad society. We need to reflect on the context and process in which the ruling elite failed to have their 'socialism' and 'developmentalism' become hegemonic ideologies in post-independence Zimbabwe. For in addition to the internal incoherence or contradictoriness of these ideologies, both the national and international bourgeoisie were consistently opposed to concepts and strategies which smacked of socialism, even of a rhetorical or populist variety.

GROWTH WITH EQUITY AND PARTICIPATION

Initially, there was some professed commitment by the post-independence state to the concepts and objectives of 'growth with equity' and 'participation.' Although these concepts were not precisely defined nor lent radical content, they served a useful political purpose to the new state. The objectives of social equity and popular participation in the economic and political life of the newly independent were laudable. They enshrined the possibilities of redressing colonial legacies of glaring social inequalities and undemocratic political structures. An economic policy statement of the Zimbabwe Government outlined the rationale for equity in these terms:

> economic exploitation of the majority by the few, the grossly uneven infrastructure and productive development of the rural and urban and distribution sectors, the unbalanced levels of development within and among sectors and the consequent grossly inequitable pattern of income distribution and of benefits to the overwhelming majority of this country, stand as a serious indictment of our society.[18]

The barriers to equity and participation were defined as the 'exploitation of the majority,' 'uneven development,' 'inequitable income distribution,' 'predominant foreign economic control' and 'historic dispossession of land and other assets.'

The primary objectives of the growth with equity policy were spelt out as the achievement of a sustained high rate of economic growth, the raising of incomes and standards of living 'of all of our people,' the development and restructuring of the economy in ways which would promote rural development and the creation of high levels of employment 'in all sectors and at all levels of skills.' Furthermore, the policy objectives included the provision of such social services as housing, health and education to lower-income groups, and reform of fiscal and monetary systems to achieve greater equity and efficiency. The more radical sounding objectives were 'the ending of imperialist exploitation' and 'the democratization of the work-place' in all sectors by encouraging worker participation in decision-making from the shopfloor upwards. These relatively ambitious goals, if achieved, would have resulted in the establishment of a society 'founded on socialist, democratic and egalitarian principles,' according to the government policy statement.

Pressed to define more clearly what growth with equity entailed, the leading architect of the policy remarked: 'our development strategy goes beyond the mere increase in the material wealth of society. Equity in the distribution of wealth and income is one if the cornerstones of our economic policy.'[19] Not only were the modalities of achieving equity not spelt out but the question of the compatibility between economic growth and equity was not addressed. The assumption that a simultaneous pursuit and achievement of growth and equity were possible in the Zimbabwean context proved somewhat naive. Other assumptions understandably more difficult to understand twelve years later, were that capitalist growth could usher in socialism, and that foreign investment could finance the economic modernization necessary for the transition to socialism.

If economic growth and equity proved impossible to achieve simultaneously through this ill-defined development strategy, what progress was made towards the goal of 'participation?' In this there was a similar lack of clarity and consistency in conceptual definition. One notion of participation related to involvement by the national bourgeoisie and state in the ownership and control of the economy.[20] Such participation was presumed to act as a counterweight to the dominance of international capital in the economy. Yet the sought participation was more reflective of economic nationalism than a means of ensuring involvement of social classes apart from the national bourgeoisie in the control and ownership of the economy. Still less was the envisaged 'participation' necessarily conducive to the attainment of equity.

Yet another notion of participation – and a relatively radical one – related to the 'democratization' of work-place relations through enhanced worker participation at all levels and the establishment of democratic and profitable cooperative enterprises. Voluntary popular participation and democratic procedures were stated to be imperative criteria for state support for cooperatives. It was envisaged that small and medium-sized enterprises in urban and rural areas would be 'cooperatively owned and run, thereby extending socialist and popular democratic participation in the ownership and management of the nation's resources.'[21]

In order to better understand the theoretical subscription of the Zimbabwean state to the objectives of equity and participation we need to set it within a broader international context. It was a context in which major international financial and aid institutions subscribed to these concepts without drawing the potentially radical logical conclusions that would have flowed from a consistent pursuit of the objectives. The World Bank, for example, referred to the imperative for the next generation in Africa to build sustainable and equitable growth:

> sustainable, because care must be taken to protect the productive capacity of the environment, and equitable, because this is a precondition both for political stability and ultimately for sustainable growth.[22]

This postponement into the future is a tacit admission that growth did not necessarily reduce poverty nor provide food security (in short, equity). In fact, the report admits that it had been a mistake to divert attention in the 1980s from programmes to meet basic needs of populations and goes on to suggest that future development strategies of African countries 'needed specifically to address poverty alleviation and better income distribution as issues in their own right.'[23]

Yet in spite of its seemingly renewed commitment to 'sustainable growth,' 'equity' and 'basic needs' it is difficult to see the consistency in World Bank programmes which address these issues. The structural adjustment programmes (SAPs) which it designs and sponsors in most African states have actually undermined the possibilities of attainment of these objectives. In reality, the genuflection to 'equity' and 'participation' do not amount to much more than lip-service to a political vocabulary which camouflages a development agenda for unbridled free-market capitalism.

Similarly, the endorsement of 'participation' by international development institutions has not stretched much beyond fashionable rhetoric. Schmitz has observed that the orthodox discourse on participation tends to skip over the critical linkage to equity as a primary determinant of the capacity of people to participate in more than superficial ways. For Schmitz, the crucial issues of who participates when, how and to what effect, are enormously important to the depth and durability of democratization.[24] The Arusha Conference of 1990 spelt out in more forthright terms what 'popular participation' should entail. It should entail the empowerment of people:

> to effectively involve themselves in creating the structures and in designing policies and programmes which serve the interests of all as well as to effectively contribute to the development process and share equitably in its benefits. Therefore, there must be an opening up of the political process to accommodate freedom of opinions, tolerate differences, accept consensus on issues as well as ensure the effective participation of the people and their organisations and associations.[25]

Popular participation is both a means and an end. As an instrument of development, popular participation provides the driving force for collective commitment for the determination 'of people-based development processes' and as an end in itself, it is 'the fundamental right of the people to fully and effectively participate in the determination of the decisions which affect their lives at all levels and at all times.' This radical definition of 'participation' was absent in the Zimbabwean state's policy statements.

In the Zimbabwean context, the concept of participation implied different objectives and processes for the bourgeoisie on the one hand and for the working and peasant classes on the other. As the years went by, the gap between the requirements for accumulation and participation would also grow wider, as would class polarization. Like equity, 'participation' became a casualty of the exigencies of an accumulation model in which accommodation with both international and national capital was an imperative. Revealingly, the official discourse on equity and participation did not permeate beyond the bureaucracy and the circle of political speechwriters. The discourse was not transformed into a popular discourse; there was no wide dissemination of the objectives of equity and participation nor debate on the modalities of achieving them.

IDEOLOGICAL SHIFT AND CHANGE OF DEVELOPMENT STRATEGY

In this section I seek to explain the pressures which contributed to an ideological shift, and abandonment of a development strategy hinged on social redistribution, towards the end of the 1980s. We will see that in the process any lingering pretence to subscribe to 'equity,' 'participation' and 'socialism' diminished to make way for the structural adjustment paradigm sponsored by international financial institutions, principally the World Bank and International Monetary Fund.

What specific form did the ideological shift take? It was basically a public renunciation of 'socialism.' By the late 1980s, fractions of the emergent bourgeoisie within the ruling elite sought a guarantee of their material interests in a shift from the original objectives of 'socialism' and 'egalitarianism.' The Senior Minister of Finance and Economic Development remarked that 'socialism could not work' in Zimbabwe[26] (some believe he had thought this ever since 1980). Another cabinet minister with extensive business interests criticized 'adherence to nonsensical and bankrupt ideologies' (principally socialism) adding that 'there must be no doubt as to the only ideology that works. Everyone must embrace pragmatism.'[27] Other senior ZANU-PF figures also pointedly advised emergent indigenous entrepreneurs to accumulate: 'since there are no black capitalists, we are asking you to go out and become capitalists.'

Finally, President Mugabe himself acknowledged the widespread denunciation of socialism within the upper hierarchy of ZANU-PF. In a widely publicized statement, he seemed to prepare the party for the eventual renunciation of socialism by his apologetic assessment of the party's long-standing ideological ambiguity:

> we have not, in our possession, as a party, a clear definition of socialism as we would want to see it applied in our society . . . Our former parties, ZANU-PF and PF-ZAPU were established and developed in an environment which, on the one hand, was national and on the other, was international. But as the parties established themselves externally and began relating to socialist countries, the Soviet Union and China, being the largest and most influential of them, they not only derived the many thousands of tons of weaponry for the national struggle but their political ideology as well.[28]

Mugabe argued that policies relating to land and social redistribution were 'nationalist,' not socialist-oriented.

The ideological revisionism, facilitated by the débâcle in Eastern Europe and the former Soviet Union in 1989–1991, is thus complete. In Zimbabwe, the boycott (or investment sanctions) by international financial institutions (IFIs) strengthened the hands of forces which championed economic liberalization. Lingering pretence and genuflection to 'socialism' disappeared.

There is, of course, need to place this ideological change within a broader context. This is a context in which a changing balance of forces – international and national – contributed to increased pressures on the post-independence state to change its development path. Let us briefly examine the roles and changing interests of international and domestic capital in the shift of economic policy in the late 1980s. First, there was concerted opposition by both international and domestic capital against the relatively large social expenditure (principally on education, health and peasant re-settlement) by the state. The corporate interests organized in such influential bodies as the Commercial Farmers' Union (CFU) and the Confederation of Zimbabwe Industries (CZI) decried the rationale for such policies and their substantial expenditure. However, sections of the intelligentsia suggested that in spite of these critiques the ruling party was in fact allied with such interests.

Through the policy of reconciliation, (the ZANU-PF leadership) built economic alliances with the ex-colonial settler bourgeoisie and the international capitalists.[29] The rhetoric of socialism and equity could not camouflage the hidden agenda and accumulation project of the acquisitive wing within the ZANU-PF leadership which from the end of 1987 was enlarged through the merger with PF-ZAPU.

Although ZANU-PF sought to play down the growing wealth of its leadership, it was generally known that some of its figures had become landlords through their purchase of farms, while others had invested in commerce and industry. Some reports convincingly demonstrated that ZANU-PF itself possessed a major entrepreneurial firm, the Zimbabwe Development Corporation (ZIDCO) with interests in vehicles, duty-free merchandise, retail operations and the production of steel products and blankets.[30] ZIDCO, on whose board sat two ministers, exports building materials to SADCC countries, has contracts to supply government ministries including that of defence, and supplies text-books and stationery to schools in Zimbabwe. This 'enterprising' party firm is estimated to generate an annual turnover of Z$350 million. The origins of the firm have been traced back to 1979 when M and S Syndicate was established as an investment vehicle for the Muzenda and Sumbureru families.[31] Additional institutions through which the state-and party-based bourgeoisie accumulate include the Development Trust of Zimbabwe, established in the late 1980s under the chairmanship of Vice-President Nkomo, the former leader of PF-ZAPU. Several ministers are board members of the Development Trust of Zimbabwe (DTZ) which seeks to invest not only in agriculture but also in commerce and industry. Revealingly, both ZIDCO and DTZ have collaborative ventures with international corporations such as Lonrho.

On the international side of the equation, the IFIs, principally the International Monetary Fund, criticised social expenditure as being detrimental to the 'productive sector.' As early as 1981, the IMF was urging the Zimbabwe government to accept its usual package of conditions, including substantial cut-backs on social services and other distribution measures. By early 1983, Zimbabwe had reduced some subsidies, including those on food, and devalued its currency by twenty percent, as part of a package involving a $375 million loan from the IMF.[32] However, as IMF pressure for further changes such as the liberalization of foreign-exchange and import controls increased; so did resistance from the Zimbabwean state. It was not yet ready to completely abandon its social democratic face:

> eventually, as internal resistance to cuts in government spending grew, and there were no signs of an improvement in the balance of payments, direct action to reduce outflows was taken in 1984 by the freezing of dividends and profit remittances, by acquiring the pool of external securities, and other measures. This naturally produced an immediate suspension of the IMF programme which, despite further negotiations and the eventual restitution of profit remittances during 1986, was not restored.[33]

The opposition to Zimbabwe's post-independence economic and social policies was quite concerted, and that to its populist 'socialism' and 'developmentalism' virulent. Thus the bourgeoisie was uncompromisingly tough towards an ideological position which, nevertheless, did not threaten the capitalist accumulation model; and towards social redistribution measures, some of which (such as human resources development) were congruent with capitalist growth. There was keen interest within the bourgeoisie to rein in the 'wayward' small country of 10 million so that it could conform to the broad agenda of international capital: in that process, it was required to renounce its inchoate 'socialist' ideology and redistribution programme. The post-independence regime was caught in the 'worst of both worlds:' its diluted socialism and incoherent development strategy failed to attract the much-needed foreign investment. The sustainability of its economic growth and social programmes were placed in doubt.

This is the broad background against which the Zimbabwean regime made a decisive policy shift in the second half of the 1980s. Although the opposition by the national and international bourgeoisie was critical to the shift, there had also emerged other internal social forces (sections within the state-based bourgeoisie, as we have seen) which were also supportive of a shift from populist 'socialism' and redistribution. It is instructive here to observe that a leading architect of post-independence economic policy, Finance Minister Bernard Chidzero, has periodized the process of accumulation since 1980 into four phases.[34]

The first phase, between 1980 and 1982, was 'a honeymoon period' which represented a change of focus from the liberation struggle to reconstruction and development. Minimum wages were introduced, as were controls over prices and other aspects of the economy. There was also an intensification of controls inherited from the Smith regime.

The second phase (1983–1985) was:

an exasperating one which coincided with nearly three years of drought, the sharp drop in commodity prices and recession. We borrowed everything during that period to sustain our programme, in order to maintain the normal function of government. And that created problems for us.[35]

During this phase, there was a significant squeeze on incomes and tighter controls on the remittance of profits.

In the following phase, in 1986–87, there was instituted a policy review against the background of increased unemployment, rising production costs and debt servicing. A study team commissioned by the government concluded that:

we had to do certain things to generate more wealth. We had to attract investment, domestic investment as well. People feared nationalisation of everything, in the light of socialist ideology. Our policies were not conducive to profit-making because the prices were very low, and the profit margin was being eroded . . . Looking at the budget, government spending was too much, where 43 per cent of recurrent expenditure was on salaries of government employees . . . Furthermore, patterns between productive investment and expenditure on social services was frightening. So we decided on structural adjustment, and this marked the fourth phase.[36]

The accumulation crisis in the mid-1980s was the outcome of the combination of domestic and external structural constraints, policy mistakes and climatic vagaries. The causes of the crisis were decidedly not simple. However, incoherent development planning, the lack of a balance between expenditure on productive and social sectors and the half-hearted pursuit of equity and participation certainly contributed to the crisis. Opposition from entrenched domestic forces and international capital (and by the countries from which the latter originated) included the withholding of investment, a form of an ideologically motivated economic embargo. This compounded the crisis.

However, even within the ruling elite (concentrated in the ZANU-PF party and government), there were discernible divisions on ideology and development strategy. Some fractions within the petty bourgeoisie which were heavily represented in this elite came out clearly and strongly against the lip-service to socialism and to redistribution policies in the second half of the 1980s. These sections of the petty bourgeoisie were in the process of transformation into a bourgeoisie proper through utilization of opportunities made possible by access to state resources. Their acquisitive tendencies contributed to a stalemate on the terms of a Leadership Code for ZANU-PF leaders which sought to restrain those tendencies.

The lengths to which this emergent bourgeoisie (including five cabinet ministers) went to exploit accumulation opportunities provided through the state were evidenced in their profiteering from the car racket known as the 'Willowgate scandal' in 1988. Cars bought by the cabinet ministers from a state-owned assembly plant were later resold at high prices, fetching them substantial profits.[37] But even as early as 1982 and 1983, personal aggrandizement by some politicians had provoked public demonstrations by women and students against their proclivities to corruption. In 1988 and 1989, the critique against the acquisitive tendencies of the politicians by students and trade unions became much sharper. The student movement condemned what it termed 'monopolistic politics of domination, corruption and petit bourgeois primitive accumulation.'[38]

THE ECONOMIC STRUCTURAL ADJUSTMENT PROGRAMME (ESAP) MODEL

In the preceding section, we observed that the political leadership's diagnosis of Zimbabwe's economic crisis in the late 1980s convinced it that adjustment measures were the only viable option. The ESAP model which Zimbabwe began to implement in 1990 bore the familiar hallmarks of SAP measures being enforced in more than 40 African countries at the behest of the World Bank and the IMF. These measures include substantial cuts of public expenditure (including social services), devaluation, trade liberalization, removal of subsidies, de-regulation of prices and labour controls and the privatization of state-owned enterprises. The agenda of the IFIs lends credence to the argument that the free-market orientation of adjustment programmes benefits international capital in general to the extent that its operations require mobility and freedom from potentially hostile nationalist states.[39] The main consideration behind ESAP-like programmes is the integration of individual economies into a capitalist world economy based on 'free markets.' Thus, the object of Zimbabwe's ESAP is to incorporate it more firmly into this global capitalism.

The proponents of ESAP argued that it had become imperative because overall economic growth and the gross domestic product (GDP) at 2.7 per cent per annum lagged behind population growth in the 1980s. Export growth increased by only 3.4 per cent per annum in real terms, and imports had declined by 0.4 per cent also in real terms between 1980 and 1988.[40] Furthermore, the fiscal deficit of the central government was in excess of 10 per cent of the GDP during much of the 1980s. In sum, the principal cause of the sluggish economic growth was low investments in the productive sectors of the economy. Thus, it was argued that in order to create a favourable investment climate, risks associated with fiscal deficits, uncertainties and 'high costs' stemming from the 'relatively high cost' of doing business in Zimbabwe's regulated business environment due to price controls, labour regulations and investment control procedures, should be removed.[41] The objective of ESAP measures centred on this opening up of the economy to market forces. Once this process was underway, it was claimed that faster economic growth and therefore higher employment levels and incomes would ensue. The growth target of the ESAP programme, which runs from 1990 to 1995, was 5 per cent per annum.

Here it is necessary to show the contradictory outcomes of Zimbabwean ESAP measures to date. First, the empirical evidence refutes the major argument that ESAP would usher in a greater growth of 5 per cent per annum in 1990–95 as against 4.8 per cent between 1985 and 1990. Second, the arguments for an unregulated opening up of the economy to market forces are contested. Full-blown trade liberalization, especially when its associated measures are fully adopted in 1995, has the likely potential of opening up the sluice-gates to a flood of non-essential consumer goods over and above the intended inputs for industry, thereby worsening the balance of payments position and outweighing any benefits to be derived from increased exports.[42] Indeed, evidence emerging from the first year of the implementation of SAP suggested speculative over-importation of goods under the Open General Import Licence (OGIL) system.[43] Zimbabwe incurred a huge trade deficit during the 1991/92 financial year; the OGIL bills have turned out to be three times higher than the government's initial estimates.[44] The country's capacity to provide adequate foreign exchange allocations for imports, especially capital goods for the modernization of industry, has therefore become questionable.

It is useful also to make a brief observation of the differentiated impact of the measures on various economic sectors. The conditionalities woven into ESAP affect different sets of producers in different ways: some become beneficiaries of the programme while others lose out. In the first one and a half years of its implementation, the Zimbabwean SAP has entailed substantial price de-regulation, interest rate increases, devaluation and import liberalization. Some categories such as the mining industry and cash crop production (mainly tobacco and horticulture rather than food production) have been beneficiaries of devaluation while other sets of producers have been forced to shelve their investment projects due to the substantially increased costs of devaluation and interest rates hikes. The inflationary spiral set in motion by the combination of fiscal and monetary measures has had a dampening effect on social consumption: housing and basic wage goods have escalated in cost. These contradictory outcomes appear to be inherent in most SAPs being implemented in Africa. As has been argued cogently elsewhere in Sub-Saharan Africa, indiscriminate import liberalization has been partly responsible for deindustrialization, improved incentives for primary products have led to competitive supply expansion and consequently falling world prices, a fall in investment has accompanied adjustment policies reducing growth potential, and cuts in public expenditure invariably affect long-term development prospects (health, education and training), research and development in priority areas and infrastructure.[45]

RESPONSE OF SOCIAL MOVEMENTS TO THE POLICY SHIFT AND ESAP

Let us now consider the response of major elements within civil society – in this case, social movements – to the shift from concerns with 'equity,' 'participation' and 'socialism' to the free-market strategy of ESAP. I begin by examining the response of the labour movement.

Broadly speaking, the labour movement has had uneasy relations with the post-independence state given the latter's vacillation between benign paternalism, coercive measures, and co-optative objectives.[46]

Instructively, here has existed a thread of continuity in the labour movement's ideological position. Whereas in the first few years after independence, the organized labour movement broadly endorsed what existed as the 'socialist' policy of the regime, sharp criticism of the latter's ideological inconsistency began to be made in the second half of the 1980s. The leadership of the Zimbabwe Congress of Trade Unions (ZCTU) challenged ZANU-PF's 'Marxist-Leninist credentials.'[47] The continued espousal of 'socialism' by the labour movement and rejection of ESAP put the former and the ZANU-PF government at ideological loggerheads. The government is viewed as having been converted to 'free-market' capitalism and to have ceded national control of the economy to international financial institutions.

The labour movement's critique of ESAP has been as sharp as its criticism of the party. It contends that ESAP has substantially eroded workers' rights, especially employment security. Under the ESAP regime an estimated total of 50,000 workers were liable to retrenchment in both the public and private sectors. The collective response of the labour movement at the abandonment of any pretence at socialist-oriented redistribution policies and ESAP induced job losses has been one of increasing anger and alarm.[48] The hefty price increases on basic wage foods as a consequence of price de-regulation, removal of subsidies and the spiralling of inflation have led to a substantial erosion of income. In an open letter to President Mugabe, the ZCTU has asserted that:

> workers and their families have little property or financial reserves to buffer them against economic hardships taking place. We are concerned the ESAP does not have the consensus amongst the affected social partners needed if it is to proceed with a common understanding. The lack of public support around ESAP will undermine its progress.[49]

The ZCTU called for a national economic convention aimed at building national consensus for an economic strategy which, unlike ESAP, took the social interests of labour into account.

A spate of industrial action in such sectors as transport, telecommunications, and the public services in 1991 and 1992 confirmed the disenchantment of the working-class and sections of the middle class with the new labour regime under ESAP.[50] Women and contract workers bear the heavier brunt of retrenchment in such sectors as clothing, and leather industries as employers take advantage of liberalized labour laws.[51] Increasingly, the labour movement believes that its economic struggles require an explicit political expression. The labour movement, it has been argued, cannot afford 'to shy away from politics since by its very nature it has to fight both government policies and employers' actions.'[52]

The intelligentsia, especially its student component, is another social force which has become increasingly critical of the regime's development model. The student movement has played a prominent role in the opposition against the one-party state and legislation which undermines academic freedom and university autonomy. The alliance between national and international capital and the inability of the regime to resolve demands for equity through land redistribution, control and management of the economy and the betterment of the material conditions of the working class and peasantry has been attacked.[53] The intelligentsia is directly affected by ESAP measures which have resulted in shrinking job opportunities in both the public and private sectors and deteriorating standards of living. The broad thrust of ESAP has resulted in the alienation rather than the cooptation of articulate sections of the middle class, especially the intelligentsia. Professional associations such as those representing teachers and doctors have begun to develop ties with the organized labour movement.

There has been a notable expansion in the numbers of students receiving tertiary education. In 1991, two additional universities were established in Bulawayo and Mutare. The University of Zimbabwe itself had witnessed its student population treble to about 10,000 in the late 1980s, creating an enormous strain on services within the university. A national student organization to which different university and polytechnic student unions could affiliate was formed and called the Zimbabwe National Student's Union (ZINASU). ZINASU has made forceful statements regarding the handling of student demonstrations by state authorities; it has been scathing about such police methods as the tear-gassing of students. During the May Day celebrations in 1991, 1992 and 1993, students participated in demonstrations organized by workers and gave solidarity speeches.

The hardships associated with ESAP and the unabated rise in unemployment have dented the ideology of capitalism; the capitalist system is increasingly viewed as incapable of sustaining conditions of growth and putting basic commodities within the reach of most people. Nevertheless, the labour and student movements, in spite of their radical critique, have not succeeded in constructing a coherent and credible alternative ideology. There exists a clear need for a counter-hegemonic ideology. The challenge of mobilizing workers and students in a counter-hegemonic project relates to the construction of an alternative ideology which incorporates the struggles and aspirations of not only these movements but those of other social classes.

Let us now consider the role of other social forces – the cooperatives, liberation war veterans, and peasants – whose critique of the regime's economic policies is steadily getting sharper. The proposals on cooperatives contained in the 'growth with equity' policy statement were conveniently ignored by the regime. In addition to the basic problems of policy and infrastructural constraints, the cooperative movement strives to hold itself together in the ideologically less favourable context of ESAP:

> the coops find themselves having to fight even harder to keep pace with the demands of ESAP. Whatever this brings us, we as a cooperative movement still have to be convinced that the programme accommodates us as weak enterprises.[54]

As the initial equivocal commitment to cooperatives has receded in this era of economic liberalization, there has been a cutback on the already marginal budget allocated to them. The ideological thrust is supportive of individualism in small-scale capitalist enterprises as against cooperatives espousing a 'socialist' model. There are, however, indications that the cooperative movement finds its future increasingly tied up with necessary linkages with the labour movement in the common opposition against the ESAP strategy.

The liberation war veterans were a staunch support base of the ruling ZANU-PF party, but in recent years they have expressed a sharp critique of the party's ideological *volte-face*. They formed the Zimbabwe National Liberation War Veterans Association in 1991. Their critique claims that ZANU-PF has accommodated 'opportunists' and 'bourgeois elements' who have in turn 'systematically destroyed the party from within while the people who fought for the liberation of this country watch on the sidelines.'[55] The critique extended to blocked access to jobs, resources and training facilities for the veterans in post-independence Zimbabwe. The problem of blocked mobility is experienced by millions of other Zimbabweans for whom some commitment and progress towards equity and participation might have provided some hope.

It is much more difficult to assess the peasantry's reaction to the policy reversal from populist 'socialism' to unabashed capitalism under ESAP. It is the least well-organized social class and its political weight has weakened in spite of its critical role during the national liberation struggle. However, the ripple effects of ESAP have begun to provoke criticism of the regime, especially in relation to spiralling prices of basic consumption goods and of inputs such as fertilizer and seed. Peasants are also restive over cost-recovery measures in education and health. Recent elections primaries in the provinces indicate massive apathy but also a swing away from ZANU's official candidates to those with roots and proven standing in local areas.[56] In the 1990 elections (before ESAP was launched), the bulk of the ZANU-PF vote came from the peasantry. That support may be beginning to wane.

CONCLUSION

This paper has provided a somewhat pessimistic account of the prospects of a small developing society veering from an orthodox development paradigm defined by international financial institutions and development agencies. Neither the lip-service to 'socialist-oriented' goals of 'equity' and 'participation' nor the swing to economic liberalization seem to offer a feasible strategy for sustainable national development. As we observed in the paper, the thrust towards redistribution was soon deflected by limited resources, not to speak of the sustained opposition from national and international capital to socialist-inclined measures, however innocuous might have been. The projected growth rates under ESAP are unlikely to be met.

For the first time since Zimbabwe's independence, a broad coalition of social forces has emerged to oppose government policies, resulting in the Mugabe government encountering its most serious legitimacy crisis. The loss of legitimacy, like that of hegemony, is speeded up in conditions of an economic crisis. A crisis of subsistence has the potential to undermine the obedience of dominated classes, for:

the maintenance of clientelist relations and of the persuasive capacity of lineage-type discourse becomes difficult when patrons have nothing to offer, because their resources (funds, jobs, land, houses, etc.) are exhausted. Likewise, clientelist systems can break down from excessive exactions by the dominant classes.[57]

The patronage base of the ruling ZANU-PF party steadily shrinks as liberalization measures undermine the size of the public sector.

The current global conjuncture is unfavourable to development strategies which deviate from those which accord a decisive role to 'market forces.' Attempts by small developing societies such as Zimbabwe to place some accent on populist measures of social distribution and pacts with labour become an object of censure by the IFIs which wield leverage as a source of substantial amounts of capital and balance of payments support.

Zimbabwe's short-lived flirtation with populist-laden 'socialism' gives credence to the somewhat pessimistic prognosis of similar 'socialist' experiments in the developing world:

> the combination of these elements – weak material base, a small working class, petty bourgeois leadership – usually introduces strong tension between the democratic dimension of the revolutionary process and the urgent need for efficacy and control, usually aggravated by economic pressures from the former colonial and imperialist powers.[58]

A major source of challenge to the development paradigm whose discourse extols 'market forces' are those social forces which least benefit from economic restructuring. Such restructuring has resulted in retrenchment, falls in income and living standards, and diminished access to basic social services such as education and health. The crystallization of the movements of protest and critique against the painful austerity measures built into ESAP-like programmes provide ground for hope that an alternative discourse (however unsystematized at this stage) of social initiative and democratic participation is emerging. It is to this discourse of critique, protest and democratic participation that progressive intellectuals should show sensitivity and contribute.

Notes

1. David Moore, 'The Crisis in Developmental Discourse and the Concepts of Sustainability, Equity and Participation,' Paper Presented to the Canadian Political Science Association Annual Meeting, Queen's University, Kingston, Ontario, 2–4 June 1991.
2. Frantz Fanon, *The Wretched of the Earth* (Harmondsworth: Penguin, 1963).
3. Amilcar Cabral, *Unity and Struggle: Speeches and Writings* (London: Heinemann, 1980).
4. Andre Astrow, *Zimbabwe: A Revolution that Lost Its Way?* (London: Zed Press, 1983); David Moore, 'The Ideological Formation of the Zimbabwean Ruling Class,' *Journal of Southern African Studies*, 17, 3 (September 1991).
5. Moore, op. cit., pp. 494–5.
6. Quoted in Michael Charlton, *The Last Colony in Africa: Diplomacy and the Independence of Rhodesia* (Oxford: Basil Blackwell, 1990) pp. 36–7.

7. Robert Mugabe, 'The Unity Accord: Its Promise for the Future,' in C. S. Banana (ed.), *Turmoil and Tenacity: Zimbabwe 1980–1990* (Harare: College Press, 1990) p. 345.
8. Loc. cit.
9. Lord Carrington, the chair of the British sponsored Lancaster House negotiations of December 1979 which paved the way for Zimbabwean majority-rule and the elections of April 1980, quoted in Charlton, op. cit., p. 119.
10. A. Kiondo, 'The Nature of Economic Reform in Tanzania,' in H. Campbell and H. Stein (eds), *The IMF and Tanzania* (Harare: SAPES, 1991).
11. Peter Gibbon, 'Structural Adjustment and Pressures towards Multi-partyism in Sub-Saharan Africa,' in P. Gibbon, Y. Bangura, and A. Ofstard (eds), *Authoritarianism, Democracy and Adjustment: The Politics of Economic Reform in Africa* (Uppsala: Scandinavian Institute of African Studies, 1992).
12. Ibid., p. 164.
13. Loc. cit.
14. Craig Charney, 'Political Power and Social Class in the Neo-Colonial African State,' *Review of African Political Economy*, 38 (1987), p. 52.
15. Loc. cit.
16. Ibid., p. 57.
17. Issa Shivji, 'The Politics of Liberalization in Tanzania: Notes on the Crisis of Ideological Hegemony,' in H. Campbell and H. Stein (eds), *The IMF and Tanzania* (Harare: SAPES, 1991).
18. Zimbabwe Government, *Growth with Equity: An Economic Policy Statement* (Harare: Government Printers, 1981), p. 1.
19. Bernard Chidzero, 'Development Overview,' *Report on Conference Proceedings, Zimbabwe Conference on Reconstruction and Development* (Harare: Government Printer, 1981), p. 53.
20. Zimbabwe Government, op. cit.
21. Ibid.
22. World Bank, *Sub-Saharan Africa: From Crisis to Sustainable Growth* (Washington: World Bank, 1989).
23. Ibid.
24. Gerald Schmitz, this volume.
25. See the resolution contained in the Arusha Conference Report on Participation and Democracy, February 1990, Arusha, Tanzania.
26. *Sunday Mail* (Harare), 28 April 1991.
27. Minister Zvogbo, as quoted in the *Financial Gazette* (Harare), 30 May 1991.
28. Robert Mugabe, 'President Mugabe's Address to the ZANU-PF Central Committee in March 1991,' *Financial Gazette*, 28 March 1991.
29. Kempton Makamure, 'The Struggle for Democracy and Democratization,' in I. Mandaza and L. M. Sachikonye (eds), *The One-Party State and Democracy* (Harare: SAPES, 1991), p. 106.
30. 'ZANU-PF's Capitalist Empire,' *Horizon* (Harare), April 1992.
31. Ibid.
32. Colin Stoneman, 'The Economy: Recognizing the Reality,' in C. Stoneman (ed.), *Zimbabwe's Prospects* (London: Macmillan, 1988), p. 56.
33. Loc. cit.
34. Bernard Chidzero, 'Interview,' *Southern Africa Political and Economic Monthly* (Harare, April 1992).

35. Ibid.
36. Ibid.
37. Sandura Commission, *Report of the Commission of Inquiry Into the Distribution of Vehicles Under the Chairmanship of Justice Sandura* (Harare: Government Printer, 1989).
38. A. Mutumbara, 'The One-Party State, Socialism and Democratic Struggles in Zimbabwe: A Student Perspective,' in I. Mandaza and L. M. Sachikonye (eds), *The One-Party State and Democracy*, p. 139.
39. Lawrence Harris, 'Conception of IMF's Role in Africa,' in P. Lawrence (ed.), *World Recession and the Food Crisis* (London: Review of African Political Economy and James Currey, 1986).
40. Zimbabwe Government, *Second Five-Year National Development Plan* (Harare: Government Printer, 1991), pp. 1–2.
41. Ibid.
42. Lionel Cliffe, 'Were they Pushed or Did They Jump?', *Southern African Report* (March 1991).
43. *Financial Gazette*, 26 September 1991.
44. *Financial Gazette*, 19 December 1991.
45. F. Stewart, 'Are Adjustment Policies in Africa Consistent With Long-run Development Needs?', *Development Policy Review*, 9 (1991), pp. 427–8.
46. We have assessed the historical dimension of the initial fragmentation, subsequent reorganization and growing assertiveness of the labour movement elsewhere at some length. See L. M. Sachikonye, 'State, Capital and Unions,' in I. Mandaza (ed.), *The Political Economy of Transition: Zimbabwe 1980–1986*, 1 (Dakar: Codresia, 1986), and 'The New Labour Regime Under SAP in Zimbabwe,' *Southern African Economic and Political Monthly*, 5, 7 (1992).
47. M. Tsvangirai, 'Workers Should Not Be Neutral,' *Southern African Political and Economic Monthly* (September 1990).
48. *The Herald*, 2 May 1992.
49. M. Tsvangirai's letter as quoted in *The Worker* (March 1993).
50. L. M. Sachikonye, op. cit., 1992, and 'An Industrial Relations Crisis?', *Southern Africa Political and Economic Monthly*, 3, 11 (1990).
51. M. Pswarayi, 'The Effects of ESAP on Working Women,' *Journal of Social Change and Development*, 28 (1992).
52. *The Worker*, 4 March 1993.
53. Mutumbara, op. cit.
54. R. Gwebu, 'ESAP: Will Coops Survive?', *The Vanguard* (Harare), February–March 1992.
55. *Sunday Mail* (Harare), April 26, 1992.
56. *Sunday Times* (Harare), 3 May 1992.
57. Charney, op. cit.
58. C. M. Ramos, 'Is Socialism Still an Alternative for the Third World?', *Monthly Review*, 42, 3 (1990), p. 103.

7 NGOs and the Problematic Discourse of Participation: Cases from Costa Rica
Laura Macdonald

INTRODUCTION

In both North and South, skepticism about the capacity and willingness of both state agencies and international organizations composed of states to address people's needs has become widespread across the political spectrum. Emphasis on the role of 'civil society,' of 'new social movements,' 'participation' and 'participatory action research' among students and practitioners of development reflects this anti-statist perspective.[1] However, insufficient critical attention has been paid to the equally problematic character of many 'non-state actors.' Many have pointed to international non-governmental organizations (NGOs) as practitioners of another type of development work, in which grassroots participation flourishes, so that the poor are able to define what they receive and how. NGOs are thus presented, and present themselves, as an *alternative* model to the hegemonic ideology and methodology of the official 'aid regime.'[2] Judith Tendler refers to this belief in their own superior participatory qualities as one of the 'articles of faith' of NGOs.[3]

Because of their small-scale, grassroots, 'people-to-people' character, then, NGO projects are frequently viewed as highly participatory phenomena, almost by definition. For example, Robin Poulton outlines a simple equation which purports to represent the 'NGO model of the eighties':

Basic Needs + Participatory Development = Community Development
(over a period of 25 years)[4]

Poulton also offers a typical description of the merits of the NGO model as opposed to development strategies adopted by state actors:

Against 'top-down' urban-designed projects, NGOs are using participatory 'bottom-up' methods which pass decision-making progressively to

the people. Against the centralised models of bureaucracy, NGOs de-
centralise responsibility to local groups and community associations.
Against a short-term project approach, the NGO methodology is evolutionary and long-term. Building self-reliant village organisations is a
long, slow process: but they are and will be organisations of the people,
which can work for developing people.[5]

There are some merits to this argument. In general, most NGO projects
do involve some form of citizen participation, official agencies have been
prompted to include more forms of participation in their development
work because of the NGO example, and some NGOs are indeed very
committed to giving Third World peoples control over their own process
of development. However, to characterize NGO assistance as an inherently more participatory alternative to other forms of aid overlooks the
fact that most NGOs are dependent on state funding, are heavily influenced by (as well as influencing) official development bodies, and developed
historically as a useful complement to official development assistance.
NGO agents thus have more autonomy than most agents of bilateral or
multilateral programmes, but this autonomy is limited, and its limits are
often left unexplored. The rosy picture of NGOs also ignores the fact that
participation is a contested, problematic concept which has many different
meanings and possible outcomes.

In order to explore these issues, this paper will discuss the various
approaches to participation adopted in three NGO projects in Costa Rica
in the late 1980s. These cases illustrate the problematic nature of participation and suggest some of the factors which need to be taken into account
when attempting to implement it. I will argue that the degree and form of
participation promoted by NGOs will vary depending on the following
factors: i) the NGO's approach to participation; ii) the influence of international actors (either state donors or international NGOs), and iii) the
nature of linkages between the NGO and local groups or social movements.

While these different elements may in practice be combined in diverse
ways, two main 'ideal types' of NGOs can be identified in the Central
American context:

a)   'Mainstream NGOs,' often associated in Central America with the
     United States Agency for International Development (AID). These
     are characterized by:

     i)   Instrumental participation, in which beneficiaries' participa-
           tion is valued primarily for its contribution to the efficient

implementation of a project; participants do not have real control over the design or evaluation of a project. In the current period, this has often gone hand-in-hand with programmes complementary to Structural Adjustment Programmes;

ii) Foreign agency paternalism, in which international NGOs and/or state donors control most important decisions and act to coopt local leadership. The type of project implemented often conforms to the interests of the donor rather than the perceived needs of the recipients;

iii) Limited local linkages, in which local contacts are largely limited to state agencies, and alliances with autonomous social movements are absent.

b) 'Progressive NGOs', which are characterized by:

i) An explicitly political strategy of empowerment, involving not only at greater control by community members at the local level but also their involvement in broader social movements seeking increased political participation by excluded groups in national decision-making processes;

ii) Relative autonomy of the local NGO, in which the international NGO respects the superior capacity of Third World partners to respond to local demands as well as the need to build a strong civil society over the long run;

iii) Links with social movements are seen as a necessary element in building counter-hegemonic movements in order to challenge the existing distribution of power and resources.

The 'progressive NGOs' must compete with the 'mainstream NGOs,' both for external financing and for influence over the political allegiances and economic choices of the popular classes. However, the conflict between the two ideal types is not as clear-cut as a black-and-white portrayal might suggest. NGOs are complex and multi-faceted organizations, full of contradictions which emerge from the interaction between the (often confused) ideology and methodology of the NGO and its donor(s), and the reality which they confront in the field. In order to avoid over-simplification, I have therefore included an analysis of what I call a 'contradictory' NGO, funded by USAID, but displaying some autonomy from the donor and some elements of 'progressive' practice. The case studies also illustrate that even the most 'progressive' NGOs have, in many cases, failed to address the specific problem of women's participation.

The case studies were undertaken in Costa Rica, a country with a long and enviable record of democratic development and social welfare, although the existing economic and political model is currently under attack. The limitations encountered in the case studies point, therefore, to the serious problems encountered by NGOs attempting to promote participation even in the apparently most benevolent situations.

NGOS AND PARTICIPATION

Given the reservations expressed by many liberal democratic theorists about the viability of systems based on widespread political participation[6], and the shortage of genuinely participatory institutions in Western societies (apart from the vote), it is somewhat surprising that participation is now almost universally hailed as a key element in a successful development strategy. Moeen A. Qureshi, a senior vice-president of the World Bank stated in 1991, for example:

> The World Bank has learned from its experience of development that popular participation is important to the success of projects economically, environmentally and socially. Our most important lesson has been that participation and empowerment are questions of efficiency, as well as being desirable in their own right.[7]

Underlying this apparent unanimity, however, are some unstated differences about what participation actually means, and how it is to be achieved.

Most serious analysts of the concept have pointed out the fact that there are many types of practices which are labelled participatory, many of which are in fact manipulative or merely illusive.[8] It must be recognized that any authentic approach to participation must respect the traditions and desires of the 'target population,' and must involve the substantial transfer of power to that population. Since any form of assistance involves complex power relations between donor and recipient, implementing authentic participation has been an illusive goal for NGOs. Some skeptical voices have emerged about the motives behind the apparent embrace of the concept of participation by Western actors. According to Rajni Kothari, 'The more the economics of development and the politics of development are kept out of reach of the masses, the more they (the masses) are asked to "participate" in them.'[9] Kothari has a similarly skeptical view of NGOs. He claims that world capitalism and international organizations such as the World Bank and UNDP are discovering in NGOs 'a most effective instrument of promoting their interest in penetrating third world economies and particularly their rural interiors which neither private industries nor government bureaucracies were capable of doing.'[10] In fact, Qureshi from the World Bank has identified one of the difficult goals which World Bank-NGO collaboration can help achieve is the implementation of 'sensitive and successful adjustment programmes.'[11]

Observers of NGOs have discerned the gradual evolution of international non-governmental assistance to the Third World through various stages which can be associated with different approaches to the issue of participation.[12] Northern NGOs first emerged as the result of humanistic attempts to mitigate the effects of both poverty and warfare. Their precursors were the Christian missionary societies who offered food, medicine, and other services as well as religious inculcation to 'heathens' in far-flung lands.[13] These missions played an important role in the official legitimization of colonialism. Some would argue that the NGOs, their modern-day equivalents, perform a more sophisticated version of the same function.[14] Many important NGOs retain a religious identification, and although most of the major churches have rejected the heavy-handed religious inculcation of the past, fundamentalist Christian sects continue to adopt this approach.

Like the official 'aid regime,' many NGOs trace their direct origins to the North American response to the needs of post-war Europe. Some of the largest agencies – OXFAM, CARE, Catholic Relief Services, Church World Service, and Lutheran World Relief – were formed to provide relief and assist the reconstruction of Europe. Subsequently, they devoted their attentions to emergency situations in other parts of the world, including the partition of India, the flight of Arab refugees from Palestine in 1948, the Korean War, and starvation in Bihar in 1951.[15]

In the beginning, then, NGOs (like official development agencies) defined their role as limited to providing material relief to address short-term needs. However, also like the aid provided by official development agencies, early NGO assistance was not politically neutral. NGO development in Latin America had its roots in the Catholic church's fear of social unrest and the Communist threat, as well as spreading Protestantism.[16] Gradually, European and North American NGOs tied to the church began channelling funds to both Catholic and Protestant groups in Latin America.[17] The church, the most powerful organization of Latin American civil society, thus played a crucial role in the formation of NGOs and their linkages with international NGOs.

The emergent Latin American organizations, like their foreign counterparts, focused on relief and service activities designed to contribute to political stability as well as alleviate poverty. Because dominant approaches

to development theory in both North and South emphasized industrialization, capital formation and construction of infrastructure as the keys to
overcoming underdevelopment, participation by the poor was not viewed
as necessary or, even, desirable.[18] As in the modernization approach, indigenous values were seen as disfunctional; the goal of missionaries was therefore to spread Western values rather than to encourage local participation.

NGO assistance was thus initially provided as charity, and recipients
were treated as objects rather than subjects of the process. This charity and
relief approach has certainly not disappeared. Food for work schemes, for
example, are a common form of coerced participation implemented by
NGOs. By the 1960s, however, the inability of charity to overcome underdevelopment gave rise to new strategies which began to explicitly address
the need for the poor to participate in development programmes. This shift
was related to the gradual consolidation of a basic needs approach within
the official aid agencies. A volume prepared for the International Labour
Office makes this connection between participation and basic needs:

> [I]t can be argued that broad-based participation, in particular – but not
> exclusively – at the local level, has an important role to play in the
> successful implementation of a basic needs strategy. The validity of this
> argument hinges mainly on the potential of popular participation to
> contribute both to the generation and articulation of effective demand
> for mass consumption goods and essential services on a sustainable
> basis and to the operation of an efficient system of supply-management
> (i.e. the production and delivery of basic needs goods and services).[19]

This version of participation has a strongly instrumentalist and technocratic character – i.e., participation is desirable in order to create effective
demand and efficient implementation of the international organization's
basic needs strategy, not to increase popular power.

There was, however, substantial resistance to the implementation of a
basic needs approach on the part of both international organizations like
the World Bank and Third World states. As a result, the buck was passed
to NGOs to become the main agents of this form of participatory grassroots development. While there was thus some change in the rhetoric of
bilateral and multilateral aid agencies, there was little change in their
actual practice. Latin American theorists referred to the models adopted in
the 1960s and 1970s as 'developmentalism.' In the developmentalist approach, the state, private industry and international donor agencies play
the leading role in national development, but NGOs can play a complementary, though subordinate, role at the local level in overcoming local
inertia.[20]

As a result of this assigning of an important, but marginal role to local participation, most Northern state development agencies established formal mechanisms for cooperation with NGOs during the 1960s and 1970s. Government funding of NGOs considerably increased their resources and scope. However, as we will see below, the acceptance of government funding often places real limitations upon the action of NGOs, although the constraints may be either subtle or blatant, depending on the government involved[21]. The main form of operation is development 'projects' which support self-reliance at the local level and promote the incorporation of 'marginal' populations into the national economy. 'Participation' by the 'target group' is seen as a cheaper and more efficient way of ensuring project success (defined in technical and economic terms), and thus requires greater organization of the beneficiary community.

The emergence of a Women in Development approach within development studies in the 1970s led to awareness that attempts to increase community participation often exclude women. During the United Nations Decade for Women (1976–85), many NGOs (as well as state donors) put greater emphasis on the effects of development programmes on women, recognizing that previous approaches often had unintended detrimental affects on women. Gender-blind approaches tend to ignore the factors (such as domestic responsibilities, lack of self-confidence, domination of organizations by men, and male controls over women in the family) which limit women's participation. However, according to Sally Yudelman, NGO projects specifically targetted to benefit women have not attempted to increase women's access to education and training, credit and land, nor challenged women and men's domestic roles:

The developmentalist approach is still dominant among Northern NGOs. However, the hegemony of developmentalism was gradually undermined by attacks from divergent forces during the late 1960s and the 1970s. On the one hand, in the North, some international NGOs, still frustrated by their inability to attack the root causes of poverty and underdevelopment, began to recognize that community development projects could only benefit a few favoured communities, and that the success of local development efforts was frequently undermined by broader national and international forces. At the same time, dependency theory gained popularity among some Latin American and Northern NGOs. Dependentistas rejected modernization theory's dualist conception of Latin American societies and claimed that 'backwardness' was the result of the systematic exploitation of the periphery by the core since colonial times. Some Northern agencies began to include development education and lobbying among their activities in order to influence the policies of the North which had a negative effect upon the South.[22]

As well, changes occurring in the Catholic Church, inspired by Vatican II and the Medellín meeting of the Latin American Bishops' Conference and the coming to power of military juntas in many countries of the Southern Cone led to new approaches to participation. Significant sectors of the Latin American church attempted to transform the church in order to push for social reforms.[23] The so-called 'popular church,' often in opposition to the conservative church hierarchy, began to organize the poor in Christian base communities (Comunidades Eclesiales de Base). By encouraging the poor to critically reflect on the nature and causes of their oppression, these church reformers hoped to stimulate organized political action. According to Chilean NGO leader Rodrigo Engaña, the result was the establishment of new 'paradigms' among Latin American NGOs, signified by ideas like 'conscientization,' 'popular education,' and 'support to organizational processes': 'In this conception were combined Freireian ideas about cultural action, Marxist ideas about society and the state, and the visions of the dependentistas about the relations between developed and underdeveloped countries.'[24]

While these new approaches to NGO activity made an important step away from instrumental conceptions of participation toward wrestling with the crucial issue of empowerment of the poor, they were not without potential pitfalls. As Rahnema points out, Freire underlines the inability of the oppressed to understand their situation, but he does not recognize that the perceptions of the conscientizers are also distorted:

> The assumption that there are such important differences in the levels of consciousness of the participants creates an almost unsolvable problem for the author's proposed dialogical action. The exercise is intended to be a learning experience for all. However, it implies that the participants are not really equal and, therefore, the persons with a 'primitive' or 'semi-transitive' consciousness have to learn from the few with a 'critically transitive consciousness' before being able to make any meaningful contribution to the debate.[25]

Despite the best intentions and the most participatory techniques, these new-style NGO efforts may thus retain substantial elements of paternalism. Consciousness-raising techniques may also become an end in themselves, without leading to effective strategies for change.

NGOS AND PARTICIPATION IN COSTA RICA

All of these dilemmas of participation and development were confronted by the NGOs I examined in Costa Rica. Unlike most Third World countries, the democratic context in Costa Rica means that individuals are free to participate in politics without excessive fear of repression. However, the legacy of a paternalistic, interventionist state has meant, paradoxically, that participation has occurred in forms that are directed from above, rather than in organizations which spring from the grassroots. Individuals are therefore accustomed to voting in free and fair elections, and often participate in cooperatives or community associations formed by the state. This type of organization tends to foster personalistic and clientelistic forms of relationships.

Because of the role of the 'benefactor state' in Costa Rica and the climate of relative social equality and respect for human rights NGOs developed less rapidly in Costa Rica than in other Latin American countries where repression was a spur to this type of organization. During the 1970s, then, as many Latin American NGOs became aligned to the cause of social transformation, Costa Rican NGOs remained focused on the provision of charity and relief to fill in the gaps of state action. The reluctance of the Costa Rican Catholic church in the post-war era to promote a social action philosophy undoubtedly contributed to this charity-orientation.

Economic Crisis, Adjustment, and NGO Response in the 1980s

In general, the NGOs which existed prior to the debt crisis of the 1980s were charity-oriented, paternalistic and apolitical. The effects of the crisis led to a dramatic increase in the number of NGOs and their access to foreign funding, and a radical reorientation in their operations. The US government's response to the Costa Rican crisis was not limited to stabilization funds and economic adjustment at the macroeconomic level. The Reagan administration's concern with Central America led to an influx of funds to Costa Rican NGOs, and also instilled a new approach to the role of NGOs in civil society. The precipitous decline of living standards amongst the poor led to a concern for the stability of Costa Rican liberal democratic institutions. The director of USAID in Costa Rica believed that the unemployment and other social problems that would result from structural adjustment meant that a 'shock absorber' was necessary to prevent violent social unrest. NGOs were explicitly promoted as a private-sector alternative to state paternalism.

In 1987, the AID created a separate organization called ACORDE (the Asociación Costarricense de Organismos de Desarrollo) to take charge of AID funding to the NGO sector. The board of directors was initially chosen entirely from the private sector by AID.[26] The criteria of eligibility for funding were also established by the AID. Control over US funds was given not to ACORDE, but to Private Agencies Collaborating Together (PACT), a consortium of 21 US NGOs, which is almost entirely funded by the AID. PACT administered the grants in US dollars to US agencies operating in Costa Rica, and appointed a technical advisor to ACORDE. Through support of NGOs in Costa Rica, the United States hoped to ease social tensions, diminish the reliance of lower-class groups on the state, and promote market-oriented production systems.

NGOs were seen as a means not only to supplement incomes for the poorest groups but also to promote the new entrepreneurial attitudes among the poor. ACORDE's eligibility criteria states that priority will be given to projects which contribute to socio-economic development through 'generation of employment, and the increase of productivity and the level of income of the beneficiaries.' While projects may contain other (social or cultural) components, the productive aspect is paramount. ACORDE's approach thus clearly supports the economic strategy of structural adjustment promoted by the AID and other international donors, encouraging greater emphasis on short-term market-oriented development, and a greater role for the private sector as opposed to state-led development schemes.

In addition to the multiplication of Costa Rican agencies compatible with AID objectives, the 1980s also saw the emergence of another form of local NGO associated with new Costa Rican social movements which emerged in the 1980s. The effects of the economic crisis on the popular sectors and the decay of the traditional organizations of the left led to the rise of new NGOs which sought to ally themselves with, and to spur the development of, independent popular organizations. Led by Costa Rican intellectuals, often linked to the universities or churches, or formerly to state agencies, these 'organic NGOs' or 'centres' were funded primarily by European NGOs.[27] These progressive NGOs engaged in a wide variety of activities, including popular education and conscientization, communications, research, organizational support to the popular sector, and promotion of appropriate technology, as well as productive projects. As elsewhere in Latin America, these progressive NGOs wished to distance themselves from the vanguardism of the traditional left.

How can the activities of the progressive and mainstream NGOs be distinguished in practice? A statement signed by members of the 'Concertación

Regional de Organismos de Desarrollo,' a grouping of like-minded Central American NGOs, states:

> What is the fundamental difference that distinguishes an NGO with a popular orientation from an NGO linked to the neoconservative strategy? Both implement small projects; they both link themselves with the most vulnerable social groups. Both even display participatory pedagogical techniques and approaches to promotion which seek to consolidate a capacity for economic self-management. In reality, what distinguishes a neoconservative wave of NGOs from an NGO movement committed to promoting the leadership of popular groups lies in how they view the problem of power. In the first case, the activity of the NGO is oriented at provoking changes in order to avoid modifications in the structure of power. In the second case, the NGOs try to promote changes in order to achieve transformations in the relation of social forces, in a manner which favours the majority.[28]

According to the Concertación, then, 'participation' alone is not enough. Popular participation at the grassroots level must be linked with participation in social movements attempting to change the balance of power in the country. The question is, however, how this general orientation can be translated into action at the local level which genuinely empowers the beneficiaries, given the structural constraints with which all NGOs must contend.

COSTA RICAN CASE STUDIES

During field work in Costa Rica in 1988 and 1989 I examined three NGO development projects. Two of them are directed by US-based NGOs and funded by the AID, one (OEF International) directly from Washington DC, and the other (Catholic Relief Services) through an institution established by the AID to channel funds to NGOs in Costa Rica. The third project is directed by a Costa Rican NGO (CECADE) which is part of the alliance of progressive NGOs (or 'centres'), and funded by a West German NGO. All three of the projects work with small peasants; the majority of the peasants live in remote, underdeveloped areas of the country and have received land under the agrarian reform process. The agencies examined all claimed to contribute to popular participation and democratization at the grassroots level. However, the conception of meaningful participation varied between the agencies, as did the strategies used to promote it.

i) 'Mainstream' NGO: Catholic Relief Services (CRS)

NGO ANALYZED	Catholic Relief Services
TYPE	'Mainstream'
PROJECT STUDIED	Support for cacao production by cooperative in Osa Penninsula
MAIN FUNDER	USAID (through CRS, ACORDE AND PACT)
PARTICIPATION STRATEGY	Instrumental participation of coop members; no participation by women
DEVELOPMENT STRATEGY	Promotion of non-traditional exports
ROLE OF INTERNATIONAL AGENCY	Paternalist
LINK WITH LOCAL GROUPS	Coopealianza, a credit and service cooperative is the implementing agency. Cooperation with IDA, state agrarian reform agency.

CRS is the second largest US development agency, with many years of experience throughout the world. It is the foreign relief and development agency of the US conference of Catholic bishops but receives the majority of its funding from the USAID. Like other established mainstream NGOs, CRS has gone through an evolution away from its initial charity and relief emphasis toward a more developmentalist approach. In addition to its secular development activities, however, CRS also provides institutional support to the Catholic church in Latin America. Because of the disinterest of the Costa Rican hierarchy in social issues, however, CRS actions in Costa Rica are perhaps more heavily shaped by the philosophy and procedures of head office and US staff than in other countries where the local church is stronger.

In 1989, CRS's work in Costa Rica was focused on rural and urban income generation. The rural projects were located in the three poorest areas on the country (the Nicoya penninsula, the Atlantic and the Southern regions). CRS established a new rural programme in 1986 with a convention signed by CRS, ACORDE and PACT (each agency provided part of the financing, ACORDE in colones and PACT in dollars, and CRS played the main operational role). The primary goal of the programme was to provide organizational, technical and financial support to small producers, primarily in the area of non-traditional agricultural products. The programme was thus consistent with the 'agricultura de cambio' programme initiated by the Costa Rican government as part of its structural adjustment measures. This programme was designed to encourage farmers to switch away from the production of basic grains and traditional exports toward non-traditional exports such as fruits, spices and ornamental plants.

The project which I examined was based in the town of Uvita, on the coast of the Osa Peninsula, in the southern region of Costa Rica. The project was initially designed to provide financing, training and technical assistance to local peasants for the production, processing, and marketing of cacao, one of the non-traditional crops being promoted by the government. Unfortunately, world cocoa prices had declined dramatically since the project was conceived, with very negative implications for the economic viability of the crop.

When the project began, the beneficiaries were organized into a 'pre-cooperative.' Since the beneficiaries were not legally incorporated and lacked experience with maintaining accounts, COOPEALIANZA, a credit and services cooperative located in the nearby town of San Isidro de El General, was designated as the implementing agency. This arrangement was planned to end once the community gained the legal and technical capacity to manage their own finances. The group gained formal cooperative status in mid-1988, but as of mid-1989, financial control remained in San Isidro.

Instrumental Participation
The CRS approach can be characterized as 'institutional support' rather than concern for the quality of participation at the grassroots level or for participation in broader social and political processes. CRS did base its selection of the Uvita community on the level of organization and commitment of the group (as reported by the state agrarian reform agency). The level of community organization did appear to have advanced, at least in formal institutional terms. However, the design and implementation of the project were largely top-down in character and showed little popular input. This type of participation is quite compatible with the traditional patterns of Costa Rican society and does little to advance the interests of small and medium peasants at the national level in an era when the state is less disposed to meet the needs of the poor.

The Uvita group was initially brought to CRS's attention by the state agrarian reform agency, IDA. The settlement was formed by peasants who had invaded lands in IDA's possession. Members of the community had formed a neighbourhood committee after the invasion which had been working together in a more or less permanent form for six or seven years. Because the group displayed 'much capacity and determination,' IDA decided to seek financing for them.[29] Both CRS and IDA were very satisfied with the level of participation and organization in the cooperative. A June 1988 CRS progress report evaluated progress in group organization as good, based on two criteria: the formal inauguration of the cooperative, and the provision of training and technical assistance in cacao farming techniques by an IDA agronomist. According to the report, '[t]his assistance has also promoted an integration of the group and a positive collaborative attitude toward working as a collective.'

However, a closer examination reveals many problems with the CRS approach to participation. Most importantly, the way in which the project was implemented and designed showed more attention to state and international donor priorities than to the needs identified by the group itself. The first two years of the initial three-year CRS-ACORDE-PACT project were spent on an academic study of economic, geographic, and social conditions in three regions of the country, with no popular input and little attention to political considerations or popular movements. The orientation of the project was decided in advance with the 1986 decision of the Costa Rican mission to promote non-traditional export production among campesinos. As a result of this orientation, groups could not expect CRS support unless they conformed to this strategy. The dominant attitude to participation was displayed in the response of the IDA promoter when asked how the decision was made to produce cacao:

> That was the idea of the members themselves. They had heard that CRS offered financing if they produced a product like that [a non-traditional export]. It seemed to them that they could grow cacao, a permanent crop.

Peasants clearly recognized that they would not receive funding for other types of activities. Community control over the nature of the project was thus limited to the selection of the crop.

It also appears that the introduction of the project created some divisions within the community as a whole. Some residents opposed the project and were boycotting the group. One male member of the Vigilance committee of the cooperative stated:

There is a minority sector of the community which hasn't been in agreement with the cooperative. They are people with a low level of education. They believe the cooperative is bad because it's only for the leaders and not for the good of the community. Besides, there are people who don't want to leave basic grain production.

This community division created by the orientation of the project shows there was inadequate attention to the range of community needs and objectives prior to project design.

There was a well-consolidated leadership group in the cooperative, but little sign of broader participation (apart from labour in the cacao crop and agricultural training). General meetings were held only twice a year, providing insufficient opportunity for community control over the project. Even basic knowledge of the project appeared limited outside of the leadership structure. One coop member stated that he thought he would leave the cooperative soon because the coop accounts were not explained to the members and because he did not understand how control was kept over project funds. He believed that he had been charged more than he had received. Even if this was not true, the belief shows a serious lack of confidence in and knowledge of the functioning of the organization.

At the evaluation session held in 1989 it was concluded that training had been successful with regard to productive requirements but that there had been no training in the administration of the cooperative.

Apart from the limitations on participation within the cooperative, the exclusive focus on cacao production also placed a serious limitation on community involvement. Farmers who did not wish to produce cacao, as well as landless peasants, were automatically excluded (although IDA obtained lands for a few men who expressed interest in joining the co-operative – unusual behaviour on IDA's part, displaying the state agency's degree of commitment to this project). Women were also virtually excluded, since under IDA regulations only single or widowed women were eligible to receive entitlements for plots, and only landowners were eligible for coop membership. According to the IDA officer, '[Women] are indirect beneficiaries. Because it's a cooperative of producers and that's fundamentally men's work. There is only one woman in the cooperative.' Many studies indicate, however, that projects need to be aimed directly at women's specific needs and to incorporate women directly if they are to benefit. Apart from links with state agencies, CRS, other international donors, COOPEALIANZA, and COOPESANCARLOS, the group has few outside contacts. No ties were established with any peasant union, and there was no attempt to influence regional or national policy, apart from gaining land titles for members from IDA. This lack of broader political involvement, in fact, may be one reason why the group received special attention from both IDA and CRS.

ii) 'Contradictory' NGO: OEF International – Programme for Education in Participation (PEP)

NGO ANALYZED	Oef International
TYPE	'Contradictory'
PROJECT STUDIED	Programme for Education in Participation (PEP) Organizational support to community banks created by FINCA (Fundación Integral Campesina), another US-based NGO
MAIN FUNDER	US AID (through OEF in Washington)
PARTICIPATION STRATEGY	Local Empowerment and increased participation by women
DEVELOPMENT STRATEGY	Mixed strategy: Basic needs + exports
ROLE OF INTERNATIONAL AGENCY	Donor–NGO Conflict; substantial autonomy of Costa Rican office from main office in Washington, D.C.
LINKS WITH LOCAL GROUPS	None

OEF International (formerly known as the Overseas Education Fund), is a US-based NGO founded in 1947 by the League of Women Voters which works primarily with women in developing countries. Like CRS, OEF is very dependent on AID funding: in 1987, almost 80 per cent of its total budget came from AID grants[30]. In the 1960s, OEF's primary activity was leadership training among upper and middle class women; in the early 1970s, though, the US New Directions legislation made this approach politically unsaleable, and with some difficulty, the agency made the transition to working primarily with lower-class women.

In 1985, OEF launched two Costa Rican programmes with very different goals and methodologies: Women in Business (WIB) and the Programme for Education in Participation (PEP). I chose to focus on the latter programme, because of its emphasis on participation and community development. PEP was part of a broader OEF programme titled 'Women, Law, and Development' which had the stated goal of advancing 'the understanding of women's subordinate and marginal status and provide them with forums through which they can build more responsive political and social structures.'[31] While the WIB programme followed the AID's encouragement of micro and small enterprise in the Third World, the PEP programme had a much more political orientation involving the promotion of social and political change. I therefore call OEF a 'contradictory' NGO both because of these very different programmes within the organization itself, and because of the differences between AID's general approach and the PEP programme.

Among the results hoped for in the Central American programme were that participants would 'take concrete action to: a) demand their share of public resources and services, and b) participate in the municipal and national political processes.'[32] These are classic goals of liberal pluralism. However, the programme also relied heavily on the use of participatory educational techniques, based on the philosophy of 'conscientization' of Brazilian educator Paolo Freire, typical of an 'empowerment' approach.

PEP was funded by a special AID 'Democracy Programme' established on the recommendation of the Kissinger Commission, and primarily designed to promote electoral processes in Central America and candidates favourable to US foreign policy objectives. Because of this special status, funds were transferred from the AID to OEF International in Washington and then to San José rather than through the normal route of ACORDE. In the project I studied, OEF provided training and participatory education for peasants in the southern region of the country who were members of community banks established by FINCA (Fundación Integral Campesina) International, another US-based NGO. This collaboration with FINCA was one of the elements contributing to the project's contradictory profile, since FINCA has a much more mainstream orientation.

The groups with which PEP worked primarily consisted of small peasant producers of basic grains and contained a high proportion of women. Participants received small loans from FINCA on an individual basis, but repaid the loan to a rotating fund managed by a 'solidarity group' of community members receiving FINCA support. The objectives of the PEP component of the project were to strengthen the 'organizational capacity,' 'collective consciousness' and community orientation of the groups.[33]

When I visited OEF-PEP in Costa Rica in 1989, the initial three year project had been completed. Another broader proposal had been made to AID, but had not been approved. When I visited the communities, therefore, the project had just ended.

Local Empowerment and Increased Women's Participation
As its title indicates, OEF's Programme for Education in Participation had a deeper commitment to promoting grassroots participation than CRS, where participation appeared as a secondary objective. OEF literature defines 'education for participation' as:

> ... a global and integral process of education, in which men and women will analyze and critically interpret their world and their problems, and will be able to acquire the skills necessary to respond to them in a cooperative and democratic way.

> Thus, education for participation transcends a determined modality to become a general theoretical-methodological orientation. The aim is to affirm the responsiblity of members of community organizations to promote full, democratic and cooperative participation in the decision-making process.[34]

This statement displays a Freireian philosophy of education. The programme is also influenced both by the liberal feminist orientation of OEF's 'Women, Law and Development' programme, which focuses on addressing legal obstacles to women's equality, and by the consciousness-raising methods of Western feminism in the 1970s. The result of these mixed origins was that PEP appeared very successful in increasing popular participation (especially by women) at the community level, but had trouble developing a clear strategy for promoting broader forms of participation and a deeper insertion into Costa Rican popular struggles.

The PEP methodology involves extensive use of participatory techniques and popular education methods such as socio-drama, drawings, poetry, songs, folk-sayings, etc., to increase the level of participation by all group members. An evaluation of PEP commissioned by AID states,

> The evaluations delivered by participants continually refer to what they have achieved in terms of self-esteem, and their ability to better express their problems and concerns, as well as what they have learned, in order to better organize meetings and plan activities.[35]

This evaluation was confirmed by the interviews I carried out with the community banks in the Southern zone. One woman from Las Parcelas stated,

Ivania [the PEP promoter] has helped us a lot. At the beginning, people were more afraid to participate, but now we're more confident – especially the women. Women often didn't participate much before, but participating in the meetings gives you more confidence.

She also stated that she and other women get out of the house more through PEP activities (campesinas on dispersed parcels of land are often isolated from community activities because of household responsibilities and machista ethics which insist women should stay in the home), and that some of the men help more with household tasks because of Ivania's involvement. Ivania attempted to address problems of machismo within the groups, so that women gained greater confidence to participate, and men allowed them to take on positions of leadership. Of course, not all men were amenable to this change in women's status, and undoubtedly many women were prevented from participation because of child care and other responsibilities, and of their husbands' unwillingness to permit them to take on a more active role.[36] The PEP promoter also focused on creating more egalitarian forms of decision-making within the groups. The groups met as a whole at least once a month, showing a higher level of regular participation by all members than in the CRS project.

PEP's encouragement of the groups to move beyond the narrow focus on financial aspects of the banks to greater community involvement also succeeded to some extent. The various groups took on such community projects as constructing a soccer field and a meeting house. A male member of the Las Parcelas group stated:

We've changed a lot, through participation in the project. Before there was a community problem. We have now united a lot. Also, within the family, there's more unity. There's more agreement between spouses. The women have their own projects, a clearer idea of what they want, so women's work is valued more.

PEP was less successful in linking this project with broader regional and national issues, partly because of the constraints imposed by FINCA. PEP had hoped to encourage the groups to look beyond their communities and to create greater unity by supporting a 'sectorial committee' with representatives of each of the 120 groups with which FINCA was working in Costa Rica. Through this organization, OEF hoped to strengthen the grassroots groups through feedback and support. Despite an initial agreement between OEF and FINCA that OEF would carry out educational work with the sectoral committee, FINCA subsequently decided that the committee would only deal with narrow economic issues. Thus, the groups with which OEF was working in the southern zone had no organized connection to other communities. It may also have been difficult for OEF to form open associations with peasant unions which were viewed negatively by AID. There was therefore the danger that these would become isolated experiments in participation at the local level. Increased individual capacity to participate would not be channelled into cooperation with other groups in similar positions in order to challenge the problems which confront them all. As well, the fact that OEF's work in the communities ended with the cut-off in AID funding, while FINCA's activities in this area continued, meant that the more individualistic and capitalistic orientation may tend to predominate.

iii) 'Progressive' National NGO: CECADE

NGO ANALYZED	CECADE (Centro de Capacitación y Desarrollo)
TYPE	'Progressive'
PROJECT STUDIED	Support for cacao production and small income-generating projects, organization of local producers' associations.
MAIN FUNDER	Agro-Action (West German NGO)
PARTICIPATION STRATEGY	Support for Social Movements. Little participation by women.
DEVELOPMENT STRATEGY	Basic needs + non-traditional exports
ROLE OF INTERNATIONAL AGENCY	Non-intervention
LINKS WITH LOCAL GROUPS	Support for UPANA\CIONAL (Costa Rica's largest peasant union). Member of the Concertation of Central American NGOs.

The third project examined was directed by a progressive Costa Rican centre, CECADE (Centro de Capacitación para el Desarrollo), and funded by the West German NGO, Agro-Action. Like OEF-PEP, CECADE's approach heavily stressed the use of participatory techniques, but, like CRS, CECADE was supporting productive projects rather than focusing primarily on education. Because it was founded by intellectuals who had for many years been associated with the Costa Rican left, CECADE had a much stronger identification, however, with peasant organizations than either of the two US-based NGOs.

I chose to study one of CECADE's productive projects, which was being implemented among small producers in the northern region of the country. The project was funded by Agro Action, a West German NGO, which had little direct involvement in the project design or implementation. CECADE began working in this region in 1986 on the invitation of UPANACIONAL, the country's largest peasant union. The main focus of work was on San Jorge, a remote settlement 75 kilometres north of San Carlos, which was formed by precaristas who occupied a large plantation there in 1976. In San Jorge, CECADE chose to support three separate activities: the production of cacao, the establishment of a concrete block factory to be used for the construction needs of the community, and a model pig farm. In each of the communities, the goal was to establish a rotating fund which would permit the projects to become (at least partially) self-sustaining. CECADE was politically opposed to the principle of structural adjustment but felt that given the cutbacks in subsidies to basic grain production, non-traditional exports represented the main alternative available to small farmers. However, like CRS, the CECADE project was negatively effected by the decline in cocoa prices.

Support for Social Movements
CECADE, less constrained by donors, and with a clearer orientation toward political change, placed a greater emphasis on the participation of beneficiaries in national social movements. However, while local participation was also seen as a goal, it was not yet sufficiently developed. Because of the emphasis on productive strategies, and, specifically, on the launching of the cacao project, group learning and empowerment were to some extent sacrificed to productive efficiency. CECADE itself recognized the need to expand community participation. For example, a 1988 project report stated:

> The size of the nursery was very large and required a great deal of work which had to be done in very little time (one month) in order to take

advantage of the rains. This meant that the process was carried out in
a very directed manner, sacrificing more reflective and democratic styles
of work.

There is therefore some evidence to support the view of critics of productive projects that such projects inevitably lead to emphasis on technocratic
concerns and detract from more purely political and participatory work.
Part of the problem, as in CRS, was the initial heavy emphasis on a
single export crop. A 1987 report by CECADE stated:

> ... the participation of the farmers has been neither constant nor mas-
> sive, given that until the present the project has basically focused on the
> production of cacao, and not all of the farmers are interested in this
> crop. This has suggested the need to begin providing other alternatives
> which make possible a broader form of participation from the families
> involved.[37]

In San Jorge, there was relatively large participation in the initial phase
of the cacao nursery by all social sectors (male farmers, women, and
youth) because of the opportunity for paid labour, but some of those who
participated were frustrated because labour was not immediately reimbursed.
Participation in the project subsequently dropped off because job opportunities in the project were limited, and farmers struggling to survive
found it difficult to leave their land to participate in the block and pig
projects.

The pig project offered employment to only three teenage girls, and
about eight to ten day labourers worked in the block factory. The projects
were not offering opportunities for participation on a regular basis to small
farmers or to women involved in childcare and household labour. The
heavy emphasis on production means that other opportunities for participation did not exist. It also limited the participation of women, whose
household labour is generally not recognized as productive.

The fact, however, that the CECADE promoters were aware of these
problems of participation at the local level and from the beginning were
seeking strategies to overcome them, shows that the organization takes the
problem of participation very seriously. CECADE had initiated a radio
project for the northern zone, financed by the Canadian Catholic Organization for Development and Peace. This communications project would
permit dissemination of information about the problems of the peasantry
in this region and allow peasants to participate in the mass media. A
literacy project was also contemplated (a preliminary needs identification

study had been initiated) because of the low level of education in the community which limited the ability of the Association to take over full control of the project (particularly financial aspects).

The field staff also wished in the future to put more emphasis on projects which could be carried out on the participants own parcels, in order to broaden the opportunities for participation. As one promoter stated:

It has been difficult to break with the paternalistic mentality; the people expect us to arrange everything. They still don't feel like the project is their's. Because they are projects which are carried out outside of their parcels it is difficult for them to participate more actively.

Even though progressive NGOs may wish to develop a more collective orientation among Costa Rican peasants, they must learn to come to terms with peasant survival strategies given the existing land tenure system which makes collective work difficult on a regular basis.

CECADE's work also benefits from a close association with the peasant union, UPANACIONAL. The project was initiated partly on UPA's request, and all members of the Asociación de Agricultores established in the villages were also members of UPA. While UPA was not the most militant of the peasant organizations in Costa Rica, having been established by relatively well-off coffee farmers, the connection with UPA ensured that CECADE's work had a connection with wider struggles of peasant producers. As well, CECADE's work to increase the organizational capacity of small producers may have acted to increase the political weight of more marginalized sectors within UPA.

CECADE also assisted the peasants in increasing their political power vis-à-vis the Costa Rican state. Unlike the parceleros in Uvita, the group in San Jorge had received little support or attention from IDA after the initial land invasion. When the project began, although the settlement had been in place for twelve years, only five of the original 44 (male) parceleros had received official land titles. Along with the local Asociación de Desarrollo Comunal, the Asociación de Agricultores pressured IDA to either process the remaining land titles, or to act as a guarantor with COOPESANCARLOS for the residents to obtain loans from the coop and allow them to participate in that group's cacao project. As a result, 16 farmers received the guarantee, and IDA agreed to send a group of topographers to map out the dimension of the parcels.

Unlike the Uvita project, the CECADE project did not accept the problems associated with cacao production passively, but promoted a political response. The CECADE promoters held workshops with farmers and technicians involved with cacao production in the northern zone, in order to share information about problems of the crop and possible solutions. Some of the responses proposed to the government included increased financing, debt forgiveness, freezes on the price of inputs, establishment of support prices for cacao, and discouragement of cacao imports. The document produced by the CECADE promoters as a result of their encounters with cacao producers states that:

> The implementation of these proposals, some of which clash with the government's economic policies, will depend on the strength and the power of negotiation developed by peasant organizations, and on the contradictions which exist within the government with respect to the economic adjustment plan, from which peasant groups may obtain some benefits.[38]

CECADE's strategic orientation thus created the political framework for transformatory political action, turning the people from the objects to the subjects of their own development. However, participation at the grass-roots level needed to become more authentic in order to sustain national social movements with the necessary strength to force changes on the plans of the state (and the international financial institutions).

CONCLUSION

These case studies from Costa Rica show that the view which presents NGOs as inherently and unproblematically participatory is naive and inadequate. As indicated above, NGOs display very different understandings of what participation means and how it is to be achieved. The problem of dominant models of development has not been that the concept of participation has been entirely lacking, but that it has been marginalized and depoliticized. Most NGOs have contributed to this process by accepting the apolitical vision of NGO work. As a result, participatory initiatives have all too often had only an instrumental value in ensuring the efficient promotion of the interests of dominant powers, rather than actually empowering the poor. In the present context, as the case of Costa Rica shows, the ideology of community self-reliance as basis for NGO activity is perfectly compatible with the current drive toward privatization and the dismantling of Third World states.

This does not mean that the concept of participation must be rejected, but that it must be reclaimed, and explicitly linked with national and international processes of democratization. If this link is not made, even the most participatory of NGO projects runs the risk of following the path of isolated nineteenth century utopian communities in Britain and North America which were eventually extinguished by internal conflict and hostile external forces.[39]

However, even those NGOs which adopt broad-based democratization as a goal lack a systematic analysis of the relationship between participation and democratization. Some assume that increased organization at the local level will necessarily contribute to democratization. There are some reasons to support the idea that personal empowerment is a necessary element of democratization, but it is only a first step. Personal empowerment does not necessarily lead to the decision to participate in the political system as a whole, nor does it guarantee the conditions for greater participation. For example, the organization of cooperatives in Guatemala in the 1940s brought about increased state repression and the annihilation of local organizations and enforced popular passivity.

On the other hand, some analysts of democratization in Latin America entirely discount the role of grassroots organizations. The influential 1986 study by O'Donnell and Schmitter, *Transitions from Authoritarian Rule*, portrays the democratization which occurred in the Southern Cone in the 1980s as primarily a process of elite accommodation.[40] Studies of and by NGOs could contribute to this debate by examining the relationship between participation at the community level, participation in social movements, and national processes of democratization. Under what conditions is this connection made?

Finally, supra-national forces have to be confronted in order to make this connection possible. How can the internationalization of the state which has occurred under structural adjustment be confronted? NGOs must avoid cooptation by the World Bank, IMF and other international actors which see them as useful allies in anti-popular projects. National and international NGOs can play an important role in representing popular interests on the global stage, but they must make constant attempts to make sure their efforts are rooted in popular experiences. NGOs themselves must be democratized in order to contribute to successful democratization of Third World (and First World) societies.

Notes

1. For a discussion of the diverse ideological perspectives on the role of NGOs in strengthening civil society, see Laura Macdonald, 'Turning to the NGOs: Competing Conceptions of Civil Society in Latin America,' paper presented to the annual meeting of the Latin American Studies Association, Los Angeles, September 1992.
2. The term 'aid regime' comes from Robert Wood, *From Marshall Plan to Debt Crisis: Foreign Aid and Development Choices in the World Economy* (Berkeley: University of California Press, 1986). Wood does not include NGOs among the institutions of the aid regime. I would argue that NGOs should be considered part of the regime, although as actors less rigidly controlled by the dominant norms and rules.
3. Judith Tendler, *Turning PVOs into Development Agencies: Questions for Evaluation, Programme Evaluation Discussion Paper No. 12* (Washington, DC: United States Agency for International Development, 1982). Among other supposed qualities of NGOs (or 'private voluntary organizations' as they are referred to in the United States) which have become articles of faith, according to Tendler, are that, in contrast to aid institutions they are: more likely to be able to reach the poor; more concerned with process than outcome; more able to be flexible and experimental, and have a special ability to strengthen local organizations (pp. 4–5).
4. Robin Poulton, 'On Theories and Strategies,' in Poulton and Michael Harris, *Putting People First: Voluntary Organisations and Third World Organisations* (London: Macmillan, 1988), p. 4.
5. Ibid., p. 32.
6. See Carole Pateman's excellent review of the view of participation in classic liberal theorists, *Participation and Democratic Theory* (Cambridge: Cambridge University Press, 1970).
7. Quoted in Mark E. Denham, 'The World Bank and NGOs,' paper prepared for presentation at the Annual Meeting of the International Studies Association, Atlanta, April 1992, p. 5.
8. One influential formulation was provided by Sherry Arnstein reflecting on her experiences with citizen participation in urban programmes in the United States in the 1960s ('A Ladder of Citizen Participation,' *Journal of the American Institute of Planners*, 35, 4 (July 1969), pp. 216–24). She describes a 'Ladder of Participation' in which each of the eight rungs of the ladder corresponds to a different extent of citizens' power in the political process. These range from 'Manipulation' and 'Therapy' which are, in fact, 'non-participation,' through 'Informing,' 'Consultation' and 'Placation,' up to the highest rungs, 'Partnership, 'delegated power,' and, at the highest level, 'citizen control.'
9. Rajni Kothari, 'Party and State in Our Times: The Rise of Non-Party Political Formations,' *Alternatives*, 9 (Spring 1984), p. 542.
10. Kothari, 'NGOs, the State and World Capitalism,' *Economic and Political Weekly*, 21, 50 (13 December, 1986), p. 2178. Robert Cox also views the rural development project aimed at self-sufficiency (of the type promoted by the World Bank but often implemented by NGOs) as the response of managers of the world economy to the recognition of the fact that the world capitalist

system 'would not absorb more than a fraction of the world's rural populations', *Production, Power and World Order: Social Forces in the Making
of History* (New York: Columbia University Press, 1987), p. 388.

11. See International Bank for Reconstruction and Development, 'Meeting of
the World Bank-NGO Committee and Recent Progress in Bank-NGO Cooperation,' Internal Memorandum, Washington DC, 13 February 1989, p. 5.

12. In an influential typology, David Korten describes the changes in NGOs
as characterized by three 'generations' ('Third Generation NGO Strategies:
A Key to People-Centred Development,' *World Development*, 15 (Supplement, Autumn 1987), pp. 145–59). According to Korten, an initial relief and
welfare approach in the early post-war period was followed in the 1960s and
1970s by a shift by many NGOs to focus on small-scale, self-reliant local
development. Korten describes a third, more recent NGO strategy as involving
commitment to 'sustainable systems development'; that is, recognizing the
limits of impact of community development projects, some NGOs have
attempted to influence broader systemic factors, including government policy.
Korten has subsequently developed a conception of a fourth generation
strategy under which NGOs would 'become facilitators of a global people's
development movement' (*Getting to the 21st Century: Voluntary Action and
the Global Agenda* (West Hartford: Kumarian Press, 1990), pp. 113–32).
However, Korten's description of this fourth generation is vague and not
accompanied by specific examples of development agencies working in this
area.

13. The emergence of liberation theology in the Roman Catholic church, as well
as related theological approaches in other churches, partly reflects a conscious
effort to overcome this legacy of cultural imperialism.

14. Stewart MacPherson notes that the term 'community development' (which
became a key feature of later NGO activities) was first coined by the British
Colonial Office in 1948. (See his *Social Policy in the Third World: The
Social Dilemmas of Underdevelopment* (Brighton: Wheatsheaf Books, 1982)).
Community development was defined as 'a movement designed to promote
better living for the whole community with the active participation and if
possible on the initiative of the community but if this initiative is not forthcoming spontaneously by the use of techniques for arousing and stimulating
it in order to ensure its active and enthusiastic response to the movement'
(quoted on page 164).

15. Organisation for Economic Cooperation and Development, *Voluntary Aid
for Development: The Role of Non-Governmental Organisations* (Paris:
OECD, 1988), pp. 18–19.

16. Part of the hierarchy's response to these perceived threats was the establishment of Cáritas, a social assistance organization composed mainly of Catholic laypeople, in various countries of the region. See Philip J. Williams, *The
Catholic Church and Politics in Nicaragua and Costa Rica* (London: ,
1989), for a description of the political motivations of the Central American
bishops.

17. FAO-FFHC, 'NGOs in Latin America: Their Contribution to Participatory
Democracy,' *Development: Seeds of Change*, 4 (1987), pp. 100–5.

18. This top-down approach was typical not only of modernization theory, but
also of the structuralist theory developed by Raúl Prebisch at the United

Nation's Economic Commission for Latin America. However, ECLA's emphasis on the importance of the expansion of the internal market lay a basis for the shift to the basic needs approach.

19. Franklyn Lisk, 'Introduction,' in Lisk (ed), *Popular Participation in Planning for Basic Needs* (Aldershot: Gower House, 1985), p. 22. The Programme of Action adopted by the 1976 World Employment Conference of the ILO states 'A basic-needs-oriented policy implies the participation of the people in making the decisions which affect them through organizations of their own choice.' (Quoted in John M. Cohen and Norman T. Uphoff, 'Participation's Place in Rural Development: Seeking Clarity through Specificity', *World Development*, 8 (1980), p. 213n). In a 1974 article, Robert Cox offers a (former) insider's view of the internal politics of the ILO and its shifting position on basic needs ('ILO: Limited Monarchy,' in Cox and Harold K. Jacobson, *The Anatomy of Influence: Decision-Making in International Organizations* (New Haven: Yale University Press), pp. 102–38.)

20. 'Desarrollismo' was strongly influenced by the structuralist school developed by the United Nations Economic Commission for Latin America, headed by Raúl Prebisch. For a discussion of this ideological current, see Cristobal Kay, *Latin American Theories of Development and Underdevelopment* (London: Routledge, 1989), pp. 25–9.

21. Cf. Jorgen Lissner, *The Politics of Altruism: A Study of the Political Behaviour of Voluntary Development Agencies* (Geneva: ILO, 1977).

22. Agencies which opted for this approach viewed participation by citizens in the North in order to overturn the unjust structures of the international system as of equal importance to participation in the South.

23. However, Philip Williams in *The Catholic Church and Politics in Nicaragua and Costa Rica* (London: 1989) notes that the degree of radicalism varied greatly according to different national contexts, tending to be greater in countries with more authoritarian forms of government.

24. Quoted in Leilah Landim, 'ONGs y Estado en America Latina,' unpublished document, February 1988, p. 9.

25. Majid Rahnema, 'Participatory Action Research: The "Last Temptation of Saint" Development,' *Alternatives*, 15 (1990), pp. 207–8.

26. A new board was chosen in 1989, selected by members of the previous board. The new board was slightly more diverse in background, including academics and professionals as well as businessmen.

27. Most progressive Canadian NGOs did not view Costa Rica as a priority for funding because of the relatively high standards of living there.

28. Concertacion Centroamericana de Organismos de Desarrollo, 'Memoria: Reunion de Organismos No-Gubernamentales para la Constitucion de la Concertacion Centroamericana de Organismos de Desarrollo,' San José, Costa Rica, November 1988, pp. 24–5.

29. Interview with Alvaro Chanto, IDA 'promotor', San Isidro, 1989.

30. OEF International, 'Documento del Programa Educacion para Participacion (PEP) para Centroamerica,' San José, Costa Rica, December 1986, p. 11.

31. Ibid., p. 9.

32. Robert F. Arnove, 'Resumen de la Evaluacion hecha al Programa de Educacion para la Participacion,' unpublished document, n.d., p. 1.

33. OEF–PEP, 'Informe de Actividades del 88, Sub-proyecto Bancos Communales – FINCA,' draft, 22 December, 1988.
34. OEF (1986), op. cit.
35. Arnove, 'Resumen de la Evaluacion hecha al Programa de Educacion para la Participacion,' p. 2.
36. In addition to the other contradictions between OEF's and FINCA's approaches, they also differ over their approaches to women's role in society. While FINCA does promote women's participation in community banks, they do not conceive of this participation as contributing to broader emancipation or challenge traditional family structures. In fact, small projects for women are seen as a response to the economic crisis which will maintain traditional structures. According to the FINCA President in Costa Rica, 'We haven't tried to get women to do activities outside of the home – so as not to create conflict, because the men are *machista*. We want to help so the men feel that the women can help economically, but still be around the house, to make lunch, take care of the kids, and so on. If the women go out to work in a factory, that could hurt the stability of the family.'
37. CECADE, 'Proyecto – Diversificacion y Capacitacion para el Desarrollo de Pequenos Agricultores – Informe de Labores, II Semestre,' San José, Costa Rica, 1987.
38. José Ramirez and Angel Villalobos, 'Los Riesgos Economicos y Sociales de los Productores de Cacao de la Zona Norte,' CECADE, unpublished document, n.d., p. 8.
39. Although the experiences of nineteenth century socialist communities based on the ideas of Robert Owen and others are in many ways distinct, several interesting parallels might be drawn between contemporary NGO efforts these earlier experiments in personal, political and economic transformation. In *Eve and the New Jerusalem* (Virago Press, 1989), Barbara Taylor examines the link between Owenite socialism and nineteenth century feminism in Britain, and details how conflicts over gender roles contributed to the downfall of several of these communities.
40. Guillermo O'Donnell and Philippe C. Schmitter, *Transitions from Authoritarian Rule: Tentative Conclusions about Uncertain Democracies* (Baltimore: Johns Hopkins University Press, 1986).

8 Participation: Local versus Expert Knowledge at the Environmental Public Hearings for a Pulp Mill in Northern Alberta, Canada

Michael Gismondi, Joan Sherman and Mary Richardson[1]

We cannot afford any more of the obfuscational rhetoric with which industry and government try to evade the truth with stupid, meaningless phrases like 'leading edge technology.'

(Kristin Reed, Proceedings, p. 555)[2]

I have learned that people that have the name 'Doctor' in front of their names don't always know everything. I used to be intimidated by people like that, but that will be no longer. The same with government. I always thought government was consistent, and I found that isn't the case.

(Ron Epp, Review Board member, Proceedings, p. 7633)

Such public hearings provide the only opportunity for minority groups to have their positions brought into the public domain. They are essential protection against the tyranny of the majority, and they should become mandatory adjuncts in the democratic process of informed decision-making.

(Harry Garfinkle for the Green Party of Canada,
Filed Document O-111:1)[3]

In most countries I would have been shot or jailed for what [the public criticism and environmental activism] . . . I have done, and so I feel pretty proud to have a country that allows me to take on a government, two governments, Canada and Alberta, in the way that I have and still have the freedoms that I have. So, yes, I get criticized but that's part of democracy. And, if people aren't willing to do that, then we have lost our democracy.[4]

This paper draws from a larger study of the environmental public hearings into a pulp and paper mill project proposed for northern Alberta, Canada.[5] It explores the merits and shortcomings of public participation during these environmental impact hearings with an emphasis upon how members of the public contested the professional hegemony of state managers and confronted the 'expertocracy' of specialists hired to review the pulp mill's impacts.

Citizen participation in the form of public review or public hearings to assess the environmental impacts of proposed development projects such as pulp mills or dams is currently an accepted part of Canadian democracy. Yet during the hearings on Alberta-Pacific's environmental impacts the freedom to speak out would have been mere window dressing had public participants not questioned widely held assumptions about the authority and language of experts, and challenged the fairness and mandate of the hearing process itself.

Criticisms of Canadian public participation models, such as the way that expert knowledge subordinates local knowledge, should be of use to those struggling against models of 'participation' being promoted by the World Bank and international aid agencies.[6]

INTRODUCTION

In Canada, the primary method governments use to determine the impact of large industrial projects on the environment is to require the project's proponents to produce an Environmental Impact Assessment (EIA) document, addressing both environmental and social impacts. On occasion, EIA's are subject to public hearings at which the public may express its support or concerns about the project.[7] A recent Government of Canada report, *Public Review: Neither Judicial, Nor Political But an Essential Forum for the Future of the Environment*, champions the public hearing process as 'a service requested of the public by the government to help it make an informed decision and to favour a harmonious relationship between economic and environmental protection.' According to this document the public hearing serves as 'a means to define the values which the population associates with a specific proposal' and 'a forum in which expert opinions on technical subjects as well as value judgments or the choices of society may intersect and merge.'[8]

This report makes the assumption that experts provide us with value-free information concerning the consequences of major developments, while the role of the public is to testify about their values and what they want. The task of decision-makers is to make a decision which ensures both economic benefit and protection of the environment. Finally, the title of the report indicates that the Study Group believes that environmental public hearings can be non-political, in the sense that their outcomes will be unaffected by questions of power, and will be based on fact and public choice alone. The Group sees no power imbalance between the public and the technical experts, or between the public and the proponent. And, public participation appears to be free and unencumbered. Each of these assumptions is questionable and our paper tells a different story of public participation where the nature and role of 'expert knowledge' of the environment was challenged by people in a number of communities in northern Alberta in 1989–90 during the public hearing process for the Alberta-Pacific (Alpac) kraft pulp mill.

Even though a number of participants felt that the Alpac hearing process was stacked against them, they 'participated' in public hearings in order to call into question the quality of expert testimony or 'impact science' in the EIA documents. They did this by comparing impact science unfavourably with traditional science, presenting testimony from counter-experts, that is, experts who disagreed with the company-paid experts, and by showing how impact science must be complemented by community knowledge. Public participants also seriously questioned the assumption that science, or at least impact science, is value-free. More than this, public participants demonstrated the value dimension of development decisions by insisting on talking about their responsibility to future generations, the value of preserving wilderness and forests for something more than future resource extraction, and the quality of community life they wished for themselves, in terms that went beyond the economic to the aesthetic, the ethical, and the spiritual. At each turn, the public redefined their 'participation' in the hearing process. On the other hand, given the splits in communities and the power of industry and governments, it doesn't seem likely that current provisions for public participation can guarantee devel6pment decisions which respect the integrity of communities and the environment.

BACKGROUND ON THE ALPAC HEARINGS

In August 1988 . . . we began to hear rumours about a pulp mill; first we heard it might be a kraft mill, then we heard it would be the world's biggest. Then we had guys skulking around trying to buy options on land and finally we had an announcement that in fact we would get all these things. Absolutely without public input. Well, not quite absolutely – the Chamber of Commerce, the Town Council, and the County Council were privy to all these plans, but the great Alberta public was not.[9]

In December, 1988, the premier of Alberta announced that Alberta-Pacific Forest Industries (Alpac) had been given approval in principle to build the world's largest single line bleached kraft pulp mill along the Athabasca River in the small farming community of Prosperity in Athabasca county, Alberta, Canada. At a cost of $1.3 billion dollars, the Japanese controlled mill would produce pulp from logs drawn from a wood supply area of some 74,000 square kilometres of boreal mixedwood forest (or 12 per cent of the Province of Alberta, an area approximately 20 per cent of Zimbabwe, 80 per cent of Malawi, and two and a half times the size of Lesotho). This would bring to seven the number of pulp mills on the Peace-Athabasca watershed. The Peace and Athabasca rivers flow into Lake Athabasca, through the Slave River into Great Slave Lake, down the Mackenzie River and eventually into the Arctic Ocean.

Community groups recognized that any hearing on the pulp mill occurring after the forests of Alberta were given over to developers effectively denied 'public participation' in discussions about underlying development directions.[10] Yet for many, a public hearing would provide the only forum to debate the government's forest-related development plans and to try to reverse them. Initially, the public was faced with the prospect of the mill proceeding with a cursory review of its impact, and no public hearing. Bowing to public pressure, the Government of Alberta did promise 'public involvement' and 'public input' and accepted Alpac's offer of 'open houses' where people could meet one-on-one with company officials to learn about the project and to express their concerns. The public was less accepting and disrupted these 'open houses,' demanding townhall meetings with question and answer sessions where public debate revealed the breadth of shared concerns, and identified and publicized shortcomings in Alpac's development proposal. Throughout early 1989 town hall meetings became organizing platforms for the anti-mill movement.

In response to public criticism, the Government of Alberta conducted a partial public review of the Alpac proposal in the spring and summer of 1989. When Alberta-Pacific was unable to address many questions raised by environmentalists and civil servants, rising public pressure and the threat of litigation finally compelled the federal government to get involved. In mid-1989, the federal and provincial governments jointly constituted the Alpac Review Board to examine the Alpac proposal.

The Alpac Review Board had numerous constituencies represented in its membership: four provincial government appointees (a local farmer; a local airline owner; the local school superintendent; and the Chief of the Fort McKay Indian Band); a representative of the Government of the Northwest Territories; two federally appointed scientists (an internationally respected environmental water quality scientist and a professor of environmental science with expertise in EIA procedures). The chairman was the head of the Energy Resources Conservation Board of Alberta.

The terms of reference of the Review Board were expanded beyond the Alpac mill proposal and included an examination of 'the cumulative effects on the Peace-Athabasca river system of existing discharges as well as those which would result from the Alpac and other proposed mills.' Forestry impacts, except as logging affected Indian lands, were excluded from review.[11] Public hearings on the Alpac pulp mill were held by the Review Board throughout northern Alberta and the Northwest Territories in late 1989.[12] Again, public groups pressured the Board to expand the hearings from five communities to eleven, including the City of Edmonton. Testimony from 750 individuals in the form of hearing transcripts or written submissions to the Review Board, comprised more than 7,000 pages of presentations. Our paper is built around what people said to this Review Board, as recorded in those transcripts.

IS IMPACT SCIENCE GOOD SCIENCE?

> Beak Associates [the consultants who prepared Alpac's EIA Main Report] are like the dating services in the yellow pages – they'll do anything to please a client.
>
> (Joseph Cummins, *The Athabaskan*, February 20, 1989)

Various points of view were expressed during the hearings on the quality of evidence presented in the technical documents supporting the project. On one end of the spectrum were those who recommended full, unquestioning acceptance. For example, the mayor of nearby Boyle urged the Review Board to 'have faith in the experts' and 'let the government do its job.' Toward the other end of the spectrum were those who questioned the willingness of Alpac to draw conclusions on the basis of inadequate evidence:

> [The EIA] goes on to say that 'There is a large uncertainty in the emission rate estimates for the cooling pond.' And that, 'The rates are educated guesses' . . . I am a household engineer. And in my educated

opinion, and I am educated, two degrees, this is bullshit science. Where do you get off making enigmatic predictions that will effect my lungs and that of my family?

(Merilyn Peruniak, Proceedings, p. 3330)

Critics often challenged impact science, the science contained in reports commissioned by project proponents and governments concerning environmental impacts of large projects, because it failed to meet standards and methods of natural science. A letter to the editor of *Science* was read into the record by a member of the public:

Many politicians have been quick to grasp that the quickest way to silence critical 'ecofreaks' is to allocate a small portion of funds to any engineering project for ecological studies. Someone is inevitably available to receive these funds, conduct the studies regardless of how quickly results are demanded, write large reports containing reams of uninterpreted and incomplete descriptive data, and in some cases, construct 'predictive' models irrespective of the quality of the data base. These reports have formed a gray literature of reports . . . voluminous and so limited in distribution that its conclusions and recommendations are never scrutinized. Often the author's only scientific credentials are the impressive title in a government agency, university, or consulting firm. This title, the mass of the report, the author's salary, and his dress and bearing carry more weight with the commission or study board, to whom the statement is presented, than either his scientific competence or the validity of his scientific investigation. Indeed, many agencies have found it in their best interests to employ a 'travelling circus' of 'scientists' with credentials matching those requirements. As a result, impact statements seldom receive the hard scrutiny that follows the publication of scientific findings in a reputable scientific journal.

(Bill Fuller, Proceedings, p. 2952)

The author of this editorial was unquestionably the scientist Alpac feared the most. Bill Fuller, the environmentalist and retired zoologist who read this letter into the record, used the hearing situation to draw attention to the poor quality of science in the Alpac EIA when he revealed that the author of this utterly devastating critique of impact science was none other than Review Board member Dr. David Schindler. In his letter, Schindler not only characterized impact science as being underfunded, subject to unreasonably short timelines, carried out by people who may not be qualified, not subject to peer review, and often making predictions on the basis of inadequate data, but also made the political point that governments appropriate the rhetoric but not the substance of good science to silence opposition. Fuller took the point one step further saying that because impact science has immediate practical consequences it should be even more rigorous than natural science.[13] Reading from another Schindler letter that appeared in the July 16, 1976, issue of *Science*, Fuller concluded:

> [Science] is a self-correcting endeavour . . . 'and one is confident that correct results will always come eventually, leaving only a relatively harmless pile of worthless papers, wasted manhours, and broken test tubes behind. But we cannot afford to let impact science follow tradition. The legacy will not be broken test tubes, but hopelessly and permanently crippled ecosystems.'
>
> (Quoted by Fuller, Proceedings, pp. 2952–2953)

Environmental groups also brought counter-experts to the hearings to challenge the quality of the technical documents of the project proposal. For example, James Plambeck, an analytical chemist at the University of Alberta who was hired as a counter-expert by the environmentalists Edmonton Friends of the North testified:

> Three months ago I was on the Thesis Review Board for a Master's thesis in environmental engineering. When I first sat down to read Alpac's mitigative response, I read it with the same eye which I would use in reading a Master's thesis in environmental engineering. I would have sent it back to its research director, sir. It would never have even gotten to the examination. I would like to start explaining why by quoting to you from our current elementary textbook of chemistry, *Quantitative Chemical Analysis*, by D. C. Harris. . . . about analytical chemistry and the law. 'Analytical chemists must always emphasize to the public that the single most important characteristic of any result obtained from one or more analytical measurements is an adequate statement of its uncertainty interval.' There isn't an uncertainty interval given in the Alpac report. What is worse, with respect to AOX,[14] the discussion which is truly relevant to the question of whether or not this mill should be built is that number. That number is a single measurement on a single sample, never repeated. It has no standard deviation. Mr. Chairman, in my field, it has no credence.
>
> (James Plambeck, Scientific Review Proceedings, p. 337)[15]

Plambeck's interventions help the public understand that rejecting the call for good science meant rejecting the requirement to present evidence to back up claims. In challenging the quality of the science underpinning Alpac's predictive claims, critics like Fuller, Schindler, and Plambeck did not address the shortcomings of science itself. Rather, they championed science and showed how impact science fell short of its ideals. However, others have argued that scientific methods are culturally shaped and often the issues it studies are politically moulded.[16] Similarly, some have argued that environmental fact-finding is permeated with ethical questions that cannot be answered by scientific methods.[17] We turn now to examples of how the public made these points.

NATIVE OR TRADITIONAL KNOWLEDGE

[T]he Indian person who speaks to tell you about whatever is going to happen, his word versus these specialized white people, the scientists, the environmentalist, their words are more solid, they are more powerful than the Indian speaking.

(Sal Marten Elder, Proceedings, p. 1347)

The impression left by the Alpac EIA was that scientific facts spoke for themselves and did not express values. When values were expressed by experts, they were hidden behind scientific conventions and somehow appeared above political and ethical criticisms. Cindy Gilday, a Review Board member and native from the Northwest Territories, questioned whether science had a place in it for traditional knowledge:

Gilday: [Y]ou said that the rigorous academic level should be applied to the EIA process as it is in regular science practices . . . Native people . . . have worked very hard to have the scientists acknowledge traditional management of animals and lands and waters and all those things. Does this requirement include the traditional knowledge as well?
Bill Fuller: [C]ertainly the traditional knowledge is valuable. I didn't mean that traditional knowledge shouldn't be used. But in terms of evaluating the river quality, I'm not sure that the traditional knowledge is able to do the analyses for these organochlorines. That is the sort of thing I meant. Not to leave out any source of information, but the study must be done rigorously enough, complete enough that it meets all the standards for scientific publication.
Gilday: My understanding is a lot of species of fish are missed by biologists simply because they never bothered to ask the Indian people who know the land, because of the language factor. But it's been a very

long fight by Indian people in the world to have their traditional knowledge acknowledged by the scientific community. I think if you are going to do a proper EIA that pertains to Native people, then this factor has to be included in the scientific academic rigours of science.

(Cindy Gilday, Proceedings, p. 2957)

Earlier in the hearings the Review Board had heard evidence from other presenters about the credibility of traditional or anecdotal knowledge:

It was felt by a number of scientists that people's recollections of water quality, especially those individuals who were close to the resource, could be an extremely valuable indicator of change . . . The reason I feel this is a valuable reflection of scientific indications of the quality of the water is, one, we don't have any hard data; and two, these people, whenever tested, have in fact produced astonishingly accurate qualitative reflections of water quality problems. . . . qualitative impressions by the Natives have been fully vindicated in the last three years by scientific studies done by teams of scientists . . . what this did for me was it established the necessity to listen closely to the users of this resource as very valuable indicators, qualitative indicators of change in these ecosystems.

(Ron Wallace, Proceedings, p. 1578)

Wallace was employed as an environmental consultant by Indian bands for the hearings. He was trying to convince other non-natives of the validity of anecdotal knowledge of the native people. In a world where the words of white scientists are more powerful politically, Wallace validated these qualitative findings as substantiated by 'science.'[18]

NATIONAL ENVIRONMENTAL INDICATORS

[O]ur research indicates that the impact of the pulp mill on agriculture will be minimal. Some land will be permanently taken out of production and Alberta Pacific recognizes this is an impact.

(Alpac, Written Responses, p. 47)[19]

With 'only 11 percent of Canada's total land area capable of agricultural production, and less than 5 percent (Canada Land Inventory classes 1–3) capable of producing a wide range of crops,' rural land conversion is a key environmental indicator: environmental indicators are tools for 'translating quantities of environmental data into succinct information that can . . . be used by decision-makers and the general public.'[20] The site selected for the Alpac pulp mill was located in the middle of an established farming community known as Prosperity. A pulp mill had never been built in an agricultural region in Alberta before, but the government and the company assured the residents that the impacts on their lives would be minimal. Farmers challenged these statements and raised concerns about conflicting use of roadways; pollution of soil, water, and farm produce; and disruption to the rhythms of farm life.

By local standards, the farms in the Prosperity area were productive and the sense of community was strong. The mill could have been located in a forested region, but was sited within daily commuting distance from four rural communities. Local businesses and municipal governments supported the pulp mill location because it meant the prospect of employment and economic benefits for their communities. Drawing from the Canada Land Inventory (CLI) system for soil productivity, Alpac claimed that agricultural land used for the mill was mainly lower quality:

> The lands [225 hectares] will be lost to agricultural production for the duration of the project as they will be occupied by facilities. These lands are rated under the Canada Land Inventory system as having a Class 4 capability for agriculture [severe limitations to agriculture], with the exception of 16 hectares along the route to the effluent pipeline, which has a Class 3 capability [moderately severe limitations to agriculture]. . . . The agricultural lands . . . are virtually all Class 4.
>
> (Alpac EIA, Appendix 3, 4. 2)[21]

Alpac's use of CLI classifications to emphasize the poor quality of soil taken out of agricultural production appeared to legitimate the decision to locate the mill in this farming community. Several farmers challenged the company's interpretation of the classification of their land by offering their own accounts of its productivity:

> We find it also very disturbing that the EIA and supplemental documentation released by Alpac keep referring to this area as Class 4 soil with limited agricultural production capabilities. I wish to bring to the attention of the panel our production averages for the past three years on our major crops and compare them to the regional averages based on data obtained from the Alberta Hail and Crop Insurance records. Our production average for wheat, 50 bushels per acre; Alberta Hail and Crop average 30 bushels per acre. Our production average for barley, 75

bushels per acre; Alberta Hail and Crop average 45 bushels per acre. Our production average for canola, 25 bushels per acre; Alberta Hail and Crop average 17 bushels per acre. Do these figures sound like the soil has limited capabilities?

(Eli and Nellie Cholach, farmers, Proceedings, p. 7327)

Another farmer offered similar testimony:

I am a local cow/calf producer . . . My home is about three and a half miles southeast of the proposed pulp mill . . . I would like to start with the agricultural uniqueness in the area . . . For proof of this, . . . in the year 1988 when most of Alberta had a poor crop, . . . we had a bumper crop in this area. In 1984, most of southern Alberta had a total forage crop failure; again, we had a good forage crop. In the year 1984, southern cattle producers were able to save their basic herds by buying hay from farmers in this area . . . Why is it important to save the basic herd? It takes ten years to establish a good working herd. When their crops fail, we usually still get a crop and sometimes a bumper crop. This has been true from the time the area was settled.

(Dennis Rybicki, Proceedings, p. 6856)

Local knowledge of high agricultural yields deflected Alpac's claims and tied the issue to a controversial debate in Canada: the removal of farm land from production to make room for urban growth or industry. While the provincial government and Alpac addressed in their documents the amount of agricultural land used for the pulp mill site, it became clear at the public hearings that agricultural land would also be taken out of production for bridges, rail lines, roads, and rights-of-way. Questioning by a local farmer provoked re-assessment of the additional land lost to agriculture:

Emil Zachkewich: I wonder if you could comment on . . . the road impacts? . . . What amount of agricultural land will each one of these three alternatives [the company proposed three routes to the mill] be taking out of production?
Jack Phelps, Alberta Transportation representative: With respect to agricultural lands, the total acreages required for Alternative 1 from Class 3 lands, . . . would be 14.6 acres; Class 4 lands would be 16.5 acres. For Alternative 2, from Class 3 would be 58.5 acres; from Class 4 would be 13 acres. For Alternative 3, from Class 3 would be 20 acres;

from Class 4 would be 22.9 acres. According to the inventory maps, there is no land of Class 1 or 2 on any of the routes.

(Proceedings, p. 3752)

These government calculations were then challenged by a Review Board member who was also a farmer:

Mike Franchuk: I was never that good at math and I was just wondering, could you please add the amount of acres taken out of production as far as agriculture is concerned?
Jack Phelps, Alberta Transportation representative: The numbers I gave were total kilometres of length, not acres. I am not sure of the total number of agricultural areas that will be removed. The total acreage required for additional right-of-way over what exists is 287 acres for Alternative 1; 293 for Alternative 2; and 207 for Alternative 3.

(Proceedings, p. 3760)

These speakers forced recognition that the government had erred in reporting length (kilometres) instead of area (hectares or acres) underestimating by a factor between five and ten times the actual acreage of land to be taken out of production. One strength of the public hearing was that local knowledge operated as a feedback and evaluative check on official/expert knowledge, in this case revealing how experts lacked sufficient experience on the land to realize that something was wrong with their calculations. Local knowledge provided serious, reliable information about the community that drew from practical experience, collective memory, and local data to correct, verify, complement, and clarify the official knowledge.[22]

JOBS AND GENDER EQUITY

No mention is made of women [in the EIA]. Women make up nearly half, 44 per cent, of the labour force in the Athabasca area, yet no mention is made of women in the company's hiring practices.

(Diana Salomaa, Proceedings, p. 2898)

The Government of Alberta provided at least 75 million dollars in infrastructure and at least 400 million dollars in loan guarantees to attract Alpac. There was a general feeling in both government and local communities that the 440 mill jobs and 1100 bush jobs created by the pulp mill would solve the problems of unemployment in the region. Unemployment rates in Athabasca county range from 10 to 17 per cent, slightly higher than the provincial urban rate of about 9 to 11 per cent. In surrounding native communities unemployment rates range from 50 to 70 per cent. While these unemployment rates were often referred to, the EIA did not consider whether the pulp mill would create jobs for women. One presenter questioned so-called economic diversification which ignored employment for women:

> As a woman, I cannot help noticing that the Alpac panel of experts and management is all male. The only women would seem to occupy clerical positions. Now, I don't say this with any suggestion of discrimination, as I would assume there are very few women who have the necessary training for these jobs, I am just saying that I see very little evidence of good job opportunities for women here. I would like to see specific information on job opportunities. According to Statistics Canada's information for 1986, females made up 43.28 per cent of the Alberta labour force. Bear in mind that many of these women are single parents who are the sole breadwinners for their families . . . goods-producing industries, such as the proposed pulp mill, employ only 14.11 per cent, while service industries employ 85.89 per cent. Perhaps we should be concentrating on a different area of job creation so that we are not almost excluding nearly half of our work force.
>
> (Ann Stiles, Proceedings, p. 3301)

Development is often promoted by weighing the benefits to the economy from the creation of jobs against any possible environmental effects. This type of discussion is known as the 'jobs versus environment' trade-off. At the hearings it became clear, however, that the jobs side of the jobs-environment equation was complex, and needed to be examined as thoroughly and rigorously as the environment side. Public intervention, like that of Salomaa and Stiles, raised consciousness about the 'gender blindness' of Alpac's job creation.

PUBLIC HEARING: PARTICIPATION OR DOMINATION?

> I think with this [Alpac hearing] process, you have been launched into the next decade; the 1990s, when people will be listened to. The little hunter, the little trapper, the little people on the land are the ones that are going to be making decisions for people that will use our natural

resources. I think this is what you have launched with a process that's very unique. It doesn't exist too much across Canada where the considerations of a province, Northwest Territories and the national values are examined under a microscope like this.

(Cindy Gilday, Proceedings, p. 7629)

There are some basic evidentiary rules when you are dealing with complex scientific issues. In the courts, these sorts of issues are traditionally resolved on the basis of expert opinion. . . . I am not saying that the large range of opinion from individuals and companies and organizations should be totally ignored. . . . The important thing was that people be heard . . . but I don't think that a lot of it necessarily plays a major part in your [Review Board] final decision.

(Dennis Thomas, lawyer for Alpac, Proceedings, pp. 7586, 7587, 7589)

What does giving voice to little people and listening to little people imply? Surely, the suggestion is that often these groups in society are silent; that they have different views because of their role and place outside the power structures and decision-making structures of society; that by giving them voice, letting them speak, we allow their views, their consciousness, their values and ideas to enter into and contest the terrain of public debate. Or, does this occur?

Does the public hearing process, as Gilday suggests, provide a fair and equitable opportunity for the opinions and values of people in the community to challenge the authority of experts and specialists, be they politicians, civil servants, or scientists? Or will review boards tend, as Alpac's lawyer Dennis Thomas suggests is true of the courts, to listen to experts and discount the testimony of non-experts?

Despite its appeal, Gilday's is a naïve view reminiscent of pluralist ideology. Participation is a contested idea, a contested right, and, in practice, lay people have to put up a fight to ensure that Thomas' views about experts do not prevail. In the environmental public hearing process, experts, their methodologies, and the use of expert language can be a control mechanism which produces or creates the problems it then seeks to solve. Pierre Bourdieu entitles it 'symbolic domination': the process of getting ordinary people to accept the terms of the debate without really knowing that a narrowing of the debate is occurring.[23] Clearly, language or discourse plays a key role in this narrowing process. In her critique of the nuclear deterrence debate, Carol Cohn explains that professional or expert discourses can define 'how issues are thought about'; 'who may be heard as legitimate'; 'what may be credibly said'; and 'what must remain unspoken.'[24]

In the EIA, it is experts, and their words, practices, and tools like multiplier effects and scientific procedures that construct and control questions, issues, perspectives, and debates. Experts take charge, using the authority of their roles as practitioners of the disciplines to identify certain issues as problems and others as not; deciding which impacts to measure (and how) and which concerns raised by the public to analyze or not; wielding the tools of impact science and environmental indicators as if they were value-free and neutral. The 'legitimacy' of science and scientific evidence embedded in impact science 'expertise' closes off debates that require strenuous, organized political efforts to re-open.[25]

In Alberta, many people were aware of the politics of expertise, of government decision-making, and political impression-management. They worked, most often in groups, to expose the interests and values hidden in the discourse of experts and mill proponents. For example, in the impact area of the pulp mill, farmers and residents formed environment groups and worked hard to establish that specialists had made measurements and calculations based on faulty assumptions about their localities, and regional ecologies, thus poorly estimating the true impacts of the mill on these communities. They also protested that Alpac's EIA addressed impacts in isolation, and asked the Review Board to consider cumulative and synergistic effects of two or more impacts.

Raising the debate to another plane, many participants in the Alpac public hearing framed their comments in the context of a vision of their place in nature or society. By doing so, they revealed the points at which ethical and moral choices were being made by specialists (or pro-mill community people) without discussion or debate – such as the choice to favour short term profit and job creation (for males) over a serious concern for future generations.[26]

We have tried to show that the hegemony of the hearing process was not something imposed from above on a malleable and yielding public. The public invaded the hearings, contested the field, challenged the restrictive claims of specialists and experts, and, by the very act of participation, made communities aware of their local knowledge or people's knowledge.

In March 1990, when the Review Board recommended that the proposed pulp mill not be built, the public had won a victory. However, the provincial government and company were still determined to go ahead with the project without delay. In order to push through the mill, the Alberta government had to make a political decision to override environmental concerns in favour of the development agenda of capitalists. They did so and by

December of 1990 the mill was given approval to proceed using a modified pulping process. There was no hegemony in this decision. There was no acceptance by the public that the ideas of the government and the proponent were 'common sense.' There was no hiding of motives behind the mask of the hearing process. This was naked power. The company and government could not dress up the project in words like 'sustainable development' and 'environmentally sound.' The public denied Alpac and the Alberta government claim to these words.

CONCLUSION

For the last four years, the authors, as members of the environmental association Friends of the Athabasca and part of the Canada–Asia Partnership (CAP), have been working with community development practitioners from Thailand, Philippines, Nepal, and Canada to explore community based responses to the EIA and public hearing processes. Despite the outcome of the Alpac hearings, the debates led by members of the Canadian community express many issues common to people in the developing world such as: agricultural land out of production, disruptions to communities, and the failure to value local knowledge against outsider knowledge. During our workshops with the CAP participants, we have come to see that the Alpac case study suggests new emphases in environmental impact assessment such as basing assessment on the holistic approach of ecology, and integrating traditional native knowledge and the knowledge of local communities with western science. Recognition of uncertainty in all stages of scientific measurement, modelling, and prediction is important as well. Learning to identify and debate ethical and moral issues embedded in scientific studies and environmental decision-making are perhaps the most crucial considerations. Taken together these new directions should diminish the dominant role of scientists and experts and allow for greater involvement of non-scientists in environmental decision-making. However, we have also learned from this experience, and from those of development workers, that participation in public hearings is not enough. Sustained political activity is required beyond the hearing process.

Notes

1.   The research for this paper was supported in part by the Canada–Asia Project: Community-Based Environmental Protection, a Canadian International Development Agency initiative.
2.   All quotations identified as Proceedings are from the *Alberta-Pacific Environment Impact Assessment Review Board Public Hearing Proceedings, Volumes 1–55* (Edmonton, Alberta: J. G. Moore and Associates Ltd., 1989).
3.   Filed Document refers to written submissions to the Alpac EIA Review Board, a collection of Filed Documents is housed at the Athabasca University Library, Athabasca, Alberta, Canada.
4.   Interview with an environmental activist in Alberta. Brent Cuthbertson, 'Motivations for Environmental Activism: A Description and Analysis of a Sub-Culture,' Master's Thesis, University of Alberta, 1992, p. 136.
5.   Mary Richardson, Joan Sherman, and Michael Gismondi, *Winning Back the Words: Confronting Experts in an Environmental Public Hearing* (Toronto: Garamond Press, 1993).
6.   For recent discussion of participation and development theory, see Majid Rahnema, 'Participation,' in Wolfgang Sachs (ed.), *The Development Dictionary* (London: Zed Books, 1992), pp. 116–31.
7.   For an overview, see Peter Jacobs and Barry Sadler, *Sustainable Development and Environmental Assessment: Perspectives on Planning for a Common Future* (Ottawa: Canadian Environmental Assessment Research Council, 1991); and Liora Salter and Debra Slaco, *Public Inquiries in Canada* (Ottawa: Supply and Services Canada, 1981); Brian Plesuk (ed.), *The Only Game in Town: Public Involvement in Cold Lake* (Edmonton, Alberta: Alberta Environment, 1982).
8.   Study Group on Environmental Assessment Hearing Procedures, *Public Review: Neither Judicial, Nor Political But an Essential Forum for the Future of the Environment* (Ottawa: Supply and Services Canada, 1988), p. 12.
9.   Bill Fuller, 'Facing the Future – An Environmentalist's Perspective', in Kim Sanderson (ed.), *Sustainable Use of Canada's Forests: Are We on the Right Path?* (Edmonton, Alberta: Canadian Society of Environmental Biologists, 1991).
10.   For a characterization of participation in EIAs in Canada, see Frank Tester, 'Reflections on Tin Wis: Environmentalism and the Evolution of Citizen Participation in Canada,' *Alternatives: Perspectives on Society, Technology and Environment*, 19, 1 (October 1992), pp. 34–41.
11.   In Canada, native lands and native welfare are federal responsibilities, as are migratory birds, inter-governmental waters, and national parks – all of which were relevant to the Alpac proposal. Forestry is under provincial jurisdiction and jealously guarded by Alberta's Ministry of Forestry, Lands and Wildlife. In fact, the Minister refused to allow his wildlife and public lands staff to participate in the Alpac hearings.
12.   See *Alberta-Pacific Environment Impact Assessment Review Board Public Hearing Proceedings, Volumes 1–55* (Edmonton, Alberta: J. G. Moore & Associates Ltd., 1989); Alberta-Pacific Environmental Impact Assessment Review Board, *The Proposed Alberta-Pacific Pulp Mill: Report of the EIA*

Review Board, March 1990 (Edmonton, Alberta: Alberta Environment, 1990); *Alberta-Pacific Forest Industries Inc. Environmental Impact Assessment Bleached Kraft Pulp Mill Main Report* (Edmonton, Alberta: Alberta-Pacific Forest Industries Inc., 1989).

13. See Michael Gismondi and Mary Richardson. 'Discourse and Power in Environmental Politics: Public Hearings on a Bleached Kraft Pulp Mill in Alberta, Canada,' *Capitalism–Nature–Socialism*, 2, 8 (October 1991), pp. 43–66.

14. AOX stands for adsorbable organic halides, sometimes called organochlorines, which includes dioxins and furans. The source of these compounds was discovered to be the chlorine-bleaching process of kraft pulp mills.

15. This quotation is from *Alberta-Pacific Scientific Review Panel, Volumes 1– 6* (Edmonton, Alberta: J. G. Moore and Associates Ltd., 1990).

16. Robert N. Proctor, *Value Free Science?: Purity and Power in Modern Knowledge* (Cambridge: Harvard University Press, 1991).

17. See Donald A. Brown, 'The Most Important Problem for Environmental Ethics: The Failure to Integrate Environmental Ethics into Daily Environmental Decision Making,' in International Forum for Biophilosophy, *Stability and Change in Nature: Ecological And Cultural Dimensions*, Proceedings of the IFB Conference in Budapest, Hungary, March 1992; see also the distinction between risk estimates and risk management in Conrad Brunk, Lawrence Haworth, and Brenda Lee, *Value Assumptions in Risk Assessment: A Case Study of the Alachlor Controversy* (Waterloo, Ontario: Wilfrid Laurier University Press, 1991).

18. For an analysis of anecdotal evidence and the cultural biases of scientific standards for health protection, see W. A. Fuller, Mary Richardson, and Michael Gismondi, 'Ethnocentrism in Scientific Standards,' in International Forum for Biophilosophy, op. cit. See also Martha Johnson, 'Dene Traditional Knowledge,' *Northern Perspectives*, 20, 1 (Summer 1992), pp. 3–5.

19. Alpac Written Responses refers to Alberta-Pacific Forest Industries Inc., *Written Submissions and Responses, Volumes 1, 2, and 3* (Edmonton, Alberta: Alberta-Pacific Forest Industries Inc., 1989).

20. Government of Canada, *A Report on Canada's Progress Towards a National Set of Environmental Indicators*, SOE Report 91–1 (Ottawa: Supply and Services Canada, 1991), pp. 72–6.

21. Alberta-Pacific Forest Industries Inc., *Environmental Impact Assessment. Bleach Kraft Pulp Mill Main Report* (Edmonton, Alberta: Alberta-Pacific Forest Industries Inc., 1989).

22. This paper draws from a larger study funded by CIDA's Canada–Asia Project – Community Environmental Indicators: A Case Study of the Alpac EIA Hearings, Joan Sherman and Michael Gismondi, January 1992, 116 pages. This report presents a series of complementary, and sometimes opposing, community environmental indicators and values – based on local knowledge. The use of expert environmental indicators was altered by local people in at least four ways: 1) incompetent or dishonest uses of expert environmental indicators were identified; 2) the simple linear concepts of environmental impacts were replaced with concepts that recognized qualitative, incremental degrees of environmental impacts; 3) the compound or synergistic effect that often occurred when two or more indicators were combined was

recognized; 4) real, yet difficult to measure, impacts that altered the quality of life were introduced.

23. Pierre Bourdieu, 'Doxa and Common Life,' *New Left Review*, 191 (January–February 1992), p. 113.

24. Carol Cohn, 'Emasculating America's Linguistic Deterrent,' in A. Harris and Ynestra King (eds), *Rocking the Ship Of State* (Boulder: Westview, 1989), pp. 153–70. Following Foucault, James Ferguson writes 'outcomes of planned social interventions can end up coming together into powerful constellations of control that were never intended and in some cases never even recognized, but are all the more effective for being "*subjectless*",' *The Anti-Politics Machine: 'Development,' Depoliticization, and Bureaucratic Power in Lesotho* (Cambridge: Cambridge University Press, 1990), p. 19.

25. See Raphael Sassower, *Knowledge without Expertise: On the Status of Scientists* (Albany, New York: State University of New York, 1993).

26. See Roger Hutchinson, *Prophets, Pastors, and Public Choices: Canadian Churches and the Mackenzie Valley Pipeline Debate* (Waterloo, Ontario: Wilfrid Laurier University Press, 1992).

Index

Index